The Massey Lectures are co-sponsored by CBC Radio, House of Anansi Press, and Massey College in the University of Toronto. The series was created in honour of the Right Honourable Vincent Massey, former Governor General of Canada, and was inaugurated in 1961 to provide a forum on radio where major contemporary thinkers could address important issues of our time.

This book comprises the 2023 CBC Massey Lectures, "The Age of Insecurity: Coming Together as Things Fall Apart" broadcast in November 2023 as part of CBC Radio's *Ideas* series. The series was produced by Philip Coulter and Pauline Holdsworth; the executive producer was Greg Kelly.

ASTRA TAYLOR

Astra Taylor is a filmmaker, writer, and political organizer, born in Winnipeg, Manitoba, and raised in Athens, Georgia; she currently lives in New York. Her latest book is *Remake the World: Essays, Reflections, Rebellions*, and her other books include the American Book Award winner *The People's Platform: Taking Back Power and Culture in the Digital Age* and *Democracy May Not Exist but We'll Miss It When It's Gone*. Her documentary films include *What Is Democracy?* and *Examined Life*. She regularly writes for major publications, has toured with the band Neutral Milk Hotel, and co-founded the Debt Collective.

THE AGE OF INSECURITY

....

Coming Together as
Things Fall Apart

ASTRA TAYLOR

ANANSI

Published in Canada and the USA in 2023 by House of Anansi Press Inc.
houseofanansi.com

27 26 25 24 23 1 2 3 4 5

Library and Archives Canada Cataloguing in Publication
Title: The age of insecurity : coming together as things fall apart /
Astra Taylor.
Names: Taylor, Astra, author.
Series: CBC Massey lectures.
Description: Series statement: The CBC Massey lectures.
Includes bibliographical references.
Identifiers: Canadiana (print) 20230473768 | Canadiana (ebook) 20230474497
ISBN 9781487011932 (softcover) | ISBN 9781487011949 (EPUB)
Subjects: LCSH: Security (Psychology) | LCSH: Uncertainty. | LCSH: Anxiety.
LCSH: Social psychology. | LCSH: Civilization, Modern—21st century.
Classification: LCC BF575.S35 T39 2023 | DDC 155.9—dc23

Series design: Bill Douglas
Cover design: Greg Tabor
Text design: Ingrid Paulson

*House of Anansi Press is grateful for the privilege to work on and create from
the Traditional Territory of many Nations, including the Anishinabeg,
the Wendat, and the Haudenosaunee, as well as the Treaty Lands of
the Mississaugas of the Credit.*

With the participation of the Government of Canada
Avec la participation du gouvernement du Canada

*We acknowledge for their financial support of our publishing program the Canada
Council for the Arts, the Ontario Arts Council, and the Government of Canada.*

Printed and bound in Canada

For Nye Taylor

CONTENTS

CHAPTER 1

CURA'S GIFT

STORIES ABOUT HOW OUR species came into being often involve mud, including the one I'm about to tell. It is the myth of the Roman goddess Cura, a figure whose name tells us she is the embodiment of care, concern, anxiety, and worry.

One day, as Cura was crossing a river, she saw some clayey soil. Thoughtfully, she took it up and began to fashion a figure. While she was pondering what she had just made, Jupiter, king of the gods, appeared; Cura asked him to give the figure life, and Jupiter readily granted her wish, breathing spirit into her creation. But when Cura wanted to give this newly living creature her own name, Jupiter objected fiercely and insisted that his name be used instead. As they quarrelled, none other than Mother Earth, Tellus herself, arose and demanded the honour be hers; after all, she had given her own body to Cura's project. Having reached an impasse, they called on Saturn, the god of time, to come settle the dispute. Saturn's judgment was swift and decisive: "Jupiter, since you gave the creature life, take its soul after death; since Tellus offered her body, let her receive its body in turn; and because Cura first fashioned the being, let her possess it as long as it lives. But since there is controversy about naming, let the name be *homo*, since the creature seems to be made from humus, from dirt."

One of the hundreds of fables collected by the Roman grammarian Hyginus more than two thousand years ago, the myth of Cura reflects on the human condition. Care and anxiety, concern and worry—the multiple meanings of the Latin word *cura*—are part of what makes us who and what we are. It is hardly a self-aggrandizing narrative. Cura's more famous Greek counterpart, the god Prometheus, for example, is said to have moulded humankind in his image, enabling us to stand upright. He went on to steal fire on our species' behalf, enraging Zeus, who condemned Prometheus to eternal torment as punishment. This tale, conflicted though its message may be, is one of human exceptionalism—it describes the origins of our "Promethean" characteristics of risk-taking and technological innovation, a story in which the possession of fire sets us apart from other animals. Cura, in contrast, doesn't give us any special traits or tools to ease our troubles. Instead, she worries over us and cares for us—she acts thoughtfully and ponders, the story says—and so fates us to worry and care and ponder in return.

At the time Hyginus transcribed his fables, the leading philosophers in Ancient Rome were the Stoics, and they were preoccupied with trying to escape the condition Cura represents. To be Stoic was to pursue a state of mind they called *securitas*, derived from the phrase *sine cura*: being without worry, free from care. The root of the modern word *security*, *securitas* meant equanimity, the mental calm the Stoics aspired to in their daily lives. Writing during the first century BCE, both Cicero and Seneca extolled imperturbability in the face of chaos and uncertainty. "What is the blessed life?" Seneca asked. "Security and perpetual tranquility," was his reply.

In Seneca's telling, true securitas involves not eliminating the concerns and anxieties that inevitably bedevil and unsettle us, but instead rising above them: "For no human virtue can rid itself of feelings. But the brave man has no fear; unconquered he looks down from a lofty height upon his sufferings."[1] For Cicero, the goal was to keep insecurity at bay: "We must keep ourselves free from every disturbing emotion, not only from desire and fear, but also from excessive pain and pleasure, and from anger, so that we may enjoy that calm of soul and security which bring both moral stability and dignity."[2] Both ambitions—surmounting emotions or being liberated from them—require willpower and hard work. In their dedication, the Stoics revealed a fundamental contradiction: securitas, care's absence, can only be achieved with effort. That is to say, with care.

The myth of Cura, meanwhile, tells us that such quests are futile, at least in absolute terms.[3] To be human is to be perpetually insecure. Real securitas, the parable implies, can only be achieved in death, when our spirits return to Jupiter and our bodies to Tellus, freeing us from Cura's influence. In other words, as long as we are alive, we are destined to exist in a condition of what I'll call existential insecurity. This existential insecurity is the kind that comes from being dependent on others for survival; from being vulnerable to physical and psychological illness or wounding; and, of course, from being mortal. It's the insecurity of randomness and risk, of a future that is impossible to control or to know. It is a kind of insecurity we can never wholly escape or armour ourselves against, try as we might to mitigate potential harms.

Like the Stoics before us, each and every one of us must wrestle with the tension this existential conundrum creates. We understandably orient our lives toward the pursuit of security, even if it is an elusive goal—I know I do. We'd all like to care and worry less. We'd all like to have a secure home and source of income, to be ensured of aid when we are sick and as we age, to feel confident in ourselves and our sense of place. But how to conceive of security in our era of unprecedented inequality, when eight billion people call our precious and collapsing planet home, presents a conceptual and practical challenge the Stoics could not have fathomed. We cannot afford to emulate Seneca, who sought his ideal of mental serenity while assisting and advising his former pupil and patron, the infamous Emperor Nero, as he brought catastrophe upon Rome. Caring for others' well-being, at some point, becomes our own self-interest. Our concern must extend beyond our personal equanimity.

How we understand and respond to insecurity is one of the most urgent questions of our moment, for nothing less than the future security of our species hangs in the balance. Insecurity can cut both ways, serving as a conduit to empathy, humility, and belonging—or it can spur defensive and destructive compulsions that protect the self instead of caring for other people, as well as the more than human world we are inseparable from and embedded within. Insecurity can bring us together or it can atomize us, it can be an impetus to reaction or to progress, but it will forever be with us.

The myth of Cura reminds us that insecurity is our birthright, but it does not instruct us in how to cope with this discomfiting gift. We can emulate the security of the Stoics, seeking private peace amid the troubles that surround us; we can retreat to the security of the bunker, fortifying ourselves and our possessions behind walls and weaponry; or we can find solidarity and resiliency in the collective, cultivating what we might call an ethic of insecurity by accepting our inherent vulnerability and seeking public-spirited protection and community to help us weather life's troubles as best we can.

Today, many of the ways we try to make ourselves and our societies more secure—money, property, possessions, police, the military—have paradoxical effects, undermining the very security we seek and accelerating harm done to the economy, the climate, and people's lives, including our own. Is another way possible? I believe it is—but we have to choose that course, both as individuals and as a society. We can run from insecurity or we can learn from it, finding connection in our common fragility and reorienting our priorities in recognition of this existential fact. Cura has given us a gift, but it is up to us what we make of it.

WELL BEFORE COVID-19 SWEPT the globe, compounding suffering and leaving greater instability in its wake, insecurity was everywhere. Millions of people had only precarious access to housing, health, food, and employment. Changing weather patterns increased the risk of fires and flooding, destabilizing communities and ecosystems, and triggering ecological tipping points that will only intensify climate upheaval. Prior to the advent of "social distancing," we hid behind doors, locks, gates, and border fences, afraid of public space and one another. Online, we fretted over information security, devising passwords to access passwords, fearful we might be hacked or exposed. We were insecure in our schools, in our homes, in our relationships, and on social media. And, of course, we felt, and still feel, insecure about our very selves—about our appearance, our intelligence, our age, our health.

Insecurity, of course, is not evenly distributed, its harshest edge reserved for the most disadvantaged and discriminated against, but it is widely felt. We are all, to varying degrees, overwhelmed and apprehensive, worried about what tomorrow will bring. Some try to hide it, papering over self-doubt with self-aggrandizement—a strategy to which we might just relate—while others wear their vulnerabilities on their sleeves. Most people are preoccupied with the stress of struggling to make ends meet, but even the comfortable and well-heeled feel on guard, anxious, and incomplete.

And so we try to cope. We give children security blankets, purchase security systems for our homes, fret over cyber-security, wait dutifully at security checkpoints, extract fossil fuels to ensure energy security, and sacrifice the lives and freedom of others in the name of our national security. We work hard, shop hard, hustle, get credentialed, scrimp and save, invest, diet, self-medicate, meditate, exercise, exfoliate. Like the Stoics before us, we engage in self-care, hoping it might help us one day care less.

Perhaps this is no surprise, given the existential insecurity the myth of Cura reveals. How else should mortal creatures, creatures who spent millennia somewhere in the middle of the food chain, feel but insecure? When you might be a tiger's next meal, a tendency toward insecurity could give you an evolutionary advantage—prompting a useful instinct that keeps you alert and out of harm's way.

And yet, even if existential insecurity is indelible to being human, the ways we structure our societies can make us more secure or less so, and in Western societies, at least, material and emotional insecurity are now on the rise. No doubt, insecurity is central to every hierarchical social system in some way. Autocratic and totalitarian regimes rule by fostering fear and threatening violence; feudal systems kept peasants toiling by limiting opportunity and mobility. And, of course, it's clear that people have long lived precarious and unpredictable lives, otherwise the Stoics and their quest for securitas would not have resonated so strongly during their time, and Buddhist thinkers would have had no need to develop the concept of Zen. But insecurity plays a unique role in the liberal capitalist order that dominates today—a role underscored by the fact that the modern word *insecurity* entered into common usage in the seventeenth century, just as our market-driven society was coming into being. Only by revisiting this history, and the central role insecurity has played in capitalism since its genesis, can we understand our present situation and see how more recent developments—particularly the decline of the welfare state over the past fifty years—have intensified insecurity and left no one, wealthy or working-class, unscathed.

Capitalism, as economists from Karl Marx to John Maynard Keynes and Thomas Piketty have understood, is prefaced on producing a profit, which can then be reinvested to make more profit in turn. It is, in philosopher Nancy Fraser's terminology, "voracious," relentless in its pursuit of new markets and growth. This means that our current capitalist system is set up less to meet and fulfill our current needs than it is to generate new ones, which, of course, can only be met through additional consumption—consumption of new lifestyles, experiences, products, upgrades, and apps with features we suddenly can't live without.

Capitalism thrives on bad feelings, on the knowledge that contented people buy less—an insight the old American trade magazine *Printers' Ink* stated bluntly: "Satisfied customers are not as profitable as discontented ones."[4] Consumer society thus capitalizes on the very insecurities it produces, which it then prods and perpetuates, making us all insecure by design. It had never occurred to me, for example, to fret over the buccal fat in my cheeks until I recently saw it described by the *Guardian* as a "fresh source of insecurity to carry into the new year."[5] No matter how much we have, we are ensnared in systems that are structured to trigger insecurity, propelling us to endlessly strive for an ideal that we will always fall short of. This is why no advertising or marketing department will ever tell us that we're actually okay, and that it is the world, not us, that needs changing.

This kind of insecurity, which I'll call "manufactured insecurity," is quite unlike the existential insecurity that is inherent to human life, as the myth of Cura underscores. Where the latter is an ineradicable feature of our being, the former is a mechanism that facilitates exploitation and profit and is anything but inevitable. Indeed, the insight that capitalism is a kind of insecurity-producing machine—that insecurity is not an unfortunate side effect but a core attribute of the system—is one that these chapters will return to and examine through different lenses.

My perspective is shaped by the years I've spent focused on the topic of inequality and its pernicious effects on culture and democracy both in my creative work as a filmmaker and writer and as an activist. Nearly a decade ago, I helped found the Debt Collective, the world's first union for debtors, which has become a bastion for people who are broke and overwhelmed. Inequality is, indeed, out of control, with ten billionaire men possessing six times more wealth than the poorest three billion people on earth.[6] But numbers do not capture the true nature or extent of the crisis. Insecurity, in contrast, describes how inequality is lived day after day. Where inequality can be represented by points on a graph, insecurity speaks to how those points feel, hovering in space over a tattered safety net or nothing at all. The writer Barbara Ehrenreich, in her 1989 study of the psychology of the middle class, dubbed the condition "fear of falling."[7] But today there's barely any middle left, and everyone is afraid of what lies below.

Part of the insidious and overwhelming power of insecurity is that, unlike inequality, it is subjective. Sentiments, or how actual people actually feel, rarely map rationally onto statistics; you do not have to be at rock bottom to feel insecure, because insecurity results as much from expectation as from deprivation. This is why insecurity impacts the well-being of people on every rung of the economic ladder, from the impecunious to the privileged (albeit in very different ways). Recent years have produced an abundance of scholarship demonstrating the negative effects of inequality on health and happiness across the board. Rising inequality, and the insecurity it causes, correlates with higher rates of physical illness, depression, anxiety, drug abuse and addiction.[8] Living in a highly competitive and consumerist society, research shows, makes everyone more status-conscious, stressed out, and sick.

Economic issues, I've come to realize, are also emotional ones: the spike of shame when a bill collector calls, the adrenaline when the rent is due, the foreboding when you think about retirement. But where my organizing work has focused primarily on the problems endured by the poor—debtors, by definition, have negative net worth—my conviction is that our current economic arrangement also harms people who have means, and that the pervasiveness of insecurity provides evidence of this fact. When we examine society through the lens of insecurity, which affects everyone, as opposed to inequality, which emphasizes two opposing extremes, we can see the degree to which unnecessary suffering is widespread even among those who appear to be "winning" according to the logic of the capitalist game. No one is totally immune to anxiety and bad feelings, no matter how high they sit on the income graph, just as no one can totally insulate themselves from the economic and ecological shocks to come.

Recognizing how we are all made insecure improves our odds of devising a just, collective response to our era's intersecting crises. Trying to cope alone, in contrast, puts us all at risk. History, including recent history, shows that hard times, or even the mere anticipation of them—the subjective feeling of being economically insecure and anticipating the worst, whether or not those fears are objectively justified—can increase the appeal of racism and xenophobia. Across the world, the reactionary far right has gained ground by speaking directly to atomized and isolated people's fears and anxieties, and offering scapegoats to blame: immigrants, Muslims, Jewish people, Black people, trans people, women seeking abortions, and so on. Too often, insecurity propels the embrace of social hierarchy and domination, much the way the threat of environmental disaster and the coronavirus pandemic have fuelled science denial and other doomed attempts to escape insecurity by taking false solace in superiority and certitude.

And yet this rightward tilt is far from preordained. Insecurity can also inspire a more hopeful response.

My own experience organizing financially insecure debtors validates research confirming that economic insecurity can also, as one recent academic paper puts it, make people "more likely to sympathize with the poor than resent them," and increase their support for redistributive policies and an expanded welfare state.[9] And we can certainly see, from the efflorescence of social movements in recent years, that the experience of shared oppression and ecological calamity can also help unite people, too, nurturing that previously mentioned ethic of insecurity. But that process of building solidarity doesn't happen automatically. This is why I believe talking about insecurity and, ultimately, organizing to address it are such urgent tasks. Even as we pay more and more attention to the problem of inequality, continuing to ignore its companion insecurity will only accelerate already grave political risks, including the already formidable anti-democratic backlash. Yet one challenge organizers like myself face is the fact that many people who would like to see progressive social change feel stuck on the insecurity treadmill, too afraid of losing what little they have to step off and challenge the status quo in a substantive way. Constant insecurity helps keep us in line, while the conventional methods of achieving security are destroying us.

Consider the hip Brooklyn café my sister worked at until a few years ago. The place has a vintage and vaguely Parisian aesthetic, retro and low-tech. There were, of course, regulars, including a medievalist who liked to chat. On a slow day, a barista on duty was exchanging pleasantries with the medievalist when her phone rang: the owner was watching the security camera live feed from his laptop and told her to stop being so talkative, despite the lack of other customers or responsibilities to attend to. When I asked my sister how many cameras were installed in the small space, she identified at least eight, and said there might be more. The charming café was, in fact, a panopticon—the boss able to tune in any time from anywhere and see from nearly every angle. Even when all they wanted to do was show a bit of kindness and community to a local eccentric, the workers were perpetually worried about being fired. The security cameras hadn't been installed to make the staff safer; they were there to make them feel insecure about holding on to their jobs.

Deploying cameras in this way is nothing new, even if today's models are networked and sometimes feature artificial intelligence. In his book *Security/Capital*, Carleton University law professor George Rigakos recounts his time working at a Toronto bakery in the 1990s. The staff regularly took home broken loaves, a perk of an otherwise exhausting and low-paid occupation. For years, management looked the other way, tacitly permitting staff to take unsaleable products. But that changed when rumours circulated that the bakery would soon close. The owners installed security cameras to catch workers in the act of taking bread, in order to have a reason to let them go without benefits. Lifelong employees were summarily fired, losing their retirement support along with their jobs. "The security crackdown must have saved the company thousands upon thousands in severance and pension dollars," Rigakos writes.[10] It also cost the workers their security in old age.

Without a doubt, the workers are the sympathetic characters in these stories, but it's important to recognize that their antagonists, the bosses looking over their shoulders, are not acting in a vacuum. They too are spurred on by insecurity, even if they don't have to endure its worst indignities: imagine being the owner of a failed business, potentially owing thousands in employee benefits, and being unable to make good on your contractual promise. What Canadian-American economist John Kenneth Galbraith called "the nerve-wracking problem of insecurity" is, he argued, a feature inherent to our competitive economic system, one that takes the form of "episodic unemployment for the worker" on the one side, and "occasional insolvency for the farmer or businessman" on the other.[11] In both instances, insecurity, as I've said, is subjective; it encompasses present ordeals as well as fear of future hardship. All it takes is a devastating enough crisis to reduce the once fortunate to a state of precarity or poverty: business could suddenly drop; the stock in a retirement account could crash; home values could plummet; a family member could be diagnosed with cancer (something that, in the United States, can eviscerate the economic security of a middle-class household overnight); a storm could wreak havoc; another, more deadly pandemic could hit. The inherent volatility of capitalism and the uncertainty of life both undermine the predictability security seeks. These stresses don't excuse unethical behaviour—including spying on or sacking employees—but they can help us understand what propels it.

Conventional wisdom would have us believe that bosses who engage in such unsavoury practices are driven by greed—by inborn mercenary and rapacious impulses and not the systemic condition of insecurity. In other words, they are said to suffer the kinds of character flaws and moral failings that children's stories often warn against. Think, for example, of Aesop's fabled goose, who lays golden eggs and is murdered by a gluttonous farmer who wants the riches all at once; or the famously covetous King Midas, cursed by his own request to increase his wealth with a touch that turns everything into gold. There is also the strange and surreal fairy tale retold by the Brothers Grimm of a fisherman who is instructed by his insatiable wife to demand a series of favours in return for sparing an enchanted fish's life. First she asks for a small cottage to replace their "dirty and stinking" shack, then a palace, and so on, until, frenzied with want, the wife demands to become God—a request that prompts the fish to restore the couple to penury.

These parables offer good advice—when you meet an enchanted fish, do not, under any circumstances,

tell your spouse—but they are insufficient and ultimately misleading guides to navigating contemporary
life under capitalism. The individualistic logic of these
fanciful tales, like Western culture's emphasis on greed
more generally, makes it seem as though all we need
is for a few deluded individuals to wake up from avarice's spell, as when Midas recognizes the error of his
ways and begs Dionysus for reprieve. Then, as if by
magic, inequality and all of its attendant miseries will
disappear.

In reality, forces less magical and more material-
ist are at work—namely, market forces. These forces
have been gathering strength for a very long time, since
well before the invention of automobiles or even steam
engines; unlike greed, which afflicts specific individuals, market forces impact us all, touching and moulding
even the most intimate facets of our lives. To understand
how these forces operate, and why insecurity is so central to them, we need to follow the historians who trace
capitalism's murky origins to the English countryside,
the place where modern insecurity first became endemic.

CAPITALISM DID NOT APPEAR fully formed, like a spirit
conjured by an incantation in a myth or legend. Instead,
it evolved slowly, taking form over hundreds of years
as England's feudal system underwent a social and economic transformation that would come to define the

modern world. For generations, the peasantry had exercised customary rights to land held in common—rights to graze their animals, to collect kindling, to glean, to plant, to fish, and to survive by accessing meadows, rivers, and woods they did not own outright but rather shared with others. Beginning in the twelfth century, these traditional rights and ways of life came under attack to make room for a new emerging order of commerce. During the prolonged and varied process now known as the enclosure movement, communal fields and forests were privatized—literally enclosed with fences and hedges—displacing commoners from the land that had sustained them and fuelling an unprecedented change.

Commoner here has a double resonance. The people in question were common, as in not aristocrats, but they also engaged in *commoning*—a word that is a verb, an action, a mode of survival, and a way of relating and being in the world. Commoners lived off land they collectively stewarded as a matter of "common right." It was commoning that helped them achieve a baseline of material security and independence, and it was the loss of commoning that made them newly insecure in the capitalist sense.

While the enclosure movement manufactured a new form of capitalist insecurity for the majority, it increased the security of the minority of landlords, who fenced and hedged their newly private property. By some estimates, even after centuries of encroachment, approximately one-quarter of the total area of England and Wales was managed as commons into the late seventeenth century, when a new wave of enclosure commenced. More and more land became the sole possession of privileged individuals, and commoners, simply doing what they had always done, were transformed into trespassers and criminals and denied access to their traditional means of survival under the threat of death. Locked out of the pastures and woodlands they had tended to and gathered in for generations, people could no longer meet their own subsistence needs and had to turn to the market for survival. Where commoners had once tilled crops and made items for personal subsistence and for their local lord and community, they now had little to sell but their own labour. The resulting social upheaval was particularly devastating for women, who had played a vital role in agriculture and who had passionately resisted enclosure. With forced migration came slums and squalor, city centres crowded with people desperate for employment, women and children among those forced to work in the dangerous new factories and commercial mills.

In 1647 Thomas Rainsborough, a witness to enclosure, called it "the greatest tyranny that was thought of in the world."[12] Rainsborough was a leader of the democratic political faction known as the Levellers, a group whose name spoke of their desire to "level off" the differences between toiling and ruling classes, and to level the fences and hedges erected to separate private parcels of land. During the English Civil War, when parliamentary forces engaged in a deadly conflict with King Charles I, another contingent calling themselves the True Levellers, or Diggers, sought the full abolition of private ownership: the earth, they insisted, "was made to be a Common Treasury of relief for all, both Beasts and Men."[13] These visionaries enacted their radical politics by setting up an occupation on a small hill, which they planted with seeds—the act of digging by which they got their name—and held their ground for four months. "England is not a free people till the Poor that have no Land, have a free allowance to dig and labour the Commons, and so lie as Comfortably as the Landlords that live in their Inclosures," they proclaimed.[14] As the bloody struggle for a more democratic political system wore on, debates about communal property rights also raged, their memory largely buried after private property became a cornerstone of the new liberal capitalist state.[15]

As the Industrial Revolution advanced, so did the intentional and methodical devastation of old ways of life. In 1735, an anonymous pamphleteer called the commons "a security for those whom fortune shou'd frown on" and noted that enclosure caused pauperism, a dire form of poverty previously unknown.[16] For landowners, this was the point. They understood that the demise of the commons and the desperation and dislocation of the peasantry would yield a more pliable labour force, and they had the power to make new laws to this end.[17] Between 1760 and 1870, the tail end of the enclosing process, over four thousand acts of Parliament changed the ownership of approximately seven million acres, one-sixth the area of England.[18] The aim was to "increase the number of hands for labour, by removing the *means* of subsisting in idleness," as one outspoken proprietor put it.[19] The cultivation of stereotypes helped their cause. Elites condemned commoners as lazy, barbaric, a "sordid race," and compared them to Muslim infidels or, as colonization advanced, to Native Americans. Enclosure was thus a kind of trial run for the dispossession of Indigenous peoples, who used a variety of communal land management practices to govern their territories.[20] English landlords, like proponents of land theft across the Atlantic, claimed that commercialization would "improve" the soil and increase its yield, while also "improving" public morals by imposing the discipline of work on the poor, a project both calculated and cruel. For example, in 1807 landowner Thomas Rudge recommended fencing with hedges that did not bear fruit, so they could not be put to life-sustaining use. He didn't want people to be tempted to eat for free: "the idle among the poor are already too prone to depredation, and would still be less inclined to work, if every hedge furnished the means of support."[21]

In her book *Commoners: Common Right, Enclosure and Social Change in England, 1700–1820*, Jeanette M. Neeson, a professor of history at York University, tracks these debates as they took place in newspapers and parliament while also recovering the culture that enclosure destroyed: the fields commoners plowed, the jokes they told, and their loss of the kind of freedom that comes from being able to provide for your own needs. The deprivation was captured by the poem "The Moors," published by the peasant-poet John Clare in 1827:

> *Unbounded freedom ruled the wandering scene*
> *Nor fence of ownership crept in between*
> *To hide the prospect of the following eye —*
> *Its only bondage was the circling sky …*
> *Enclosure came and trampled on the grave*
> *Of labour's rights and left the poor a slave,*
> *And memory's pride, ere want to wealth did bow,*
> *Is both the shadow and the substance now.*[22]

Commoners shouldn't be romanticized, of course. Their lives were hard, and they were hardly free by contemporary standards. Nevertheless, they enjoyed certain liberties that most of us have never known—namely, the freedom to make a living from the earth underneath them, despite not owning that particular piece of ground outright. If they grew food, collected firewood, picked fruit or thatch, or earned income, it was by their own hands and on their own terms. Enclosing landlords decried commoners' poverty (even as they pursued policies that would leave them much poorer) and were duly perplexed when peasants responded that they didn't want to be rich—survival was, in the words of at least one commoner, "enough," because it came with autonomy. It was the upper class who, in their hunger for more and their obsession with crop yields, productivity, and growth, were plagued by insecurity.[23] After enclosure robbed commoners of their self-sufficiency and, just as critically, the collective power that comes with community, insecurity became their lot, too, and wage labour their only option. Enclosure thus helped produce the proletariat, facilitating the transition from feudalism to capitalism.

Today we take for granted that we must work a proper job to earn a wage in order to provide for our basic needs, and we structure our entire lives around this fact. The history of enclosure reminds us that this arrangement is anything but natural. Before the wage earner could emerge as our society's paradigmatic subject, a condition historian Michael Denning calls "wagelessness" had to be imposed. "Capitalism," Denning writes, "begins not with the offer of work, but with the imperative to earn a living."[24] In other words, it begins with manufactured insecurity—insecurity in its new modern economic sense.

It would take until the early twentieth century for more secure forms of employment to become the norm, at least for a subset of mostly white men, and only after decades of sustained and often militant labour organizing. Vulnerable and exploited workers forged solidarity from insecurity, demanding better wages and treatment

from bosses and protection and assistance from government. During the Great Depression, an unlikely
assortment of trade unionists, social reformers, and
visionary politicians highlighted insecurity as a central and unjust component of laissez-faire capitalism
and mobilized to remedy it. The 1933 Regina Manifesto,
the founding document of Canada's Co-operative
Commonwealth Federation, the influential precursor to
the NDP, offered a forceful critique of labour insecurity
that helped pull the country leftward: "The spectre of
poverty and insecurity which still haunts every worker,
though technological developments have made possible a high standard of living for everyone, is a disgrace
which must be removed from our civilization."[25] In
1940, the Canadian federal government introduced
the Unemployment Insurance Act, the nation's first
national social security program.

Meanwhile, in the US, the *New Republic* magazine
opined, "For a long time now people have been saying
that perhaps the greatest evil of capitalist industrial-
ism is not its unequal distribution of wealth but the
insecurity it brings to the majority of the population."[26]
The next year, in 1935, President Franklin Delano
Roosevelt echoed the point, observing that the "civilization of the past hundred years, with its startling
industrial changes, has tended more and more to make
life insecure." Denouncing insecurity as "one of the
most fearsome evils of our economic system," Roosevelt
would go on to invoke "security" as the justification for

the New Deal. These policy measures formed the foundation of the American welfare state: the old-age social
insurance program known as Social Security, health
care supports through a mix of public and private benefits, public higher education, progressive taxation, mass
unionization, and more. Wealth inequality reached historic lows as employment stabilized.[27]

But even this modicum of institutionalized material
security for ordinary people proved intolerable to economic elites, who required social insecurity to do what
they deemed acceptable business. Over the past half
century, corporations and their allied politicians have
launched a series of coordinated attacks on the gains of
the post–World War II era in an attempt to shake themselves free from the rights and protections that labour
unions won during the 1930s, much the way proponents
of enclosure liberated themselves from the peasantry's
customary rights to the commons centuries ago. As a
result of this big-business-led backlash, a growing number of jobs today are contract gigs lacking predictable
full-time schedules; even if they are well-compensated,
as many of the gig jobs in tech or television can be, they
are short-lived and lack benefits. Most new jobs created in the wake of deindustrialization have been in
the service sector—retail stores, restaurants and bars,
health clinics and spas, entertainment venues, and so
on—where pay is middling and security non-existent.
This means that many people work multiple jobs or live
in households where everyone of age has to work. A

2019 Bank of Canada report found that almost a third of Canadians participate in precarious work, the majority doing so out of necessity, not choice.[28]

In a sense, the unsettling process of enclosure has never ended, though it has been rebranded—first as "creative destruction" and later as "disruption." Insecurity is now manufactured with the help of high-tech software and apps, which relentlessly track and rate workers as they race across warehouse floors, serve fast food, and navigate delivery routes. The Big Tech entrepreneurs who popularized the term know that disruption is not a regrettable pit stop on the road to broadly shared prosperity but rather a permanent condition for vulnerable workers. This is especially true for immigrants, who perform much of the work in the steadily expanding gig economy, which Statistics Canada defines as characterized by "short-term tasks, projects, or jobs, with no assurance of steady employment," including rideshare services.[29] Companies like Uber and Lyft financially benefit from the fact that millions of people can't make ends meet with one job, from the fact that rising housing costs mean a growing number of drivers have no choice but to live in their cars, and from the fact that most drivers are ashamed of their predicament, which makes them less likely to stand up for themselves.[30] For those positioned to capitalize on it, insecurity begets opportunity. Once again, insecurity is not a by-product of our economic system, but a desired product; as the techies say, it is a feature, not a bug.

No doubt, some members of the business community would take issue with my insistence that employers and policy makers intentionally foster job insecurity. Many tech entrepreneurs, for example, argue it's an unfortunate but inevitable consequence of innovation. In the cold-blooded language of market-friendly economists, rising labour productivity requires fewer workers to produce the same output, which means the problem is automation rather than the employers and their habit of speeding up and deskilling work. Others point the finger at globalization. Domestic job insecurity, they maintain, is an unavoidable outcome of international trade and competition—but they fail to note the way employers use the threat of offshoring to strengthen their hand in contract negotiations. How many companies have forced their employees to accept pay cuts out of fear that their jobs will be outsourced to high-tech robots or artificial intelligence or offshored to Mexico or China? With a growing number of gig or contract workers barred from joining labour unions and from engaging in collective bargaining—a privilege more readily available to "traditional" salaried employees—insecurity is used to pit worker against worker, usually along lines of race, immigration status, and nationality.

Whatever the root causes, the consequences of job insecurity are widely felt. For bosses and shareholders, worker insecurity pays dividends, while workers and their families pay the price. The academic research on employment insecurity signals a full-blown public health crisis. Losing your job earlier than expected, scholars have shown, reduces life expectancy—you literally die earlier. The mere fear of job loss causes ill health, as does the direct threat of being fired. A 2021 study of Canadian workers reported that those who feel their jobs are insecure have "significantly higher odds of major depressive disorder" than those who feel secure at work, and multiple job losses have been shown to raise the risk of heart attacks as much as cigarettes, alcohol, or hypertension.[31]

The phenomenon of so-called deaths of despair fits this woeful trend. Nobel Prize winner Angus Deaton and economist Anne Case first identified and sounded the alarm about rising mortality rates among white adults without four-year college degrees. Once again, the problem here is not poverty in absolute terms but the insecurity that comes from downward mobility, the loss of social status and community—in other words, the tearing apart of once-robust social fabrics and the loss of hope that life will one day improve. People might have the same jobs their parents or grandparents had before them—factory worker, janitor, office clerk—but they are now temps employed by a private contractor, relegating them to a kind of second-class status with no prospects for promotion or improvement in their job benefits, should they be lucky enough to have any.

The resulting desolation, Deaton and Case argue, was methodically milked by pharmaceutical companies peddling opioids as a balm for the pain caused by this dislocation. Systemic job insecurity proved a massive windfall for drug companies, while costing the public far more in lost lives, family and community devastation, and, also, money. The US Congress Joint Economic Committee estimates the public cost of the opioid epidemic was nearly $1.5 trillion in 2020 alone, while Canada's annual estimates soar well into the billions.[32] In Canada, where the opioid crisis has intensified apace, people who live in poverty are four times more likely to die opioid-related deaths than their affluent counterparts. As a 2018 study published in the *Canadian Medical Association Journal* noted, Indigenous communities are particularly hard hit, representing a disproportionate percentage of fatalities—a direct consequence of the ongoing legacies of colonialism, racism, and intergenerational trauma.[33] And in 2022, a team of epidemiologists released a report documenting spiking opioid-related deaths among Ontario construction workers. "There's a lot of job insecurity, which leads to a lot of underreporting of injuries or pain and a lot of pressure for people to return to work, because if they're not working, oftentimes they're not being paid," one of the lead researchers explained.[34]

Despite the obvious social risks and the harms to worker health, the captains of industry continue to manufacture insecurity to increase their advantage. Consider Jack Welch, the former head of General Electric, who made his reputation advising companies to intentionally stoke the fear of job loss to keep employees on their toes. Companies, Welch maintained, should lay off ten percent of their workforce year after year to "improve performance"—an insecurity-producing tactic used on middle management as readily as on blue-collar workers.[35] In 2022, *Fortune* reported that Meta CEO and Facebook founder Mark Zuckerberg told his staff he was "turning up the heat" to weed out underperformers: "You might decide this place isn't for you, and that's okay with me."[36] With the days of lifetime employment and good pensions long gone, well-paid white-collar workers can't afford to rest unless they want to risk being laid off. And they literally can't rest, either. One study of Canadian professionals found 43 percent reporting that a lack of employment stability keeps them up at night.[37]

Official monetary policy in the US and Canada adds to the pressure. While the central banks of both countries have dual mandates to promote maximum or full employment and fight inflation, worker insecurity remains a pillar of both countries' economic policies, and secure jobs a pipe dream.[38] In the 1990s, Alan Greenspan, the influential long-serving head of the US Federal Reserve, made job insecurity an official matter of Fed policy, enthusiastically noting that it checked wage growth. A 1997 article in the *New York Times* summarized his remarks to Congress: "Workers have been too worried about keeping their jobs to push for higher wages," he said, "and this has been sufficient to hold down inflation without the added restraint of higher interest rates." The article added that it wasn't enough for job insecurity to exist—it has to be getting worse in order to ensure a fearful working population. "Once it levels off, and workers become accustomed to their new level of uncertainty, their confidence may revive and the upward pressure on wages resume."[39]

Greenspan's commentary echoed a memo written by Janet Yellen, who in 2021 was appointed secretary of the US Treasury by President Joe Biden. Writing in 1996, she approvingly reported that "job insecurity produces productivity-enhancing changes in workers' behaviour, mitigating the need for alternative controls." In other words, companies could get away with paying non-competitive wages without enduring what she called "worker backlash"—people shirking on the job. "Presumably," Yellen continued, "increased insecurity makes workers more fearful of unemployment, more desirous of pleasing their employers through improved performance and higher effort, and less apt to quit in search of alternative work."[40]

With her mention of "worker backlash," Yellen presaged the phenomenon more recently dubbed "quiet quitting," a phrase that includes both outright resignations and a more low-key refusal to go above and beyond formal work requirements—that is to say, shirking.[41] Boosted by pandemic assistance programs and an abundance of jobs as economies reopened after Covid-19 lockdowns, people felt less pressure to please and more emboldened to seek out better compensation and treatment, even as rates of inflation and costs of groceries, gas, and rent spiked. Emergency welfare measures had an immediate and remarkable impact: the Canada Emergency Response Benefit (CERB) provided millions who had lost work with a humble $2,000 a month, leading to an almost 20 percent drop in overall poverty while reducing child poverty by an astonishing 40 percent. In the US, the combination of stimulus cheques, expanded unemployment programs, and child tax credits prevented wide-scale destitution and caused child poverty to reach a record low.[42]

As a result of this sudden increase in federal income support, millions of people—including my sister—felt materially secure enough to leave jobs where they felt disrespected, abused, unhappy, bored, underpaid, or unable to advance, leading to a historic "quit rate."[43] Employers were less than thrilled. The *Financial Post* reported in late 2022 that the actions of a newly "empowered" workforce had caused "a growing sense of anxiety among bosses."[44] Part of capitalism's power has always been the insecurity induced by the pink slip, and quiet quitting was a sign that fear was diminishing.

Central banks stepped in to strengthen and secure the bosses' hand by escalating the threat of wagelessness. Citing inflation and plentiful job vacancies, US Federal Reserve chair Jerome Powell declared a need to "get wages down."[45] *Bloomberg*, hardly an ally of the working class, published a story with the headline "Fed's Inflation Battle to Strip Workers of Rare Bargaining Power." Instead of letting bosses bend to worker demands for modest concessions—raises, more humane hours and management, and maybe sick leave or remote work options—Powell moved to cool off what he called an "overheated" labour market by increasing interest rates, the tool central banks use when they want to increase unemployment and one known to increase the likelihood of a recession. In early 2023, Powell announced that he was considering additional hikes that could put two million people out of work.[46] Such "an outcome," *Bloomberg* reported, "would allow companies to revert to old habits of using job insecurity to hold down wages and rebuff workers pressing for better conditions."[47]

The Bank of Canada took a similar tack, ignoring the recessionary risks posed by higher rates. In a report on monetary policy released in July 2022, the bank warned repeatedly of a "wage-price spiral," essentially blaming rising prices on rising wages—even though wages were not keeping up with inflation, which meant that ordinary workers, despite their gains, were still losing ground.[48] In remarks made later that year, Tiff Macklem, governor of the Bank of Canada, reiterated the report's core argument. Inflation, he said, was being caused by an "increasingly tight labour market," and he described the required correction as restoring "labour market balance" by decreasing workers' bargaining power. While he acknowledged that the process of increasing rates would not be "painless," he emphasized that it would bring prices down, including the price of labour—in other words, it would suppress wages by making job insecurity so intense that employees would stop asking for more.[49]

Eight hundred years after the privatization of the English commons commenced, the old logic of enclosure reverberates from the current centres of government and high finance as they impose insecurity on ordinary people for the benefit of current and future employers. Governments shut down the pandemic assistance programs as quickly as they had started up—not because these programs were too costly or ineffective but because the material security they provided was a threat to the economic status quo, perhaps a greater threat than Covid-19 itself. Large corporations, meanwhile, have managed to mostly insulate themselves from insecurity, revelling in the image of risk-taking entrepreneurialism as they foist instability on others. A good worker remains an insecure worker, even at a moment when corporate profits break records: in 2022, after-tax profits were the highest percentage of Canada's GDP they have ever been, with margins climbing sky high in the US as well.[50] And yet those who seem to be winning are setting themselves up to lose. In the long run, no one is safe from this ravenous, growth-obsessed approach. Insecurity gnaws at the people on the very top, too.

THE POWERFUL HAVE NEVER wanted the masses to be secure. In the Middle Ages, Christian thinkers denounced security as a sin and an insult to God—"perverse security," as one seventeenth-century theologian memorably called it.[51] And as we've seen, insecurity has long been viewed as a useful mechanism to incentivize people to perform or suffer the consequences. "Along with the carrot of pecuniary reward must go the stick of personal economic disaster," John Kenneth Galbraith observed.[52] Manufactured insecurity reflects a cynical theory of human motivation, one that says people will work only under the threat of duress, not from an intrinsic desire to create, collaborate, and care for one another. Insecurity goads us to keep working, earning, and craving—craving money, material goods, prestige, and more, more, more.

But what is it, exactly, that we really need more of? In a world beset by staggering inequality, it is easy to see what poor people lack—cash, most obviously, and thus the means to acquire basic necessities. But we should also remember those ineffable and invaluable things that all human beings need and seek—connection, camaraderie, meaning, purpose, contentment, safety, self-esteem, respect. These are things that our highly competitive society makes artificially scarce, despite the fact they don't actually have to be in short supply. Indeed, far from being zero-sum, these immaterial things become more abundant the more people use them. If we're going to disentangle the insecurities we face today—distinguishing the manufactured insecurity of capitalism and the existential insecurity that is Cura's gift—in order to alleviate what unnecessary suffering we can, we must recognize the trick being played on us. Manufactured insecurity encourages us to amass money and objects as surrogates for the kinds of security that cannot actually be commodified, the kind of security we can find only in concert with others.

Accumulation has many perils beyond the spiritual emptiness we associate with materialism and the mountains of trash piling up in our landfills and oceans. The utilitarian philosopher Jeremy Bentham wrote about the "fear of losing" and how wealth itself becomes a source of worry. Assets must be guarded and grown, after all, lest fortunes and reputations be diminished or lost. "When insecurity reaches a certain point, the fear of losing prevents us from enjoying what we possess already. The care of preserving condemns us to a thousand sad and painful precautions, which yet are always liable to fail of their end," he wrote in *Theory of Legislation*, first published in 1802.[53] He was referring to money and objects, which can be ported away by thieves, but he could also have been talking about status, which is impossible to steal yet is never secure. In a world of economic extremes, even the most prosperous are afraid of losing rank, of falling in both net worth and self-worth. It is this insecurity that keeps them scrambling ever upward.

Economists call this "fractal inequality." The person who is in debt looks to the person with zero dollars, who looks to the person making fifty grand, who looks to the person who makes six figures, who looks to the person making half a million dollars, who looks to the person who has a million dollars in the bank, who looks to the person with twice as many assets, and on and on it goes. In her 2017 book *Uneasy Street: The Anxieties of Affluence*, sociologist Rachel Sherman studied fifty high-net-worth individuals. All of them avoided describing themselves as "rich" or "upper class"; despite the fact that they were firmly part of the top 1 percent or 2 percent, they described themselves as comfortably in the "middle." They were looking up, at the members of the .01 percent, and so saw themselves as comparatively lacking.[54]

At a recent party at a penthouse apartment in Manhattan, I met a woman who spoke of being caught in the fractal's vertiginous snare. I was there making a pitch to potential donors on behalf of an independent magazine. It was clear, simply from her presence, that she had means—a fact she confessed she would normally take pains to hide. When I asked what had brought her to the event, she told me she had joined a network of wealthy people who pool their funds to support social justice causes. She sought the group out after receiving a substantial inheritance—her father had been a newspaper magnate in the Midwest. Initially she had been overwhelmed by her windfall, a trust fund of money she had done nothing to earn. She wanted to be emboldened to give a good portion away. But the main effect of coming to know other wealthy people, she told me, was that she felt poor and insecure in comparison.

Her good fortune suddenly paled next to the tens and hundreds of millions, even billions, others had.

This sense of not having enough, even when you objectively have a lot, is not simply a spontaneous reaction to seeing others with more, a kind of lizard-brained lust. It is upheld as the only rational way to behave in an insecure and risk-filled world. One of my younger friends also inherited substantial wealth. When he advocated for liquidating his share of the family's portfolio, he found himself stymied by a battalion of financial advisors—what Chuck Collins, an heir to the Oscar Mayer fortune, calls the "wealth defence industry."[55] For obviously self-interested reasons, the advisors were dead set against the idea of giving away anything more than a portion of the earned interest. My friend's parents were also opposed, invoking the threat of a global recession or unexpected illness. The cost of wealth maintenance is cognitive dissonance: these are people who purport to hold progressive ideals while benefiting from a highly regressive tax code that they find morally objectionable. (In Canada, lax codes mean billionaires can pass their fortunes to their children essentially tax-free; America's billionaires use a variety of accounting tricks to achieve the same result.) Our possessions, monetary and otherwise, have a way of possessing us and turning us into people we may not actually want to be. As Diogenes the Cynic, the former-slave-turned-philosopher, observed two thousand years ago, "A man keeps and feeds a lion; the lion owns a man."[56]

Entranced by the idea that the sky is wealth's limit, the commoner's sense of feeling secure, or even prosperous, with just "enough" is shocking by today's standards, but it's especially scandalous to the landlord class. Left unchecked—or rather, untaxed—the fractal's spiral never ends, as Silicon Valley's parade of billionaires jockeying for fame and dominance makes clear. Like a modern King Midas who hasn't yet realized he's cursed, Elon Musk chased wealth, investing in electric vehicles and rocket ships, until he became, fleetingly, the richest man on the planet, a coveted position that he lost when his compulsive online displays of arrogance and bigotry caused the value of his various companies and personal net worth to suddenly plummet by a record-breaking $200 billion.[57] "Just a reminder that money will never buy your way out of insecurity," New York Representative Alexandria Ocasio-Cortez, a frequent target of Musk's ire, tweeted in response to his antics.[58]

If Musk can't buy his way out of bad feelings, what hope do the rest of us have? No wonder a growing number of people the world over report feeling profoundly distressed, including a significant portion of the well-off. According to a 2022 Gallup survey focused on the emotional lives of 150,000 people in over 140 countries, "anger, stress, sadness, physical pain and worry" have reached a new global high.[59] The same year, another survey found half of Canadians reporting that their financial woes had recently kept them up at night, while nearly 80 percent of Americans say they are worried about their economic well-being.[60] Throughout the Western world, people of all ages and class backgrounds are experiencing spiking instances of anxiety and depression, problems Covid-19 and the climate emergency have worsened. In a 2021 *Lancet* article, experts estimated a nearly 30 percent rise in cases of major depressive disorder and a 25 percent rise in cases of anxiety disorder globally due to the virus.[61] A recent survey of the attitudes of more than ten thousand individuals in ten countries found that "distress about climate change is associated with young people perceiving that they have no future."[62] Rising generations increasingly sense they've inherited a world spinning out of control.

Despite the strong correlation between insecurity and physical and psychological health, we must remember that insecurity is not a mental illness or a diagnosable disorder—this isn't a problem that can be identified or cured by physicians alone. While insecurity can lead to very real ailments and aggravate certain medical conditions, it is not, in itself, a disease.

Experiencing insecurity is a normal and understandable reaction to difficult circumstances. This means that changing people's circumstances—instead of just trying to change their minds or how they feel—could go a long way toward easing people's suffering. Providing people with stable and meaningful work, adequate shelter, healthy food, and old-age supports would relieve incalculable stress. Similarly, reducing climate anxiety requires climate action, not only prescribing antidepressants to anguished kids.

In the absence of such societal shifts and more substantial welfare support, and as formerly stable communities fragment and scatter, we are left to pursue security on our own—an often fraught and self-defeating proposition. The main mechanisms by which we are told to gain security for ourselves—making money, buying property, earning degrees, saving for retirement—often involve being invested in systems that rarely provide the stability we desire and often make other people more precarious, whether by poisoning the planet we all depend on or fostering feelings of insecurity in the pursuit of profit. Across disparate fields, from housing and pensions to the wellness and beauty industries to the education and energy sectors to policing and the military, the systems that promise us security often, in fact, undermine it. And so the quest for security becomes a kind of roundabout suicide pact.

If that metaphor seems overwrought, consider the example of the American love of handguns, which takes the logic of the individual-security mindset to a tragic extreme. Often purchased to safeguard a person and their property from intruders and other threats, the weapon itself becomes a hazard, harming the very people it is supposed to protect. A landmark 2022 study published in the *Annals of Internal Medicine* that looked at six hundred thousand California households found zero evidence of any kind of protective effects of gun ownership and ample evidence of risks.[63] People who live with handgun owners, particularly if these people are women, have a much higher rate of being fatally shot by an intimate partner than those who do not. Researchers have found that handgun ownership offers no measurable protection against being killed at home by a stranger, yet substantially increases the likelihood of dying in a domestic violence incident or by suicide.[64]

The pursuit of security can also backfire at the geopolitical level, where the risks are far more severe. Think of the Cold War, with its decades-long obsession with enemies both domestic and foreign, which inspired anti-communist witch hunts that destroyed thousands of lives and wars that left millions dead across the world. Or the advent and proliferation of nuclear weapons, driven by the logic of Mutually Assured Destruction as a deterrence strategy. In early 2023, as the conflict in Ukraine escalated, veiled threats from Russia caused the Bulletin of the Atomic Scientists to warn that annihilation was more imminent than it had been since the close of World War II.[65] International relations scholars call this conundrum the "security paradox," which is an all too common absurdity that unfurls whenever attempts to increase one's own security lead to the heightened insecurity of other actors, stimulating strong counterreactions that leave everybody worse off in the end.[66]

The fact that I spent my intellectually formative years under the shadow of the War on Terror may explain why

the security paradox speaks to me—and why the word
security, despite my commitment to rethinking it here,
still gives me pause. I was in Lower Manhattan the day
the Twin Towers fell, and watched, mouth agape, as the
dust clouds rose skyward and the city shut down in
shock. The powers that be seized that moment of insecurity, of profound fear and grief, to wage illegal and
inhumane wars in Afghanistan and Iraq that ultimately
killed more than nine hundred thousand people and displaced many millions more—all while instructing the
public to sacrifice civil liberties, democratic accountabil-
ity, and moral integrity at security's altar.[67]

A few months after the World Trade Center attack, I
got a job associate-producing a documentary about the
individuals and families trapped in the War on Terror's
dragnet. Despite my being twenty-one and lacking any
prior journalistic experience, it fell to me to find potential subjects and convince them to share their trauma
publicly for what we hoped would be the greater good.
And so I found myself sitting in living rooms and
standing outside mosques, meeting with people who
had been locked up and the loved ones of those still
being held in detention. More than five thousand Arab
American citizens and residents were detained indefi-
nitely in abrogation of their civil liberties in the name
of national security. Detainees were subject to arbitrary arrest, deportation, and solitary confinement. A
man told me how he found himself transported into a
Kafkaesque nightmare after what first appeared to be a

routine traffic stop; another spoke of being kept alone in his cell with the fluorescent lights on twenty-four hours a day. These encounters and others are why, at the time, I was skeptical of the word *security*, which gave cover to racism, nationalism, and war profiteering. September 11 and its aftermath taught me that we always must ask: Security of what? For whom? At what cost?

At the time, I did not realize this trade-off between liberty and security was a centuries-old motif, one brought to us initially, or at least most influentially, by the philosopher Thomas Hobbes. His book *Leviathan*, published in 1651, has been pivotal in shaping our modern conceptions of security, shifting the dominant understanding away from that Stoic concern with mental calm and toward the need for physical security and a strong centralized state. Personal safety, Hobbes insisted, can only be achieved by forfeiting personal freedom and submitting completely to an authoritarian ruler or sovereign who will protect us. The alternative is to exist in a brutal "state of nature" and perpetual war of all against all. "The cause of men's fear of each other lies partly in their natural equality, partly in their willingness to hurt each other. Hence, we cannot expect security from others or assure it to ourselves."[68] Hobbes was notoriously cynical about human nature and an apologist for absolutist monarchy, but his contention that political communities are essential to security, and that security can only be achieved collectively, holds true. We will not become more secure if we go it alone.

Fortunately, instead of the Leviathan Hobbes envisioned, modern states are supposed to provide us security as a matter of democratic right—a right we do not have to sacrifice any of our civil liberties to receive. And yet few people likely realize that we are all legally entitled to security, no matter where we live. The Universal Declaration of Human Rights is unambiguous: "Everyone has the right to life, liberty and security of person" as well as "the right to security in the event of unemployment, sickness, disability, widowhood, old age or other lack of livelihood" in circumstances beyond our control,[69] The International Covenant on Economic, Social and Cultural Rights further emphasizes our right to security, including the basic means of survival such as food, clothing, and housing, while the United Nations Declaration on the Rights of Indigenous Peoples, which Canada ratified as law in 2021, pledges that Indigenous individuals have "the rights to life, physical and mental integrity, liberty and security of person" in addition to "the collective right to live in freedom, peace and security as distinct peoples."[70]

The concept of being secure also runs through a good number of domestic constitutions, including those of South Africa, Jamaica, the United States, and Canada. As Section 7 of the Canadian Charter of Rights Freedoms proclaims: "Everyone has the right to life, liberty and security of the person and the right not to be deprived thereof except in accordance with the principles of fundamental justice"—a sentence ripe for philosophical interpretation and, I believe, laden with political potential.[71] This right to security, as we'll explore in the next chapter, has its roots in the long struggle over the commons and the principle of material provision for all. In Canadian jurisprudence today, security is explicitly understood to have physical and psychological dimensions, and there is a strong case to be made that it should include a right to a healthy environment, too.

As a dedicated organizer, I'm struck by how rarely this legal entitlement to security is mentioned or discussed. Perhaps it's because the incongruity between the principles on the page and the reality of our day-to-day lives is too much to bear; it feels like an impossible dream. Political types like myself tend to talk far more about the principles of freedom, equality, and democracy than security, and I've come to believe this is a strategic mistake. Security, particularly the material security of reliable access to food, water, shelter, medical care, welfare, protection from violence, and a habitable environment, must be understood as foundational to freedom, equality, and democracy, not an afterthought. Contra Hobbes, freedom does not exist in opposition to security but, rather, is one of material security's most important rewards. The security of having our needs met allows us to have real autonomy and creative agency in the world.

· · ·

IS INSECURITY SOMETHING WE always need to flee? Is
security something we should always chase? We need
to think carefully about the patterns we're stuck in and
the options before us—and then proceed with care.
Insecurity and misguided pursuits of security define
and help drive so many of the problems that plague
us today: the concentration of wealth and poverty, crises of health care and housing, looming environmental
calamity, pandemic and climate denial, racist policing,
and the revival of fascism.

To use a phrase coined by the Zen-influenced writer
Alan Watts, I believe there is a "wisdom of insecurity"
worth trying to access. Our existential insecurity,
our inevitable fears and anxieties, can be invaluable,
if challenging, teachers. But where Watts focuses on
individual awareness and acceptance, my position—
organizer that I am—is that we need to change our
outlook so that we can work together to change our
circumstances. Security is not something that we can
achieve heroically or stoically through consumption
or recycling, education, medicine, or mindfulness. We
cannot breathe our way out of our thorny social problems, nor can we amass enough wealth to wholly buffer
ourselves from them; social media sabbaths, however
appealing and temporarily soothing, do nothing to
change the insecurity-generating logic of the algorithms that deliver us content. These strategies all leave
us embedded in systems designed to generate and profit
from the very insecurities we hope to escape.

Recognizing these pitfalls—and the ways insecurity impels us to grasp for security—doesn't mean I think people are trapped or that we are automatons lacking free will, passively reacting to external forces. On the contrary, acknowledging our circumstances and how they shape us can be a catalyst to awareness and action. It can make us more empathetic by helping us understand that, unlike in the simplistic children's fables, the problem with people is rarely greed alone. Insecurity, particularly its manufactured variety, is what compels bosses to squeeze their workers, pushes self-professed progressives to engage in legal tax evasion, drives billionaires to continue competing, and coerces workers to stay in jobs that underpay and mistreat them.

Insecurity, both as a feeling and as a lived material experience, is what keeps the vast majority of people scurrying to catch up. The command to live life according to market priorities is so persuasive precisely because it is coupled with threats—threats of unemployment, destitution, shame, loss of status, and respect. Rapid economic changes and new technologies have multiplied our insecurities while also raising our expectations, increasing the risks of failure as a result. We follow the prescribed course—work, consume, save, strive—because we want to make our lives better, which is not the same thing as being selfish. In the absence of new pathways to security, we can only continue along the old routes, even as they are collapsing beneath our feet.

Rather than something to pathologize, I want us to see insecurity as an opportunity—an opportunity to come together and create alternative routes and more fulfilling destinations. An ethic of insecurity can provide a powerful moral framework to help us reimagine and reorganize our social and economic systems. The simple recognition of our mutual vulnerability—of the fact that we all need and deserve care throughout our lives—has potentially revolutionary implications. Indignation at the way insecurity is fostered and exploited under capitalism can help strengthen existing movements and galvanize new ones, coalescing powerful coalitions with the capacity to expand and fight for collective forms of security based in compassion and concern instead of desperation and fear. This communal and collaborative form of security is not something we have to create from scratch. It is here now, every time we watch out for each other: when we help and protect vulnerable friends and neighbours; when we organize against oppression and dispossession; when we resist the erosion of the welfare state; when we fight the companies contaminating air and water and encouraging self-loathing and shame. Security, in these instances, is both noun and verb, a web of material supports and social relationships. It is the security of the commons, updated for a modern age.

This is Cura's gift. Insecurity is what makes us human, and it is also what allows us to connect and change. "Nothing in Nature 'becomes itself' without being vulnerable," writes physician Gabor Maté in *The Myth of Normal*. "The mightiest tree's growth requires soft and supple shoots, just as the hardest-shelled crustaceans must first molt and become soft."[72] There is no growth, he observes, without emotional vulnerability. While Maté is speaking of individuals, the same also applies to societies. Recognizing our shared existential insecurity, and understanding how it is currently used against us, can be a first step toward creating solidarity. Solidarity, in the end, is one of the most important forms of security we can possess—the security of confronting our shared predicament as humans on this planet in crisis, together.

CHAPTER 2

BARONS OR COMMONERS?

ON A JUNE DAY in 1215, an angry King John had no choice but to bow to a rebellion organized by his barons. A notoriously incompetent, treacherous, and violent ruler, John's name today is often followed by the epithet "the worst king." This seems an accurate assessment: John's exploitation of his feudal rights and taxation powers, which he employed to fund doomed military ventures, pushed England's aristocrats to the brink. They wanted King John off their backs, their property returned, and a restoration of their privileges. Gathered in mutiny in Runnymede Field, a large meadow twenty miles west of central London, the barons demanded a drastic change in government. But this was no democratic rebellion. Incensed at their ill treatment, the barons withdrew their fealty in a kind of upper-class strike, proposing new limits on the monarch's power. These were detailed in a royal declaration of rights and freedoms, a text known to us as the Magna Carta—the

Great Charter. Since a king without loyal subjects cannot rule, his majesty reluctantly agreed to its terms.

The Magna Carta contained sixty-three clauses, the majority of which are confounding or irrelevant to the modern reader ("No town or person shall be forced to build bridges over rivers except those with an ancient obligation to do so."). But Clauses 39 and 40 became legendary and remain lucid and resonant. They contain the famous phrases "To no one will we sell, to no one deny or delay right or justice" and "No free man shall be arrested or imprisoned ... except by the lawful judgment of his peers or by the law of the land." These clauses are said to have helped establish the legal concept of due process. Most important of all, as every history textbook now states, the Magna Carta was extraordinary for arguing that the king was not above the law and that governments need to be restrained. The barons, in this conventional telling, are heroes for fighting a tyrannical king, and they did indeed accomplish something revolutionary. Claiming that citizens need protection from their own sovereign introduces a central idea of democratic governance: the power of the state must be checked for the population to be secure.

Predictably, monarchs despised this idea. King John had the charter nullified the first chance he got, aided by Pope Innocent III, another unsavoury thirteenth-century character. Together they engineered a papal bull that declared the Magna Carta "null and void of all validity for ever," and pronounced the idea that people needed security from an overweening sovereign to be "illegal, unjust, harmful to royal rights and shameful to the English people."[1]

Over the years, decades, and then centuries, the Magna Carta faded in and out of fashion, forgotten or suppressed by the powerful, only to be rediscovered by those looking to break free of monarchical power. In the 1620s, the famed legal theorist Sir Edward Coke, then speaker of the British House of Commons, helped usher in the English Revolution of the 1640s with his framing of the Petition of Right, which extended the principles of the Magna Carta for a new age. From there, its ideas drifted across the ocean, where the Magna Carta became a tool of colonial independence. The authors of the US Bill of Rights—the first ten amendments to the American Constitution—found inspiration in the charter's principles as they sought to build a government that could guard citizens against state tyranny, a kind of anti-government government. The Magna Carta directly influenced the American amendments guaranteeing the right to a jury trial and due process, as well as the right "of the people to be secure in their persons, houses, papers, and effects, against unreasonable searches and seizures."

It is this medieval document, alternately repressed and rediscovered, that we today claim as the foundation of our modern democratic societies; as the Canadian Supreme Court put it in 1998, "The evolution of our democratic tradition can be traced back to

Magna Carta."[2] It is also an early enumeration of what we now call human rights. Most notably, for our purposes, many experts regard it as the basis of the right to security, a guarantee encoded in a range of international and domestic treaties, covenants, and constitutions.[3] Today, we rarely think of ourselves as possessing a right to security—compared to, say, the right to free expression or freedom of religion or equal protection before the law—but we do. And the fact that we do, as well as what this evocative and ambiguous right might mean for our present and future, is profoundly shaped by this seemingly remote history I have just sketched, and by what we emphasize and what we leave out.

This version of the story of the Magna Carta—in which barons revolt against an abusive ruler—is not the only one we can tell. There's another tale, told less often and far less known, also worth recounting. The barons, it turns out, were not the only group incensed at King John. Commoners were angry, too, and the rights the Magna Carta is now famous for—the right to be protected from the king's tyranny—were paired with rights to subsistence and security that benefited the peasantry. Granting the commoners' rights to material livelihood helped concretize the Great Charter's revolutionary promise. Critically, it introduced a second central idea of democratic governance: the state must provide for its citizens in order for the population to be secure. Yet this second idea has been mostly erased from the illustrious history of the Magna Carta and from the understanding of a right to security that prevails in legal circles today.

The commoners had plenty of reasons to be aggrieved. In thirteenth-century England, almost one-third of the country was designated as "forest," a legal term that described land enclosed for royal use and governed by Forest Law, a system that hoarded natural resources for the crown. As time went on, more and more territory was privatized by royal decree, making it harder for regular people to survive—a prelude to the systematic enclosure of the commons four hundred years later as market capitalism ascended. Like rulers before him, King John and his enforcers capriciously infringed on peasants' customary rights to subsistence: rights to fish in the streams and let their animals forage and graze; to gather nuts, berries, honey, kindling, and herbs for medicine. Fences and hedges kept them out of land they did not own outright but had long shared and used and even lived upon. The king's adjuncts charged the needy fees to enter the woods, and fined or killed trespassers without recourse or remorse. It is no surprise that tales of the folk hero Robin Hood, living freely with a band of rebels in Sherwood Forest and thwarting the foresters and the local sheriff, first appeared in these years.

This is why, in addition to protecting the barons' interests, the Magna Carta also addressed the commoners' growing discontent. Consider Clause 47: "All forests that have been created in our reign shall at once be disafforested. River-banks that have been enclosed in our reign shall be treated similarly." And Clause 48: "All evil customs relating to forests and warrens, foresters, warreners, sheriffs and their servants, or river-banks and their wardens, are at once to be investigated in every county by twelve sworn knights of the county, and within forty days of their enquiry the evil customs are to be abolished completely and irrevocably." In plain speak: the misuse of Forest Law by the king and his minions will cease, and the forests and river-banks shall be held in common once again.[4]

In 1217, seeking to consolidate political support, John's young son Henry III, under the guidance of his regency, reissued the Magna Carta alongside a new companion document, the so-called Charter of the Forest. This addition expanded on the original Magna Carta's mention of "evil customs" and clarified the political remedies, including the restoration of a significant portion of royal forests back to the commons.[5] It was, in a sense, an early example of reparations, for it returned property that had been stolen, while also providing the peasantry an affirmative right *to* something: the security that access to the commons provided. By detailing the right to the woods, the Charter of the Forest offered commoners assurance that they could sustain themselves without fear of being drawn and quartered, or, in the charter's words, without losing their "life or suffer[ing] ... amputation."[6] McGill University law professor Pearl Eliadis described it to me as the "bread and butter charter" because it secured the livelihoods of vulnerable villagers and not only their limbs.

When I asked my friend Peter Linebaugh, one of the foremost historians of the commons, about this period, he told me that the Magna Carta and the Charter of the Forest were twin documents, often read aloud together in public spaces because the vast majority of people were illiterate.[7] Sir Edward Coke, for example, called them the "Charters of England's Liberties"; later, the famed British jurist William Blackstone spoke of the "two sacred charters."

And yet we have forgotten this pairing. In 2015, when the eight hundredth anniversary of the Magna Carta was marked by a raft of celebratory museum exhibitions and media coverage across the English-speaking world, there were virtually no mentions of the Charter of the Forest—and certainly no continued assertion of collective commoning rights. Nor was there a separate eight-hundredth-anniversary celebration for the Charter of the Forest two years later. For the Magna Carta to take on its modern form as the protector of individual and not communal liberties, it had to be severed from its companion. By the early twenty-first century, the cleavage was complete.

Why this rupture? The answer, simply stated, is that the Charter of the Forest provided material security for all: it limited private property rights, halted privatization, and returned land for common use. This makes it deeply unsettling to today's capitalist democracies and generally reviled by the business interests that currently reign, for it implies rights not only to be protected *from* something—tyrannical state power—but the right *to* something—a good life supported by the state.

Political theorists describe this as the difference between negative rights and positive rights, or rights that shield you from threats versus rights that grant you what you need. Both kinds of rights are essential to a free society; that is, we need the Magna Carta and the Charter of the Forest conjointly. But their respective urgency is class-based. If you are a baron, you want to be able to hunt in the woods without being charged a hefty fee, and to be free to exploit the peasants who dwell in your fiefdom—you just need the king off your back. You are content, in other words, with negative rights. If you are a commoner, though, what you need above all is the right to access land you can farm, fuel to heat your home, and confidence you won't be displaced—the positive right, in essence, to the means of survival and a dignified life. When we shift our perspective and view this history through the lens of the commoners, instead of the barons, we can see that the right to forage in the forest was inseparable from the right to not be mutilated while doing so. Then as now, a secure existence requires both provision and protection, subsistence and safety, in equal measure.

Today we revere the Magna Carta but ignore the Forest Charter, despite the fact it remained in force far longer than its more fabled counterpart, lasting for centuries because peasants fought to defend their commoning rights and resist enclosure as best they could. Telling the story from the barons' point of view obscures the positive rights these entwined documents were written to uphold, leaving us with a depleted and deficient conception of security and an underestimation of the collective action it takes to make laws and policies responsive to our shared interests. The question before us, then, and the challenge I want to pose, is whether we will continue to accept this division. Will we remember—or misremember—security in a limited and defensive way, as the kind of security of private property and due process won by the barons in the form of negative rights? Or can we also recognize it as something more substantive—as the material security embodied in the peasantry's rights to the commons?

What follows is an argument for recovering and re-energizing the positive conception of security found in the combination of the Magna Carta and the Charter of the Forest, for repairing the split that has persisted for far too long. We need the right to things, not just protection from threats. It is not enough to be granted the right not to be abused by our governments without the corresponding right to receive assistance; not enough to possess civil and political rights without social and economic ones as well. By exploring the examples of health care and housing, I hope to reveal the perils of taking a purely negative approach, a paradigm that compels us to seek security through individualistic, market-driven mechanisms that actually perpetuate mass insecurity in the short and long terms. By showing how we've missed past opportunities to embrace a more expansive conception of security, I also aim to show where these opportunities present themselves today and to encourage us to seize them. The question before us, really, is quite simple: Do we see ourselves as barons or commoners?

IN TODAY'S WORLD IT can be hard to tell, largely because we are encouraged to see ourselves as barons-to-be. Given the underfunded and shrinking state of many public services, the most obvious path to security for ordinary people is through the marketplace. Security, crudely put, is a function of wealth: the resources to rent or purchase property, to buy food and necessities, to pay for education, to invest for retirement, and all the rest. From this vantage point, it makes a certain kind of sense to guard what we possess, and it can seem rational to view the state as a threat and taxation as a form of theft—in other words, to adopt the anti-government framework of the barons. This blinkered perspective suits society's real barons just fine; it's the preferred approach of high-flying financiers and corporate CEOS. The high and mighty have long perceived a secure population as a threat, which is why they have worked so relentlessly to shrink the social safety net and make competition more intense. The last thing the powerful want to see is a revival of the idea found in the Charter of the Forest: a robust right to the material security of the commons for all. Such a guarantee would make it harder to manufacture the insecurity that capitalism relies on—insecurity that hounds everyone, not only the poorest among us. If we could rely on the security of the commons, we wouldn't need to aspire to be barons anymore.

A revival of the commoners' perspective is long overdue. Updated for our present age, the ancient idea of the right to the commons embraces security not as any one single thing, but rather as a bundle of entitlements that, together, help ensure individual and collective well-being. Security, in this holistic understanding, includes civil and political rights (negative rights) as well as their economic and social counterparts (positive rights): the right to a decent home; to medical and mental health care; to education; to support in disability and old age; to meaningful and remunerative work; to a healthy and habitable environment, and so forth. These are the modern equivalents of the medieval rights detailed in the Forest Charter: to herbage (grass for grazing sheep and cattle), pannage (sustenance for pigs), turbary (peat fuel from a bog), and estovers (kindling).

This linking of positive and negative liberties is neither an archaic or nostalgic ideal, nor some starry-eyed distant possibility. It is, in fact, woven into the fabric of the Universal Declaration of Human Rights. The final draft of the Declaration, crafted in the wake of the catastrophe of the Second World War and formally adopted in 1948, uses the word *security* three times:

Article 3: "Everyone has the right to life, liberty and security of person."

Article 22: "Everyone, as a member of society, has the right to social security and is entitled to realization ... of the economic, social and cultural rights indispensable for his dignity and the free development of his personality."

Article 25: "Everyone has the right to a standard of living adequate for the health and well-being of himself and of his family, including food, clothing, housing and medical care and necessary social services, and the right to security in the event of unemployment, sickness, disability, widowhood, old age or other lack of livelihood in circumstances beyond his control."

These rights, of course, have not been realized. Despite possessing such entitlements on paper, we continue to live amid pervasive and persistent insecurity. Governments near and far commit heinous acts of violence against their citizens; billions of people can barely provide for themselves, if at all. An estimated 1.8

billion people worldwide are homeless or live in grossly inadequate housing, lacking basic services including electricity, water, and sanitation.[8] Wars rage, people starve, police kill, and the climate burns. And as our societies grow more deeply unequal and our environment collapses, even the comparatively affluent never feel wholly secure.

This stark disparity between promises and reality explains why, particularly if you travel in left-wing circles, you may be familiar with the quip that the powerful decided the poor could have rights when they realized that rights were useless. Or, as a friend of mine always says, "We don't need rights, we need things!"

I take her point, but my perpetual retort is that we need both. As an organizer, I'd always rather have legal rights, particularly the right to the thing I'm fighting for, than have no rights at all. Even when they appear to be empty promises, these entitlements enable us to mount legal challenges, highlight government failures, and bring more people more easily into a fight to match words with deeds. The existence and exercise of rights means that more of us grow up believing that universal goods like freedom and material security belong to us by birth, and will for generations to come. The bailiff looking the other way as you gather herbs in the king's woods is a privilege; knowing that you can continue to do so, and that your children and grandchildren will be able to do so as well, is a right, also often referred to as a guarantee.

When we talk about insecurity and security, we are often talking about the future; we anticipate what might occur beyond the here and now. The philosopher Jeremy Bentham (who happened to be an early critic of the idea that there were inalienable natural rights, which he famously derided as "nonsense on stilts"), recognized the importance of duration in his reflections on the relationship between security, the law, and human happiness. For Bentham, a "disposition to look forward" enables our species to transform discrete moments of our lives into a cohesive narrative, linking past, present, and future. "The sensibility of the individual is prolonged through all the links of this chain," Bentham explained. What he called the "principle of security" helps our experiences coalesce, making it more likely that events will conform to our expectations.[9] In the absence of security, we unravel; the threads connecting what has happened to what will happen come undone.

This is why *food insecurity, housing insecurity, health insecurity,* and *economic insecurity* are useful terms. They may sound euphemistic—food insecurity might seem less urgent and visceral than "hunger," and housing insecurity less pressing a crisis than "homelessness"—but adding the modifier *insecurity* emphasizes the importance of time and the fact that human beings require much more than having our immediate needs met. You may have a meal on the table or a fridge full of groceries, but that does not mean you are confident the same will hold true tomorrow, or next month, or six months hence. Likewise, you might presently have a roof over your head, but you are not securely housed if you are a month or two from not being able to pay your rent or mortgage; staying somewhere unsafe or unhealthy; facing the prospect of eviction or foreclosure; suffering discrimination from landlords for your race or sexuality; or more than likely to be pushed out of your neighbourhood when your lease ends. Security means having some assurance of future stability and the ability to plan ahead.

The Universal Declaration for Human Rights and its predecessors, the Magna Carta and the Forest Charter, all contain this richer and more substantive idea of security. Should we work together and bring it back to life, our present-day selves would be better protected. Our future selves would be, too. Security could cease to be a conservative concept aimed at fortifying one's self and possessions against a hostile state and instead become a progressive principle, one that can help us make society more equitable and just. Thanks to generations past, the groundwork for this struggle has already been laid—despite the opposing efforts of those who want only the baron's negative conception of security to have sway.

IN WORDS THAT DIRECTLY and deliberately echo the Universal Declaration of Human Rights, Section 7 of

the Canadian Charter of Rights and Freedoms proclaims: "Everyone has the right to life, liberty and
security of the person and the right not to be deprived
thereof except in accordance with the principles of
fundamental justice." Compared to the Charter's more
renowned provisions (rights to peacefully assemble,
to free expression, to access government services in
both official languages, to not be arbitrarily detained)
the right to security of the person is less known and
more ill defined. But it is, I hope to convince you, no
less significant.

Does the right to security of the person promised
by the Canadian Charter oblige the state to provide for
citizens materially, or does it, in fact, only obligate the
state to step back and, in some cases, actually refrain
from taking action? In other words, does the Canadian
concept of "security of the person" guarantee just what
the barons want or, also, what commoners need? How
we answer these questions will have tremendous implications for the well-being of all Canadians and the fate
of the country's welfare state.

Since the Charter's inception, and over the objections of advocates, scholars, lawyers, and a good
number of justices, Canadian courts have consistently
refused to either affirm or deny the existence of positive social and economic rights, effectively upholding
a purely negative view. Canadian citizens, despite the
country's general commitment to welfare-state principles, have affirmative rights to remarkably little. To

date, the fight over the possibility of positive economic rights—rights to income support, health care, housing, and so on—has revolved around the Charter's promise of a right to "security." It's a fight that has been quietly raging in the background of some of the country's most heated political debates for nearly four decades.

The concept of security of the person has played a pivotal role in a startling array of society-shaping Supreme Court cases: striking down abortion restrictions, restoring funding for safe injection sites, removing laws that made sex workers unsafe, and, as we'll see, protecting homeless encampments and even facilitating the privatization of medical care. When it decriminalized medical assistance in dying (MAiD) in 2015, the court argued that leaving people to "endure intolerable suffering" impinges on their security of the person.[10] Over time, the Supreme Court of Canada has fleshed out the meaning of the phrase *security of the person*, determining that it includes physical and psychological security, bodily integrity and personal autonomy, and that it can be triggered not only by the infliction of actual harms, but also by the risk or threat of harm. But no decision has decisively embraced a positive conception of the right to security of the person—that is, one that entails substantive social and economic rights—or at least not yet. Instead, the question, in the language of a 2020 court decision, has been left "unsettled."[11] As a result, for the duration of the Canadian Charter's life, the right to security of the person has remained in a kind of legal limbo, wherein its positive attributes have never been fully affirmed nor explicitly denied. This legal indecision inadvertently puts Canadians' security in jeopardy. We can see this clearly with MAiD. Some chronically ill and disabled individuals have been driven to state-enabled suicide primarily due to their intolerable material circumstances, including a lack of adequate income and an inability to find affordable and accessible housing. As one recent news headline put it, "poverty, not pain, is driving Canadians with disabilities to consider medically-assisted death."[12] For now, the absence of a clearly defined, positive right to security of the person means that the government will help certain vulnerable people die, but will not give them the support they need to live.

That this is an unsettled matter may strike some as odd. Don't we know what words and laws mean? The truth is, far from it—and thankfully so. In Canadian jurisprudence, the Charter of Rights and Freedoms is often referred to as a "living tree," a metaphor that emerged from the famous 1929 "Persons Case," which decided that women were, in fact, persons and thus eligible to sit in the Canadian Senate. (And so, it follows, entitled to security of the person, too.) In stark contrast to the United States, where a ghoulish obsession with originalism has turned the country's Supreme Court into a reactionary bulwark, the living tree looks to the future and acknowledges the inevitability of change. The living tree doctrine means that instead of being stunted by assertions of authorial intent—and outmoded patriarchal gender roles—the Charter's precepts must flexibly adapt alongside society, branching in directions its original authors could never have foreseen.

Even so, the past still has influence. Precedent matters. Both the Charter's living tree and the phrase *security of the person* have long roots, so tracing them can help us understand where, exactly, the Charter currently stands and how we might use it. The process of patriating the Canadian Constitution, which culminated in the creation of the Canadian Charter of Rights and Freedoms in 1982, was spurred by an array of factors, including concerns about Quebec's independence and growing demands for Indigenous sovereignty. As numerous historical accounts of this period confirm, the desire to conform to the international human rights treaties that Canada had recently ratified also played an important role.[13] This is why the history of the Universal Declaration of Human Rights matters for Canadian politics today: it explains a critical part of the political context from which the Canadian Charter of Rights and Freedoms—and with it, Section 7's guarantee of security of the person—emerged.

These connections and this history are personified in the life of one man, John Humphrey, who spent most of his long career as a professor of law at McGill University before retiring at the age of ninety in 1995.[14] He was also the lead author of the Universal Declaration of Human Rights, though much of his work happened behind the scenes and his role in its creation is not well known. Humphrey would have been the first to recognize his debt to the Magna Carta, and while I have not found any definitive proof that he also drew on its companion, the Forest Charter, he was undoubtedly someone who believed in, and fought doggedly for, a positive conception of security fully in line with the medieval rights to the commons. It was largely thanks to Humphrey's vision and persistence that the final draft of the Universal Declaration of Human Rights ended up protecting both negative and positive liberties.[15]

Humphrey was born in New Brunswick in 1905. His father died when he was an infant; at age six, he had his left arm amputated after a severe burn, and cancer took the life of his mother when he was eleven. But it was the suffering of others that made him a socialist. The Great Depression radicalized him. Humphrey joined the League for Social Reconstruction, a national alliance of socialist intellectuals, to campaign for the creation of a welfare state as a remedy to capitalist insecurity.[16] ("Despite our abundant natural resources the mass of the people have not been freed from poverty and insecurity," its 1932 manifesto declared.[17]) The league evolved into the Cooperative Commonwealth Federation, the left-wing political party that jump-started Canada's eventual adoption of universal medicare. Throughout this period, Humphrey was focused on advancing equality and security for all Canadians, collectively and as individuals. The fact that he would go on to help create an international system of rights based on the sanctity of individuals was not a contradiction of his radical politics but a logical outgrowth of them. For democratic socialists like Humphrey, ensuring a baseline of material security and equality is what enables the full exercise of human freedom.

During the two years it took to compose the Declaration, Humphrey occasionally clashed with Eleanor Roosevelt, President Franklin Delano Roosevelt's widow and chair of the drafting commission, as she pushed for a document that would be palatable to the United States, which balked at the idea of binding and enforceable social and economic rights.[18] In 1944, the year before he died, her husband had proposed a Second Bill of Rights, which would have enshrined a number of economic rights into American law, including rights to adequate income, health care, education, and shelter—a combination of rights, FDR explained, that together spelled "security." Southern segregationists conspired with northern industrialists to doom the bill, incensed at the prospect of a right to security that would apply to everyone "regardless of station, race, or creed." And yet, remarkably, while FDR failed in the US, Humphrey and his allies prevailed on the global stage, winning the war for economic rights less by persuasion than through compromise and attrition. Upon the Declaration's official passage by fifty-eight UN member states, Eleanor Roosevelt trumpeted it as a new "international Magna Carta." Thanks to Humphrey's dedication, it reflects the true richness of its medieval predecessors, liberties negative and positive affirmed and entwined.

Humphrey's goal while drafting the Universal Declaration of Human Rights was to expand the Canadian welfare state to the whole world.[19] His conviction that governments had duties to provide material security to citizens hardly made him an outlier. In the words of historian Samuel Moyn, the "original public meaning of human rights" was synonymous with the "project of national welfarism." Despite their numerous disagreements and differences, most UN member states assumed at the time that social entitlements were the way of the future and would keep the world secure after the ravages of World War II.[20] But the global consensus around social welfare was short-lived. Almost as soon as the ink on the Declaration was dry, emerging Cold War fractures began to spread. American proponents of capitalism associated freedom with free markets and painted any constraint on the private sector, including redistributive policies or progressive taxation, as a form of creeping communism. Some avowedly communist countries, meanwhile, invoked economic development and social cohesion as excuses to constrain civil and political liberties. In Canada, conservative political forces and business interests regarded the Declaration with open hostility. "The Universal Declaration of Human Rights has now been adopted; but the miracle for which some of us hoped did not happen," Humphrey despaired.[21]

That a more holistic conception of security was one of the era's casualties became clear in 1966, when, following years of intense negotiation, the Universal Declaration of Human Rights was split into two legally binding treaties: the International Covenant on Civil and Political Rights and the International Covenant on Economic, Social and Cultural Rights. Western states had successfully derailed long-standing plans for a unified international treaty. Negative and positive liberties, once united in a single document, had been officially sundered, as the Forest Charter had been severed from the Magna Carta.

Canada ratified both covenants in 1976, the first year it was possible to do so. (Its neighbour to the south, more hard-nosed about Cold War dichotomies, has ratified only the International Covenant on Civil and Political Rights, and did not do so until 1992.) While ratification does not, on its own, give the covenants the same force as domestic law, it does create binding international obligations and articulates guiding standards that Canadian lawmakers must respect and promote at home and abroad. Signing on to the covenants signalled Canada's understanding of the interdependence of all human rights, and its formal acknowledgement that adequate food, housing, health care, education, social security, and fair working conditions are more than matters of government policy—they are things to which all human beings are unconditionally entitled. The adoption of the Charter six years later cemented the deep connection between Canada's constitutional principles and international law—international law that was inspired, to a significant degree, by John Humphrey's appreciation for the Canadian welfare state.[22] But the Canadian Charter was also born at the dawn of a fierce backlash against those very values. In the 1980s, a new era of market triumphalism was taking hold.

IN 1987, DURING A time of rising youth unemployment, a young woman named Louise Gosselin launched a challenge under the Canadian Charter of Rights and Freedoms. Despite the dearth of jobs in Quebec, people under thirty were not eligible for full welfare benefits, a disparity Gosselin argued violated her right to security of the person; her lack of stable income was causing her extreme physical and psychological distress. Fifteen years later, in 2002, the Supreme Court finally issued a decision, denying her claim. In the majority's view, Gosselin had failed to prove she had been "deprived" of her Section 7 right to life, liberty, or security of the person, and so there were no grounds for an increase in income support. But, they acknowledged, the matter was not "frozen." "One day," the court said, punting the question, Section 7 "may be interpreted to include positive obligations."[23] We are still waiting for that day.

Justice Louise Arbour issued a passionate dissent, countering that the Charter not only implies a duty to guarantee positive rights—but also, in fact, compels immediate action by the state. She explained: "A minimum level of welfare is so closely connected to issues relating to one's basic health (or security of the person), and potentially even to one's survival (or life interest), that it appears inevitable that a positive right to life, liberty and security of the person must provide for it."

Arbour was adamant that the Charter could not be interpreted from one side, from only the barons' perspective. "As a theory of the Charter as a whole, any claim that only negative rights are constitutionally recognized is of course patently defective," she stated. The right to vote, to trial within a reasonable time frame, to minority language education—all impose positive obligations on the state, meaning that the state must invest money and resources to implement them. "Positive rights are not an exception to the usual application of the Charter," Arbour insisted, "but an inherent part of its structure."

After retiring from the bench in 2004, Arbour was appointed UN High Commissioner for Human Rights. One year later, she gave a speech interrogating the Canadian Charter's history and connection to the welfare state, in which she asked, "What is it in Canadian society that prevents the poor and marginalized from claiming equal enjoyment to the full range of their rights recognized under law, including economic, social and cultural rights?" Arbour then called out the "timidity" of both Canadian litigants and the courts "to tackle head on the claims emerging from the right to be free from want." The timidity served a purpose, she argued: "The western bias today toward a particularly narrow strand of 'civil liberties' likely has more to do with their instrumentality for neo-liberal, market-driven policy imperatives than anything else. Such policy preferences, however, do not warrant subjugating—or obfuscating—rights labelled 'socio-economic' for their supposed incompatibility with liberalism or the so-called rules of the market."[24]

The Charter of Rights and Freedoms, Arbour effectively warned, had been cut off from its roots—captured to serve the interests of society's barons and enclosed like a royal forest, rather than used to provide for everyone.

The 2002 decision that earned Arbour's strong dissent didn't signal an end to the debate over positive economic rights, however—quite the opposite, given the court's continued indecisiveness. It remains a hotly contested issue in Canadian law, and one with life-and-death implications, as seen in the case of Nell Toussaint, a Grenadian immigrant who came to Canada in 1999. After she had been working for nearly a decade at a car parts assembler and as a general labourer, her employer suggested that she apply for permanent residency so that she could be hired full-time. As the process of trying to regularize her status dragged on, her health worsened. She was diagnosed with diabetes and other chronic illnesses, but her precarious immigration status blocked her from receiving adequate care.[25] In 2013, she was granted permanent residency on humanitarian grounds, along with the health coverage that came with it, but by then her illnesses were irreversible: blindness, kidney failure, the amputation of one leg above the knee, and a stroke. In 2018, five years after she filed an initial appeal, the United Nations Human Rights Committee informed Toussaint that Canada had, indeed, violated her rights and was obligated to provide compensation and prevent similar violations from happening to others.

After this directive was ignored for two years, Toussaint initiated a Charter challenge, arguing that her Section 7 rights to life, liberty, and security of the person had been breached and demanding the right to public health care for anyone in Canada who is demonstrably at risk of serious impairment or death. Toussaint knew the case would be less of a benefit to herself than to others. Or as she put it, "I'm still fighting, but now it's for other people in my situation to get health care."[26] In late 2022, after further setbacks, an Ontario court granted her case permission to move ahead, while expressing indignation at the "prejudicial stereotype" the federal government had leaned on in their attempt to strike down her claim—including the insinuation that hard-working immigrants come to Canada only to "milk the welfare system."[27] Shortly thereafter, Toussaint slipped into a coma and passed away at age fifty-three. While her case continues to wind its way through the court system, it now does so without its named claimant.

Barring the success of a case like Toussaint's, Canadians will continue to occupy a muddled netherworld in which many people have the thing itself without the right to it as clearly defined within domestic law: a public medicare system without a corresponding right to health care or material security for all. This ambiguity exposes the system to great risk from modern barons. Where Toussaint and other public health advocates work to expand the public health care commons, some are eager to privatize them.

In early 2023, many Canadians breathed a sigh of relief when the Supreme Court dismissed a case brought by Dr. Brian Day, a Vancouver-based orthopedic surgeon and CEO of a for-profit medical clinic, ending a high-profile fourteen-year legal battle. Day had sought to overturn key provisions of British Columbia's Medicare Protection Act by arguing that long wait times violated people's Section 7 rights. The right to security of the person, he argued, entitles people with means to jump the queue and access for-profit health care by paying out of pocket or buying private insurance—an arrangement that would enable doctors like himself to double-bill, invoicing the public insurance system while also charging patients. It was an argument that, not long ago, received a sympathetic hearing. In 2005, *Chaoulli v. Quebec (Attorney General)* repealed provincial prohibitions on private clinics and private insurance after four of seven Supreme Court justices ruled that they violated the rights to life, personal security, and inviolability guaranteed by Quebec's Charter of Human Rights and Freedoms, while a plurality found that "delays in obtaining medical treatment which affect patients physically and psychologically trigger protection" of Section 7 of the Canadian Charter.[28] By refusing to hear Day's case, the Supreme Court declined to go further down the road of defining the right to security of the person as the right to pay for faster care. But Day's loss does not quite qualify as a victory. It maintains the muddled and fragile status quo instead of affirming a positive right to security and health care based on need.

To be clear, my objection to for-profit health care provision is structural, not individual: I would never blame anyone who pays for care out of fear and desperation. The harm caused by long delays and an overstretched system is urgent and heartbreaking. Who, for example, could have blamed Nell Toussaint for pursuing treatment that might have saved her life, had she possessed the money to do so? But the point, of course, is that she, like countless others, didn't have the resources. Private options appear to offer a quick, practical path to short-term security, but over time, they corrode the public system on which most people rely. It is what the ancient Greeks called a *pharmakon*, a word that refers to elixirs both noxious and healing, simultaneously poison and cure. This is the paradox of market medicine: even as it saves lives, it is structured to benefit from insecurity and suffering, and so simultaneously aggravates these underlying conditions while soothing the symptoms.

We only have to glance into the abyss of American health care, as we will soon do, to see the risks posed by the court's doctrinal ambiguity. The judiciary's unwillingness to affirm a positive right to security is far from neutral; it aids enterprising barons and their allies, including conservative premiers eager to increase the private sector's role in health care.[29] As University of Ottawa law professor Martha Jackman told me, if the *Chaoulli* decision had determined that the proper way to respect the public's constitutional right to security was to reduce wait times by improving public medicare, instead of deregulating private insurance, the current crisis might be far less dire. But as things stand, the fear and insecurity generated by a stressed public system only strengthen the hands of aspiring profiteers, who claim that privatization will improve efficiency and outcomes, serving as a "safety valve" or offering a measure of what Prime Minister Justin Trudeau has called "innovation."[30] No matter that medical systems the world over, public and private, are facing similar capacity challenges, heightened by the strain of a historic pandemic.[31] Comparative research by health care policy experts, meanwhile, clearly shows that an expanded private sector would actually worsen staff shortages by pulling doctors and nurses from public service, while also "skimming the cream" by catering to high-revenue, low-risk patients—a situation that would cause both wait times and costs to rise, and not only for the poor.[32]

As I know all too well through my work with the Debt Collective, the union for debtors I helped found, rising costs and the prospect of bankruptcy ultimately form a kind of fence, blocking people from accessing life-sustaining care and further enclosing what should be a public good—just as the commoners were forbidden from accessing the forest's pharmacopoeia when gathering herbs in once-common woodland. The US outspends Canadians two to one on health services, while experts agree that Canadians, on average, receive superior care—and they aren't financially ruined as a result. To get sick or injured in the US is to face the prospect of spiralling insecurity. People regularly lose their savings and their homes, and they are sometimes sued and even jailed for hospital bills they cannot pay.[33] Over one hundred million Americans are mired in medical debt thanks to predatory services such as CareCredit, peddled to patients in their hospital beds—a medical credit card that takes advantage of fear and desperation to lock people into high-interest contracts when more affordable options are available.[34] Insurance under this regime is exorbitant and exasperating: in-network providers, out-of-network providers, deductibles of thousands or tens of thousands of dollars, and essential services that don't qualify for coverage. In the US, not even the wealthy are safe from the spectre of financial disaster. "Covid Killed His Father. Then Came

$1 Million in Medical Bills," a recent *New York Times* headline warned.[35] This is what security looks like when barons get their way.

In the US, advocates of universal health care—and the improved material security that would come from it—face an overwhelming uphill battle, which is a source of despondence for organizers like myself. But in Canada, a real cure, not a pharmakon, is within reach. My friend Tarek Loubani is an emergency room physician working in London, Ontario. Like many doctors, he makes a handsome living, and pandemic staffing shortages have dramatically increased his take-home pay. When I spoke to him in early 2023, I asked him how the past few years have gone. He said he would happily sacrifice his salary boost in exchange for reforms that would provide high-quality, fast, and free treatment to everyone in need. Tarek compared the public health care system to a car being stripped for parts—Canadian medicare used to be a Mercedes, he said, the envy of the world, but the less maintenance it receives and the more random bits people make off with, the less roadworthy it becomes. One day, he fears, all that will be left is a rusting chassis.

Since the adoption of the Charter of Rights and Freedoms in 1982, the number of hospital beds per thousand Canadian residents has plummeted from a high of 6.8 to around 2.5 today.[36] Deteriorating investment and capacity causes real human suffering while also providing fodder for modern proponents of enclosure.

Looking ahead, the strong financial incentives offered by a two-tier health care system all but ensure that Day's case will not be the last of its kind. Medicare will remain fragile and underfunded, the public frustrated, and the forces of privatization will continue their zombie-like march. Attending to what Tarek called the "moral injury" of a collapsing system—one that makes his patients wait in anguish for hours before he sees them, or that leaves immigrants to die for lack of care—will require restructuring and reinvestment.

Improvement will also require imagination: What does real health security actually entail? What is public health, anyway, and how can we best maintain it? Instead of a Mercedes, we could aspire to something even more ambitious—picture medicare as a state-of-the-art, emissions-free, high-speed rail system. Of course, rebuilding public health care is not something the courts can do alone. The process will require parliamentary and provincial action and sustained public engagement. Overburdened nurses will need to organize and strike, and patients will have to support strikes and protest, too. The Charter can either be a tool to assist in this undertaking—one that strengthens and expands the medicare system, and the welfare state more generally—or it can be bent to aid the dismantling of the public sphere. For now, as Justice Arbour warned, the refusal of the courts to acknowledge the existence of positive economic rights only aids the market forces that want guarantees of government provision to recede—an outcome that calls into question the very purpose of the Charter of Rights and Freedoms. What good, after all, is the right to security of the person if it only secures the right to purchase private medical care (if you have the means to do so) and not the right to a public health care system that meets everyone's needs? Or if it guarantees you medical assistance in dying should you become sick or disabled, but not the right to the income supports and accessible housing that could make your life livable? Where is the fundamental justice the Charter promises?

CRAB PARK, ON VANCOUVER'S Downtown Eastside, is currently home to around fifty people who come from all walks of life. They manage their affairs during weekly meetings held in a shared warming tent. Jobs are distributed to keep things clean, and people look out for each other; it's safe enough that they can leave their tents and belongings to access services nearby. When the community learned in the summer of 2021 that the city was going to clear their encampment, they sued—and won. In early 2022, the BC Supreme Court struck down the impending eviction on Section 7 grounds. "We're all overwhelmed," resident Clint Randen told the CBC upon getting the news. "It's a wonderful thing." Another park dweller, Andrew Hirschpold, attended the proceedings and said the judge engaged humanely.

"The question he asked to the lawyer of the parks was, 'Where does the responsibility go for these people facing displacement?'" The city didn't have a good answer, and so the judge determined they could stay.[37]

The decision provided further recognition that the right to security of the person includes a limited right to shelter, a right that lawyers such as Alexander Kirby, who worked on the CRAB Park lawsuit, have spent years slowly establishing and expanding, building off an initial victory in 2009 that ruled people could shelter on public land overnight but had to pack up their personal belongings in the morning. Case by case, inch by inch, the parameters have expanded. When I spoke to Kirby, he told me that the situation in Vancouver shows how important negative rights can be for the vulnerable; just being able to camp in one place provides life-improving stability. But the very same successes also show why negative rights on their own are insufficient. "The Charter tells us that we live in a society that considers life, liberty, and security of the person to be the most important thing," Kirby explained. "Without positive rights, including a positive right to housing, we're not actually getting to the root of the issue."

Like health care, housing is an essential component of security, and once again the legal situation is confusing and murky. As we saw, Canadians have no explicit right to health care in domestic law, but health care is provided as a matter of policy, which means citizens have the thing but not the corresponding right to back it up (and this lack of a right is partly why the thing itself is vulnerable to threat). In housing, as the CRAB Park case shows, the Charter now protects a negative right to shelter—a right not to be evicted from a tent and exposed to the elements when you have nowhere else to go—but no positive right to stable housing. Adding another layer of complexity to the mix, the passage of the 2019 National Housing Strategy Act has committed the federal government to a "human rights-based approach to housing" and to "further the progressive realization of the right to adequate housing as recognized in the International Covenant on Economic, Social and Cultural Rights." It's a reference, of course, to the Covenant ratified in 1976, and a sign that John Humphrey's spirit lives on. Under international human rights law, housing is not a commodity, and being adequately housed means more than access to shelter on any given night; it is sanctuary and secure tenure.[38] International law guarantees a positive right *to adequate* housing, both now and in the future—not just to a flimsy tent in a muddy park. And yet, so far at least, the National Housing Strategy Act, with its promise to "progressively realize" such a right over time instead of immediately granting it, has not been much help to Kirby's litigation efforts, nor to his houseless allies who are still sleeping rough.[39]

However laudable this human rights approach to housing is in theory (and it is laudable), in practice, nothing in the act disrupts our current market-driven housing system, a system that treats housing as a commodity, not a right, and thus condemns millions of people to perpetual housing insecurity. Without transforming how housing and residential land development are financed, owned, and operated, the positive human right to housing will likely remain unrealized—words without deeds, a right without the thing. Currently, 96 percent of housing in Canada is provided on a market basis, with only 4 percent provided by governments as a public good.[40] In the US, that figure is less than 1 percent.[41] A genuine human rights approach, in contrast, would rebalance these numbers by substantially investing in a robust public option for housing—in other words, directly funding and building high-quality, environmentally sustainable, and non-market housing that is available to everyone who needs it. This would ensure that a substantial portion of housing is treated not as a commodity but instead as a kind of commons.

Canadians are generally aghast at the inhumane and shocking consequences of the American two-tier health care system, and rightly so, for reasons I touched on above. And yet, where housing is concerned, both countries take a market-first two-tier approach. Both nations embrace private property as the ideal and reject the possibility of universal public provision, while providing meagre and demeaning public options to a fraction of those in need.

As a result, across North America, the cost of staying sheltered is surging so much that the housing "emergency" has by now become a permanent condition. This is a realm where Canadians out-American their southern neighbours, spending more of their income on housing than almost anyone else in the world.[42] In 2022, one in four Canadian adults polled said that their mental health had been negatively impacted by housing insecurity—by their inability to find adequate housing or to pay for it—and an estimated 235,000 people experience homelessness in Canada in any given year.[43] Like the peasants violently pushed off the commons, poor and working-class people today are routinely displaced from their homes and communities. But a market stuck in overdrive means housing insecurity is creeping higher and higher up the income ladder. Comparatively affluent people also have much to gain from supporting a commoners' approach to housing, including more generous public investment and strong tenant protections.

From sea to sea to sea, housing insecurity is highly racialized, with non-white people more likely to be housing insecure and disproportionately burdened by rent and mortgage debt.[44] In Nunavut, for instance, the number of Inuit households living in "unsuitable, inadequate or unaffordable housing" is over three times the national average, and conditions described as "abhorrent" by the United Nations Special Rapporteur are commonplace. In 2021, Mumilaaq Qaqqaq, a former MP from the region, released *Sick of Waiting*, a report documenting the shocking state—including sewage problems, holes in walls, water rot, leaking windows, and crumbling floors—of both private and public housing in five Nunavut communities; that year, over a third of Inuit in Nunavut lived in dwellings in need of major repairs. Qaqqaq laid the blame "squarely with the Federal Government" and the underfunded Nunavut Housing Corporation. "Promises don't get rid of mould," she wrote. "Words don't fix windows and doors. Empathy doesn't fix leaking pipes." These inequities are the result of explicit policy choices, not a lack of resources. They unspool from a system that refuses to treat housing as a human right, harming Indigenous communities most intensely while making housing insecure for Canadians more broadly.

The oft-proposed solution to the housing crisis is for private developers to build more housing—the assumption being that affordability will flow from abundance. The problem with this stance is that, similar to the previous example of medical care, housing markets do not abide by a mechanical law of supply and demand. Developers understand, for example, that it is more profitable to construct so-called "shoebox" condos as potential investment properties for people who already own homes than to build rentals earmarked for leasing at below-market rates, let alone at the deep discounts most people need to afford housing in our radically unequal world.[45] In a place like Nunavut, building high-end private high-rises will never yield the aggressive returns investors seek, which is why local housing activists continue to demand high-quality public housing—housing the federal government has committed to building, but not nearly at a scale or pace that meets the urgent need.[46]

Should new apartments be speculative investments or durable social goods? Should they exist to enrich developers, financiers, and wealthy individuals (today's barons) or to provide material security, dignity, and shelter for ordinary people—which, in our overheated housing markets, now means anyone who wouldn't survive a bloody bidding war? University of Toronto housing expert David Hulchanski told me that framing the issue as a problem of "affordability" as opposed to one of housing insecurity confuses the nature of the problem and effective solutions. "Affordability" implies that reducing prices at the low end of the market would fix things when the problem actually stems from rising inequality. A small minority of people are able to pay a great deal for housing, which inflates rents and prices across the board, further enriching a lucky few. As Hulchanski put it, "Canada's housing system has become a very successful mechanism for increasing wealth for some while increasing housing insecurity for many."

This problem is widespread. Even the most egalitarian social democracies tend to treat housing as a market commodity, which is why housing is sometimes called the "wobbly pillar" of the welfare state. Yet some countries have succeeded in making housing a more reliable welfare cornerstone by dramatically increasing the number of residences provided on non-market terms—by making housing a kind of commons.

Consider Finland and Austria. In Finland, where housing is constitutionally guaranteed, 16 percent of homes
are social housing, and over a quarter of new construction is supposed to fit into that category. One in
seven Helsinki residents live in the city's sixty thousand social housing units. In addition, the government
has embraced a "housing first" approach to homelessness, which means it provides stable housing before
attempting to address other needs. This has proven
both more humane and more cost-efficient than leaving people in the streets or locking them up: a home
for a single unhoused person saves the government
€15,000 in emergency health care and law enforce-
ment expenses. These policies have made Finland
the only country in the European Union with falling
homelessness rates.[47]

In Austria, 26 percent of the country's overall housing stock is non-market, with nearly half of Vienna's
homes owned and run by the municipality. Viennese
social housing shelters an estimated 60 percent of the
population, which means it serves all kinds of people: low-income earners, immigrants, the elderly,
environmentalists, middle-class families, and young
professionals. The city's rents are low across the board,
since private landlords face real competition. The average monthly price for a sixty-square-metre flat in the
city is €767 (a fraction of what something similar would
cost in Toronto, London, or New York), and social rents
are even lower.

"Having a comfortable and affordable roof over your head is critical to a sense of security and happiness—and, some economists have argued, productivity," a recent article in the *Financial Times* marvelled, before praising the socialists who spearheaded Vienna's unique housing scheme in the 1920s for their style and good taste. Those socialists believed that poor people deserved to live in beautiful, safe, and centrally located buildings, and that ethos still informs the city's approach to housing today: complexes often include saunas, swimming pools, meeting rooms, shops, and kindergartens.[48] Daniel Aldana Cohen, a professor who has studied Vienna's social housing model and advised US congresswoman Alexandria Ocasio-Cortez on her proposed Green New Deal for Public Housing legislation, told me that the municipality keeps standards high by setting reasonable budgets for its projects and inviting developers to compete on quality, not price. Aesthetics and amenities count for a lot, and ecological benefits do, too. Governments, Cohen explained, can purchase energy-efficient materials in bulk and experiment with new environmentally sustainable materials at a scale that private developers can't or won't.

Here we see the right and the thing, the combination of promise and policy, the guarantee and its full realization. In the US there is no right to secure housing at all. In Canada, as a result of the National Housing Strategy Act, the right exists, but it is still being realized, which means it has yet to actually manifest. In

Finland and Austria, both exist.[49] This is what the adoption of a positive right to material security looks like: rights, backed by policies and public investment that prevent markets from undermining everyone's well-being. And yet, across North America, social housing is generally considered inferior to private ownership and is too often stigmatized. People dream of getting a mortgage, not accommodation in a co-operatively managed or government-owned apartment building, no matter how luxurious.[50] Our very imaginations, it seems, have been enclosed.

IT'S A MEASURE OF just how steeped in economic thinking we are that the word *security* is now most familiar to us through the language of the marketplace. Think, for example, of the term *security deposit*, which indicates a sum paid to the landlord upon the signing of a lease. Or of the ironically named *securities*, the packages of subprime home loans that brought down the global economy in 2008. Securitizing is the common practice of bundling together different kinds of loans (residential or commercial mortgages, credit card receivables, auto loans, rental incomes, and so on) and then selling the package, plus the promise of future interest payments, to investors. And yet securitized financial products actually bring insecurity to us all, both because they rely on a steady supply of personal and household debt and also because they enable financial entities to play with fire by pooling credit risk and off-loading it onto others. In 2008, securitized American mortgages—subprime loans that were sliced, diced, and rated triple-A—produced a devastating financial shock, causing millions of people to lose their homes and jobs in the US and plunging other countries into crisis.

In the market utopia we now inhabit, housing is not only a commodity but a securitized commodity. The mortgage debts people owe for their housing can be bought and sold, and so can tenants' future rent payments. Across North America, mammoth corporate landlords are scooping up apartment buildings and single-family homes in order to securitize the rental streams, promising investors inordinate returns for years to come and making it harder for ordinary people to buy homes. Housing scholar and urban planner Martine August estimates that in 2020, the largest twenty-five corporate landlords in Canada held about 330,000 private rental apartments, or 20 percent of Canada's entire stock.[51] These anonymous investor-backed entities are more likely to evict tenants (or threaten to do so) than traditional landlords, and their properties are more likely to be in need of repair.[52] Steve Pomeroy, a senior research fellow at Carleton University, estimates that for every one affordable unit created by Canadian government funding, around fifteen become unaffordable because of the financial-ization of rental housing.[53] Wherever securitization occurs, systemic insecurity rises—a lesson we should have learned by now. The profits of a few financiers may balloon, but as with the aforementioned mortgage crash, when the bubble bursts, we will all be made to pay.

Securitization, to be clear, is not some accident or aberration. It is as much the product of government policy as is the present lack of social housing. And both the US and Canada have invested significant resources to encourage citizens to rely on private-sector lending, thus facilitating securitization. Consider the Canada Mortgage and Housing Corporation, established in 1946, which focuses on providing direct support for private borrowing. That institution put home ownership within reach for many Canadians after World War II, even as the overall percentage of renters in Canada remained high as compared to the US. In the eighties and nineties, Canadian mortgage and mortgage insurance markets grew, and soon banks introduced mortgage-backed securities. In the words of one MP, these changes were designed to encourage "creative ways to attract new sources of funding to respond to the housing needs of low to moderate income Canadians."[54] According to scholars Alan Walks and Brian Clifford, encouraging people to take on mortgage debt—and finding ways to securitize that debt to make it profitable for investors—provided a way of relieving pressure on government social spending.[55] The result is a lending industry that has built immense wealth and financial security for a small class of bankers and investors while fuelling one of the world's most inflated housing markets. According to a recent report on the financialization of housing, "housing has become by far the most valuable asset on Earth, worth three times more than global GDP and more than 20 times all the gold ever mined." The value of residential real estate worldwide exceeded US$258.5 trillion in 2020, increasing by $90 trillion in just four years.[56]

The astonishing wealth of today's financial sector has been built atop the insecurity of the many—and particularly, it must be noted, the insecurity of Indigenous and racialized people. In both the US and Canada, government-backed lending programs perpetuated racist exclusion to build a middle class that was overwhelmingly white. Between 1934 and 1962, a full 98 percent of the loans insured by the Federal Housing Administration went to white Americans, while Black families were pushed into urban slums, decrepit public housing, or home ownership via terms dictated by subprime, high-interest lenders.[57] Research by geographer Ted Rutland shows how similar dynamics have played out in Canada, specifically in Nova Scotia, beginning with the theft of land from the Mi'kmaq people who had called it home for ten thousand years.[58] Rutland explores the way the province's African-Canadian communities in Africville and elsewhere were repeatedly denied opportunities to reap the full benefits of home ownership and were thus prevented from building intergenerational wealth. After being consistently denied basic municipal infrastructure like sewage, street lighting, and road and sidewalk paving, Africville residents were ineligible for government-backed mortgage insurance that would have enabled them to take out loans for much-needed home improvements. Racist policies kept whole communities impoverished and insecure.

What happened in Africville affects us all, because these same racist attitudes and market-driven policies have made everyone more housing insecure by helping to destroy the possibility of high-quality social housing. During the thirties and forties, American planners and policy makers briefly looked to Vienna for inspiration as they laid the groundwork for the US welfare state, much the way a new generation of housing academics and activists are doing today. But real estate and banking lobbies worked hard to ensure that mortgage lending and private ownership would lie at the heart of America's New Deal, sabotaging a commoners' approach to housing in favour of the barons' ideal by slowing investment in public housing to a trickle. Starting in the 1970s, US government officials deployed racist stereotypes to justify the dereliction and destruction of the remaining public housing stock, destroying hundreds of thousands of units that were never replaced. Despite their separate trajectories, Canada and the US ultimately arrived at similar destinations, with funding for social housing dramatically curtailed under liberal, or rather neo-liberal, cost-cutting governments. While Canada saw a successful burst of mixed-income, co-operative, "community" housing development in the 1970s, the same fiscal belt-tightening that would cause the number of hospital beds to plummet in the 1990s also precipitated a dramatic decline of the federal social housing supply. Authority devolved to the provinces, which have failed to meet demand.[59] Today, the waiting list for social housing in Toronto runs to more than eighty thousand households, while the average wait time for a one-bedroom unit is twelve years.[60]

Both the US and Canada have the financial resources to create abundant, attractive, ecologically sustainable, and secure social housing, but instead both countries prioritize tax credits that incentivize private ownership. American housing researchers estimate that the US federal government loses an astonishing US$600 billion annually to mortgage-interest tax deductions that disproportionately subsidize rich homeowners, an amount that exceeds Washington's total affordable housing expenditures by a factor of fourteen.[61] In Canada, the capital gains tax exemption on principal residences disproportionately benefits the wealthy and costs upward of $10 billion in foregone revenue every year—over five times what the federal government currently spends on all social housing and more than triple the $3 billion needed over the next decade to solve the housing crisis in all traditional Inuit territory, including Nunavut.[62] Should we ever follow Vienna's lead and get rid of regressive

tax exemptions, ample money will exist to fund environmentally sustainable social housing units, capitalize
zero- or low-interest loans for co-operative alternatives,
and retrofit and beautify decaying public housing stock.[63]

For most North Americans today, home ownership
is not only about the security of shelter, but also about
material security in a broader sense. Purchasing property is a way to compensate for the absence of a robust
and trustworthy welfare state, particularly the lack of
adequate public pensions in old age. Houses, in our current paradigm, are both places to live and investments:
they are our de facto retirement accounts, emergency
funds, and inheritable wealth. I can't help but wonder
what things would be like, and how I might live differently, if my material security were guaranteed. Would
I have recently bought a house, for example, if my town
were dotted with green and inviting social housing
complexes for rent? Or if I weren't afraid of joining the
growing ranks of the elderly and destitute? My point is
that, for all the free market's chatter about "choice," in
the absence of accessible non-market options for housing, real choice is something we rarely possess. Rather
than sharing in the abundant material security of the
commons, each of us is forced to grapple for our own
corner of the enclosure or be left out in the cold.

Now that I own a house, I receive regular email
updates from a real estate app, one seemingly designed
to remind me that my home is actually a commodity.
The alerts feature an arrow next to a number indicating

whether prices are rising or falling in my zip code and how much they are expected to rise or fall in the year ahead—an index of my future security. It is, however, an impoverished version of security, with no guaranteed future and a steady dose of anxiety. Commodities have values, and values, in our speculative economy, can rise or fall; conventional home ownership means consigning ourselves to living in something that always could, financially speaking, collapse. This is the source of the housing market's power, the grip that keeps property owners vigilant, insecure, and on edge—and, in too many cases, oblivious or hostile to the needs of others, as the not-in-my-backyard, or NIMBY, movement shows. Insecurity prods us to care which direction the arrow points on an app, and that prevents us from realizing that security may better be gained another way—not by going it alone, but by providing for one another.

So far, in my case, the app's arrow rises, briefly dips, rises again, but never dives. My relief at this fact makes me painfully aware of my conflicted allegiances and of insecurity's power. Of course I don't want the value of my house to crash—who would? But I am also aware of the ancillary costs of my home's steady appreciation. The app does not tally the collateral damage of long-time residents displaced from my neighbourhood, the number of families sharing cramped rooms or relying on food banks, the people living out of their cars or in doorways, the teachers and nurses and retail workers commuting longer and longer distances, the people trapped with abusive partners because they can't afford to move out on their own, and the loss of community, local character, and creativity that escalating home values inevitably entail. (I am, for one, a firm believer in a correlation between artistry and cheap rent.) The app isn't programmed to care about the political harm caused by spiralling wealth inequality and racial disparities, which an overheated housing market only aggravates; nor does it appraise the ecological harm of a sprawling system of single-family fiefdoms. It certainly doesn't factor into its assessment the fact that my friends and loved ones may have to move out of town soon, because the rent is too high for them to stay. But where will they go? Everywhere you look these days, the arrows shoot relentlessly skyward.

A FEW YEARS AGO, I found myself wandering the English countryside, where I felt the commons beneath my feet. I was exploring some of the veins of meadowland that were spared from enclosure and remain open today for everyone's use and enjoyment. In 1865, the Commons Preservation Society was formed; early members included such luminaries as the philosopher John Stuart Mill and William Morris, the radical author and textile designer. The group got to work protecting footpaths and rights-of-way, and, after various name changes, the organization still campaigns for their preservation today. At first, it felt strange to be traipsing through areas that, where I live, would be designated as private property. I traversed fields and what felt like backyards, but as I passed people by, they greeted me, putting me at ease—I had a right to be there. Later in the day, ambling around a Derbyshire churchyard, I saw a grave with an unusual marker, which I bent down to read:

> *Here lies buried*
> *Little John*
> *The friend & lieutenant of Robin Hood.*
> *He died in a cottage (now destroyed)*
> *to the east …*

It hadn't occurred to me until that moment that there might be real history behind the fable—even if, despite the grave I stumbled upon, it remains unclear whether the Sherwood Forest rebels were real individuals, amalgamations, or pure myth. As a child, I understood that Robin Hood stole from the rich to give to the poor, but the account I'd heard portrayed their struggle as an anti-tax revolt, not a fight for the commons—a fight for the very paths I had just strolled. The barons' rebellion that birthed the Magna Carta has also been narrated in a way that reinforces an anti-government worldview. The story of the barons, in its conventional telling, implies that we're all rich-people-in-waiting, all men near the top of the feudal hierarchy who just need the state to leave us and our property in peace. The barons, though, were not ordinary folks but landlords whose vast holdings included castles or entire villages, and their immense power and wealth came from living off the labour of others and taxing them into deprivation. These barons, unlike most of us, controlled private armies, courts, and officials. No wonder the common people flocked to Robin's free band of merry men, real or imagined as they may have been.

This baronial, anti-government world view tells us our homes are our castles, an analogy first suggested by Sir Edward Coke, the jurist who did so much to popularize the Magna Carta. But many of us who technically own property hardly qualify as mini-monarchs. A mortgage means we're effectively renting from the bank, in my case for thirty years; I'll be seventy-two when I'm free and clear. In North America, this is undoubtedly a privilege, given that the alternative is to rent for my entire life and thus be consigned either to paying someone else's mortgage or contributing revenue to corporate landlords' swelling cash reserves. But that shouldn't cause me to forget where my true interests lie—with the commoners and the ideals of the Forest Charter, and a future that offers material security for all as both a reality and a right, instead of a lifetime of debt.

What material security entails precisely is something ordinary people should have the opportunity to decide democratically. As I was writing this book, I took to asking

people what security meant to them. Security, they told
me, is:

Safety

Safety nets

Having basic needs met

Food

Universal health care

Having health care

Mental health services

Community

Family

Friends

Money

$25 million, to which someone else said that
only $50 million would suffice

Delusion, said a person who studies
propaganda for a living

Illusion, said a former war correspon-
dent who spent years reporting in US-occupied
Afghanistan and Iraq

Not living in a war zone, said a Syrian
refugee now residing in Montreal

Knowing someone will be there to help me if
my wheelchair breaks, said my disabled sister

Housing

Having a home with no landlord

Not worrying about rent

Freedom from want

Freedom from fear

Peace of mind
A state of being that enables creativity

In these responses, I hear echoes of both the Magna Carta and the Forest Charter, John Humphrey and FDR, Nell Toussaint and Louise Arbour, the Commons Protection Society and Robin Hood. I hear the desire for a web of welfare supports capable of sustaining a good and dignified life and a reimagining of the security offered by a thriving commons. I also hear a useful dose of skepticism, a reminder that, for vulnerable creatures like ourselves, it is unlikely that security will ever be absolute. This list is, of course, just a beginning, but it is a reminder that the quest for material security is less about owning specific goods than embracing an expansive understanding of well-being, as well as an awareness that no one can be secure on their own.

Across North America, class mobility has diminished or disappeared entirely, and economic insecurity has risen apace, keeping the future uncertain. As I'll discuss in the next chapter, the result is a perilous situation—rising material insecurity poses the risk of turning a sizable portion of the population toward authoritarianism. But it can also have the opposite effect: like John Humphrey, awakened by the economic insecurity of the Great Depression, many younger people are turning to democratic socialism, looking to the state as a possible solution to their problems, not as a threat to their private interests. This revival of socialism is evidence that some people are transforming their experience of insecurity into an opportunity to build solidarity, and doing so by embracing the ethos of the commons.

The question, again, is whether we adopt the perspective of barons or commoners—will we recognize the importance of both negative and positive rights to a good and dignified life or continue to leave one half of this essential democratic equation by the wayside? Are our personal interests really served by a model of security that envisions the government simply as a threat to our freedom, and taxation as theft? By a health care system that allows people to jump to the head of a price-gouging queue? Or by a housing system so bloated that only the rich can compete? Or would a more dependable and durable form of security come from a state that delivers collective care and provision—the provision of herbage, pannage, turbary, estovers; of social security, housing, health care, education, and meaningful, fairly compensated work. Today, insecurity haunts everyone, even the affluent; finally realizing our economic and social rights would benefit the privileged, too.

We all have and deserve the right to security. It is written into declarations and constitutions, proclaimed as an entitlement that belongs to every human being. But rights require action, as thirteenth-century peasants knew. Like the barons who gathered on Runnymede field, the peasants also rebelled, asserting and reasserting their right to sustenance and survival time and again. Maintenance of the commons required constant care and regular doses of civil disobedience. When their rights were threatened, commoners fought back, protesting their abuse with great defiance, trespassing, taking what was theirs, jumping fences, and making "rough music"—the era's charming term for the clanging of pots, banging of drums, and shouting of chants that still ring out at demonstrations to this day. People who were considered lowly subjects demanded the ability to live with some measure of autonomy and dignity. As a result of their efforts, the rights enumerated in the Forest Charter endured in various forms for centuries.

The right to security, like all rights, is not only a technical term for lawyers and courts to interpret and decree. The idea that matters of law and policy should be left to experts is a myth today's barons want us to believe. Like the medieval commons, the law is something that belongs to everyone; it is political terrain we can struggle over and change. The right to security—whatever we decide security is—is ours to debate, reimagine, proclaim, and make real.

CHAPTER 3

CONSUMED BY CURIOSITY

MY MOTHER, MARIA, WAS born in the spring of 1960, at the dawn of a decade that would come to be synonymous with social change. Her parents were an unlikely pair of outsiders: my grandfather, a Hungarian refugee with a penchant for existentialist philosophy, soon to return to Budapest and rarely be heard from again; my Ontario-raised grandmother, her own birth circumstances so scandalous that she spent time in an orphanage as a toddler. When given the chance, Grandma severed all attachments to middle-class social mores and embraced a life that was freewheeling. My mom and her sister spent their early years hanging out in Toronto's bohemian enclaves, frequenting beatnik cafés and bookstores, be-ins, and happenings. One morning, on the bus to school, the kids pointed excitedly out the window, screaming in disgust, "Yuck, a hippie!" My mother turned to look. Her mom's latest boyfriend was strolling by.

In 1969, my grandmother fully committed to the countercultural path, heading west and then north with daughters in tow. The day they arrived in the Yukon Territory, it was so frigid that my grandmother's coat, made of some fashionable synthetic fabric, split apart. But they weren't there to be fashionable. My grandmother had come to help a small group of spiritual seekers establish a Buddhist outpost near Whitehorse, a town she would grow to love and would never leave. Faith that she was helping to usher in a shift in consciousness sustained my grandmother through the hardship of those initial years. For her young daughters, the move was an adventure but also a challenge. At one point they lived in an old shed with an outhouse (hardly the pinnacle of comfort), and being constantly broke took its toll. Freedom also had its risks. The typical childhood guardrails were nowhere to be found—rock and roll and psychedelic drugs were deemed appropriate for kids and adults alike.

As intrepid as my grandma, my fourteen-year-old mother added a year to her age and enrolled herself in an experimental school fifty miles south of Whitehorse on the outskirts of Carcross, a village formerly known as Caribou Crossing for the herds that passed through on their semi-annual migrations, and the long-standing home of the Carcross/Tagish First Nation. Founded in 1972 and surrounded by 1,600 acres of wilderness, the Carcross Community Education Centre was an alternative boarding school, one of the thousands of free schools sprouting up across North America during that period—free, in this context, meaning that they were concerned with freedom, with the authentic and uncoerced expression and development of students. Born of an unusual partnership between the Yukon Territorial Government and the Anglican Diocese of Yukon, the Carcross centre catered primarily, though not exclusively, to white students and occupied the recently abandoned site of an old residential school—a disturbing history we'll return to. The new experimental school, to be clear, was not religious; instead, it was suffused with a countercultural spirit: a belief that people could establish more egalitarian and satisfying modes of coexistence. Students arrived from across Canada, as well as a few from the United States, a good number of whom had been labelled "troubled" in their local schools and marked for "rehabilitation." The Carcross centre offered them not punishment and discipline but the possibility of thriving in a wholly different educational environment.

In the late sixties and seventies, many people—an entire movement's worth—were attempting to rethink education from the ground up. Bestselling books like A. S. Neill's *Summerhill: A Radical Approach to Child Rearing*, an account of the legendary anti-authoritarian boarding school in England; Paul Goodman's *Compulsory Miseducation*; Ivan Illich's *Deschooling Society*; and Paulo Freire's *Pedagogy of the Oppressed* all signalled the zeitgeist and sold millions of copies. These ideas began to influence public policy and teaching methods: *Living and Learning,* an Ontario government report released in 1968, shocked the Canadian education establishment by advocating for child-centred, democratic, and grade-free instruction.

At Carcross, teenagers like my mother put these radical ideas into practice by running the school alongside teachers and so-called parent-members. Lesson plans evolved according to participants' interests, each class a collaborative and open-ended endeavour. Though the school was accredited, grades were regarded as retrograde and arbitrary. (One teacher solved the problem by throwing darts at a board to come up with random marks.) The most important learning came from managing the community—from figuring out together how to solve problems and live in common. Young people talked philosophy while repairing the buildings and constructing log cabins, farming and occasionally hunting, cooking, and cleaning. They baked bread and made crafts that were sold to help keep the school financially afloat. The school's decision-making process required endless meetings, as democracy always does. At one of these long sessions, my mother and a small gang of pranksters, calling themselves the Wooden Plank Committee, spoofed the painstaking quest for inclusion and consensus by pretending to represent the interests of carpentry supplies.

My mother enrolled at Carcross in 1974 and stayed for a year. In a charming thirty-minute CBC documentary about the Carcross centre made during that time, the narrator marvels at both the school's outlandish methods and remarkable success. The film shows sweet-faced, long-haired students sitting in a circle, deliberating over how to fairly share cleaning responsibilities and thoughtfully discussing power differentials with the parent-members. In one interview, a girl reflects on the school's commitment to breaking down the traditional hierarchy between teachers and students to facilitate learning through authentic interest and mutual respect, not obligation or fear. "There's a lot of care here," she says. "It's none of this 'Mrs.' and 'Mr.' and bow-to-the-ground for your teacher ... and that sort of helps you work harder."[1] It was this ethos—the idea of education's connection to autonomy, curiosity, and security—that would leave the largest mark on my mother. By extension, it profoundly marked my childhood, too.

ONE DAY IN 1968, the year before my grandmother and her daughters left Toronto, a young political scientist named Ronald Inglehart found himself surrounded by protesters. The month was May, and Paris buzzed with rebellious energy. Students occupied their universities and workers waged wildcat strikes; paving stones were ripped from the street and tear gas hung heavy in the air. As the economy ground to a halt, rumour had it the president had fled the country (in reality, he attended a secret meeting in Germany to ensure he had support from his armed forces). Everything, it seemed, was up for debate. Demonstrators denounced consumerism, American imperialism, outmoded gender roles, and deadening teaching methods—and demanded a new way of relating and being. "The barricade blocks the street but opens the way," popular graffiti proclaimed. "We want nothing of a world in which the certainty of not dying from hunger comes in exchange for the risk of dying from boredom."[2] Inglehart knew that what he was witnessing was not unique. The French demonstrations were part of a global wave of youth rebellion, surging from Mexico City to San Francisco, from Vancouver to London to Tokyo.[3] This wave changed the course of Inglehart's career.

In 1977, he published his first book, *The Silent Revolution: Changing Values and Political Styles Among Western Publics.* It would become a classic in the field. Using survey data from North America and Western Europe, Inglehart argued that a generational transformation in outlook was "gradually but fundamentally" remaking Western society for the better—rendering it more open-minded, democratic, and free.[4] Inglehart called this new outlook "postmaterialist." In essence, *The Silent Revolution* analyzed the cause and political impact of the 1960s' social movements. What conditions, he wanted to know, had catalyzed the sea change that swept up millions of people in such bold new cultural and political experiments, my grandmother and her daughters among them?

Inglehart didn't believe that younger generations were somehow intrinsically more enlightened, unprejudiced, or innovative than their predecessors, as some hagiographic accounts of the swinging sixties might lead one to believe. Rather, he argued, they had come of age in a very different world than the one their parents and grandparents had been raised in—specifically, in one that was far less economically and physically insecure. The relatively egalitarian conditions of the post–World War II era encouraged millions of people in North America, Britain, and Europe to become less reactive than prior generations, for intuitive, even obvious, reasons: people's basic needs were being met and, critically, they believed they would continue to be met in the future. Thanks to rising wages and expanded welfare systems, even poor people like my grandmother felt secure enough to take risks and try to live in new ways. They could, in capitalist parlance, afford to experiment.

Inglehart's great innovation lay in extending the psychologist Albert Maslow's famous hierarchy of needs from individuals to society writ large. Maslow described this framework as a "theory of human motivation." With it, he sought to describe what makes us tick. As Maslow put it, "It is quite true that man lives by bread alone—when there is no bread." Material necessities such as food and water and physical and economic security take first priority, Maslow thought, and meeting those frees us to focus on non-material needs, culminating in what he called the need for self-actualization. Inglehart believed this process was playing out on a vast scale. Those who came of age amid the Great Depression and two world wars valued safety and subsistence most of all, because they recalled a time when both were scarce. But a booming economy had raised expectations from "a chicken in every pot" to "a car in every garage."[5] Younger people grew up in newly built suburban homes stocked with consumer wonders: vacuum cleaners, curling irons, lawn mowers, Jell-O packets, radios, and TVs. Accustomed to the affluent society's warm embrace, Inglehart argued, masses of young people felt secure enough to prioritize autonomy and personal growth, and to question consumer culture's stifling embrace. People like my grandmother looked at those cookie-cutter houses with those car-filled garages, all watching the same four television channels and purchasing identical products, and thought: Maybe people in those houses were comfortable, sure, but were they actually happy?

The generational divide was stark. Older people, Inglehart's survey revealed, valued "maintaining order in the nation" and "fighting rising prices." Their offspring, in contrast, valued "giving people more say over political decisions" and "protecting free speech." Inglehart described this as a shift from "survival values" to "self-expression values."[6] A growing sense of material security, he believed, was allowing so-called "higher" needs to rise in salience for a rapidly growing percentage of the population: needs for love, esteem, intellectual and aesthetic satisfaction, belonging, and purpose.[7] At the same time, increasing access to post-secondary education helped make people more open to new ideas and to other lifestyles—attitudes conducive to the emergence of movements for peace, racial equality, women's liberation, gay rights, Indigenous sovereignty, and environmentalism.

What *The Silent Revolution* demonstrated was that varying levels of insecurity and security can have profound cultural and political consequences. Security or its absence can usher along the forces of reaction or of progress. It can stifle democracy or strengthen it.

In the years that followed the book's publication, Inglehart went on to become one of the most cited political scientists in the English-speaking world. Over time, he expanded his research to over one hundred countries, attracting collaborators on every inhabited continent. For years, the data they collected showed a rise in post-materialist attitudes across the globe, an encouraging, predictable, and progressive trend. Democracy looked to be spreading, prejudices slowly fading, secularism on the upswing. Then, around the turn of the millennium, things began to slowly backslide. In the Western world, authoritarians entered (or re-entered) the electoral mainstream. England's alarming Brexit vote in 2016 was followed by newly emboldened autocratic leaders in the United States, Hungary, Brazil, and Italy. Across the liberal democratic world, conspiracy-driven movements gained converts and influence.

Inglehart, who passed away in 2021, believed that spiralling insecurity helped explain today's authoritarian tide. Insecurity, he maintained, tends to spark an "authoritarian reflex": the closing of ranks behind strong leaders in reaction to perceived threats and grievances. But contemporary insecurity, he noted, differs markedly from the insecurity of the past. During the relatively secure conditions of 1928, the Nazis took less than 3 percent of the vote in national elections, only to become the strongest party in the German Reichstag in 1933. This, of course, was four years into the Great Depression, which had financially devastated the electorate. The grim scarcity of economic collapse fuelled fascism in Europe.

Today, in contrast, we live amid astonishing and incredibly lopsided material abundance: the world's richest 1 percent now capture almost two-thirds of all newly generated wealth. This maldistribution leaves most people feeling economically insecure despite high levels of overall societal prosperity. This insecurity, in turn, has been shown to make some people more susceptible to racist, reactionary, and sexist appeals. Here we have to remember that insecurity is always subjective; it has as much to do with one's objective circumstances as one's sense of the future. Far-right foot soldiers, research finds, are typically better off than their neighbours, but still feel vulnerable, and not always without reason. For example, an analysis of the protesters who stormed the US Capitol in early 2021 found that while they tended to be more affluent than average, a disproportionate percentage of participants who were arrested had also experienced significant money troubles at some point—bankruptcy, evictions, unemployment, and the like. The insecurity of an unequal and volatile economy tilts some people rightward.[8]

In 2019, Inglehart reflected on the state of the authoritarian reflex in Canada, a country where, as in the US, "about a third of the population expresses conformist sentiments such as the belief that obedience and discipline are keys to the good life." While Inglehart and his co-authors were reassured that "more Canadians embrace open, flexible sensibilities that may serve as a check on the political expression of authoritarian impulses" than their American counterparts, they also warned that status anxiety and anger at perceived outsiders were on the rise.[9] Only time would tell, they wrote, whether the authoritarian reflex would manifest "as a passing spasm or a more significant seizure." Less than two years later, the country was gripped by the so-called Freedom Convoy in Ottawa, a massive protest against Covid-19 vaccine mandates, supported by one-third of Canadians and cheered on by right-wing movements around the globe.[10] The protesters were by no means the poorest or most oppressed citizens—insecurity's subjective dimension once again on display.

Ours is a strange and scrambled political moment, at once prosperous and precarious, encouragingly open-minded and dangerously reactive. Like Inglehart, I believe there is a correspondence between insecurity, security, and social change, but I do not believe this relationship is preordained. Human beings do not live by reflex alone, and the forces pushing some people toward authoritarianism are more than automatic expressions of our essential nature. They are products of a co-ordinated attack on our economic and emotional well-being—an attack, as discussed in the previous chapter, aimed at privatizing and commodifying the welfare commons, strengthening the hand of the market, and making our societies more competitive and individualistic. The resulting insecurity has left us feeling like we are never enough, have enough, or know enough; pulverizing our self-esteem, stoking consumerism, and corrupting education. Today, we are caught between two conflicting theories of human motivation: one that sees material security as the basis for personal and social growth (a view held, for example, by Inglehart and Maslow), and another that is committed to manufacturing insecurity to keep people compliant, anxious, and striving.

And yet insecurity is also a complicated thing. It can shut us down, close us off, and threaten egalitarian values. Or it can open us up, nurturing our habits

of curiosity and social connection, facilitating democratic renewal. It was the shared condition of insecurity,
for example, that bonded struggling workers with the
unemployed during the Great Depression, enabling
them to form coalitions and push states to adopt the
redistributive policies that, if we're to believe Inglehart,
set the stage for postmaterialism. While it is true that
disasters and instability can be fertile ground for
authoritarian strongmen, ordinary people just as often
come to each other's aid. The more we can understand
the nature of insecurity—the systems that manufacture it for power and profit, and the existential forms
of insecurity that shape us—the more capable of forg
ing solidarity and caring for each other we will be.

WHEN I WAS EIGHT years old, I had a rude awaken-
ing: I realized that I actually lived in the 1980s. Until
then, I had happily inhabited a kind of countercultural,
postmaterialist 1960s time warp. My parents drove two
beat-up VW vans, and the kids wore homemade tie-dye
T-shirts and ran around barefoot, true to every hippie
cliché. There were no bedtimes, no morning alarms, no
schedules, no classes, no curricula or teachers or tests in
our eccentric, ramshackle household. Instead, there was
just us, my siblings and me, doing what we wanted to do.
We wandered the nearby creeks and woods, unsuper-
vised and unafraid, hands in the mud, clothes stained

with red dirt or green streaks from rolling in grass. We played, squabbled, sang, hung out with the dogs, fought over video games, or watched the two channels that came through on our TV. We spent endless hours reading books or staring at the walls, bored, and then found something to capture our attention again.

My mom never forgot her time at the Carcross Community Education Centre, with its beguiling ethos of youth empowerment, and she put those ideas—and new ones she encountered or developed herself—into practice through her parenting. I have long admired how my mother replicated the good parts of her countercultural girlhood (the playfulness and lack of judgment) without the bad or, frankly, dangerous elements. Unlike Grandma before her, my mother would never have bid me a nonchalant farewell as I set off to hitchhike thousands of miles as a teenager with no intention of returning home. My siblings and I were given autonomy, not abandoned. Our home life, however chaotic and unkempt, was fundamentally secure, and my sense, looking back, is that this security made me open to learning on my own—to trying, failing, and trying again.

This process of learning, of being supported to explore whatever we wanted or needed to know, was usually circuitous and spontaneous. There was no attempt to replicate school in the home, to set up a little row of desks facing a wall and follow a predetermined course with Mom or Dad in the role of disciplinarian— that is to say, as the person who enforced boundaries on knowledge while also meting out punishments. We were not homeschoolers but unschoolers, a term coined by the educator and author John Holt. My parents shunned coercion and relied instead on our curiosity to drive us, which they understood to be the most basic human characteristic. This belief was core to Holt's philosophy: "The human animal is a learning animal," Holt would say. Infants learn to speak by being spoken to and wanting to speak back, not by being tutored in sixty-minute sessions with a quiz at the end. Curiosity, in this view, is one of the most powerful forms of motivation our species possesses, and the goal of education should be to nurture and unleash it.

It was a happy arrangement for me, but with one glaring downside: I was lonely. In Athens, Georgia, the sleepy college town we had recently moved to, unschoolers were few and far between, while Christian homeschoolers, far more prevalent, were openly hostile to heathens like us. "Red Rover, Red Rover, send Jesus right over!" the children screamed the first and only time we tried to join their playgroup. Out of desperation, I decided to go where the remaining kids spent their days: Gaines Elementary School.

The first thing I learned was that I was always doing the wrong thing. I would line up in the hallway or sit in the lunchroom only to have the tiny humans I had hoped to befriend scold me for whatever grievous social error I had most recently committed. I spoke to the wrong classmates (girls were not supposed to talk to boys), turned in my work too fast or too slow (Goldilocks I was not), had a bad haircut (my mom did it herself), and was not wearing deodorant (I didn't need to, I explained earnestly, because I hadn't even gone through puberty yet—a response that, quite predictably, only made my tormentors mock me more). Most of all, I heard about my clothes. My "outfits," I was told, were bad, out of style, did not match. Other kids, it turned out, did not appreciate Albert Einstein, and certainly not enough to wear the same shirt with his face on it three days a week. But it was shoes that were the real source of grief. When I reflect back on that period, I can still feel my longing for Keds sneakers. In place of my off-brand thrift store shoes, a pair of white Keds, I came to believe, would have bought me respect, and respect would have bought me peace.

Toward the end of the school year, when it was clear that I was on the verge of dropping out, the principal called me into her office to see if I would reconsider. I was a good kid, and she wanted me to stay and learn. But she had no idea that the lessons I was learning were all wrong. Gazing at me across her large desk, she tried to explain how social hierarchies work. The kids who were picking on me most intensely, she said, were some of the most disadvantaged. They were poor and came from broken homes, and some of their parents even used drugs. The implication was that my bullies were also being picked on by the richer kids, who were probably being picked on by the kids above them, and that this was just what kids do; I needed to toughen up. I sat in silence, unsure of how to process this information. At least I had enough sense not to tell her that I was pretty sure my parents had used drugs, too. She made me feel guilty enough that I stayed until the end of the year. And then I quit.

Looking back, of course I recognize that the teasing I was subjected to was hardly extreme; I wasn't crammed in a locker, my head wasn't dunked in a toilet, and no one taped an insulting sign on my back—nor was I subjected to the online abuse that makes school unbearable for so many young people today, driving a distressing number of them to suicide. What made my experience unusual was the fact that my sheltered life caused me to find my peers' behaviour not just cruel but bizarre—and that I had enough remove to be curious about it, too. I simply could not figure out why little kids with allowances of a couple quarters a week were judging each other for what they did or did not possess. I was thinking like a postmaterialist in a survivalist era. Back home for what would have been fifth grade, I felt unschooling to be a reprieve. I returned to relating to objects as ends—toys to play with, bikes to ride—instead of means—to social acceptance, to self-esteem.

NEVER AGAIN WOULD I approach people so openly, so guilelessly, as I had walking into that first day of fourth grade. I lost a bit of trust in other people that school year, which meant that I had also lost some measure of trust in myself. But that, I now believe, is what our educational and economic systems are too often designed to do: make us feel as though we are lacking and inadequate. Fourth grade was my first encounter with what I call manufactured insecurity, the kind of insecurity generated to keep us competing and consuming, nudging us to act like materialists and compete for scarce resources, even if we might prefer to try to live another way.

Little did I know back then that a backlash against the countercultural values I was raised with was in full swing. In a roundabout way, postmaterialists had prompted a right-wing resurgence. As Inglehart ruefully observed in 2017, paraphrasing Marx and Engels, postmaterialism had become "its own gravedigger."[11] Focused on making society more open, less discriminatory, and free during the 1960s and 1970s, postmaterialists ignored the first levels of Maslow's pyramid of needs. Taking a baseline of material security for granted, they emphasized the importance of social inclusion and environmental sustainability over rudimentary bread-and-butter concerns. But many people were becoming more materially insecure as the economy entered a new crisis. In the early seventies, oil prices spiked, inflation rose alongside layoffs, and economic growth lagged across North America and around the world. During the 1930s and 1940s, a broad and militant labour movement fought for redistributionist policies, ushering in the material security and middle-class stability of the post–World War II period and laying the ground for the flowering of self-expression values. But by the 1970s, the old labour coalitions that safeguarded economic security for working people were fragmenting and under assault.

The postmaterialist challenge to established notions of patriotism and nationalism, family life, and social hierarchy had unsettled as many as it had inspired, and this unease only increased as the economy contracted. More traditionally minded people, overwhelmingly white and older, clung to survival values in the face of disorienting social change and diminishing opportunities. Political conservatives, backed by big business interests, capitalized on their anxieties. They fuelled resentment by railing against racial, religious, and sexual minorities—all while implementing policies that made ordinary people's lives even more miserable and tough. In this way, the social movements of the sixties—emboldened Black and brown people, uppity feminists, unashamed queer people, entitled students, and know-it-all professors—became the scapegoats for the new-found insecurity of the white working class, obscuring the true culprits: an increasingly cutthroat capitalist regime and the rise of corporate globalization.

In 1979, two years after the publication of *The Silent Revolution*, Margaret Thatcher became the prime minister of Britain by taking advantage of precisely these dynamics, a role she would hold until 1990. Ronald Reagan, playing a similar game, became president of the US a year later. Together, they remade the global economy—and reshaped mainstream attitudes as well, their influence trickling all the way down into my fourth-grade classroom. As Thatcher put it in a 1981 interview, "What's irritated me about the whole direction of politics in the last thirty years is that it's always been toward the collectivist society. People have forgotten about the personal society." By changing economic doctrine, the then–prime minister explained, people's priorities and outlooks could be reoriented: "Economics," she said, "are the method; the object is to change the heart and soul."[12] Thatcher's goal, bluntly put, was to use policy to manufacture in order to nudge the public rightward. Instead of looking for help from government programs or joining a labour union to collectively bargain for better treatment, citizens were encouraged to go it alone.

By failing to fully account for the connection between personal freedom and material security, the 1960s emphasis on self-expression smoothed the way for Thatcher's claim that there is "no such thing as society," only isolated men and women and families whose foremost "duty" was to look after themselves.[13] Thatcher's version of individualism—which involved shrinking the social safety net and weakening organized labour—left people even more atomized and scrambling.

By the time I was growing up, this new supercharged brand of capitalism was ascendant. To varying degrees, it reshaped liberal democratic governments around the world—they deregulated key industries, privatized public goods, and lowered taxes on the rich— as it channelled the individualism of the counterculture into the consumer frenzy of the 1980s. In the Cold War logic of the era, democracy became synonymous with an abundance of consumer choice; freedom was access to commodities, not access to the welfare commons. As social provision shrunk, striving became a form of personal insurance against future risk; as employment became more precarious, education was advertised as the most reliable path to upward mobility. Competition was extolled as the most effective way to keep afloat, and the purchase of new products the surest path to self-expression. Wealth and power concentrated at the top, but everyone was free to buy—if not with cash, then with credit. Unhinged from the material security that once sustained it, the postmaterialist emphasis on personal freedom and self-expression began to take on a desperate, darker, and more insecure edge. According to this new paradigm, by valuing objects and seeking status through them, the elementary school children who so confused me were only doing their civic duty.

HUMAN BEINGS HAVE LONG had a penchant for things. The archaeological record brims with evidence of our appreciation of objects and adornment. The oldest known jewellery, carved shell beads found in what is now southwest Morocco, date back an astonishing 150,000 years.[14] I will allow, then, that the schoolchildren's insecurities about matters of attire were partly a reflection of a drive both old and profound. Consumption—of essentials such as food and water, of art and culture, of tools and ornamentals—literally sustains us; if we don't consume, we die. But different cultures can have very different modes of consumption, and there is a difference between consumption for utility or pleasure and consumption that creates feelings of inadequacy that can only be allayed by an endless stream of commercial goods. The Potlatch gift-giving ceremonies long practised by Indigenous peoples of the Pacific Coast, including the aforementioned Tagish community in Carcross, for example, have an element of status competition, but one based in the generosity of giving things away, the giver's prestige measured by communal munificence instead of private accumulation.[15]

Rooted in insecurity rather than magnanimity and hoarding rather than sharing, capitalist modes of consumption are always fraught—a conflict contained within the etymology of the word itself. The term *consumption* emerged from the Latin *consumere*, which means to use up, exhaust, waste, destroy, or devour. Consumption thus initially referred to a kind of physical expenditure, like a log or a candle consumed with flame, or a person consumed by desire, and later, a disease that wastes the body away. There was also a related word, *consummare*, that conjures not depletion but wholeness—to sum up, finish, or perfect, as in to consummate. Thus *consumption*, when we trace its roots, evokes more than mere acquisition. The word holds out the promise of completeness while also acknowledging the possibility of sickness and destruction. Thus, we can understand consumption as both a wanting and a wasting disease, one that has now covered the earth with North American refuse.[16]

Yet despite our modern excesses, we are hardly the first to worry about material desire getting out of hand. In the sixth century B.C., Chinese philosopher Lao Tzu warned: "Fill your bowl to the brim, and it will spill. Chase after money and security and your heart will never unclench."[17] Around the same time, the rise of Buddhism called attention to the suffering caused by desire, describing a realm of hungry ghosts condemned to an eternity of insatiable longing for food or things. Soon, Plato linked excessive consumption to immorality, arguing in the *Republic* that rulers of a just society must be indigent, owning no property whatsoever, if they were to truly serve the common good.

In his magisterial book *Empire of Things*, historian Frank Trentmann reveals how similar concerns about consumption and desire, including fears of what he calls "emulative spending," were present at the dawn of modern consumer culture in the fifteenth century. Even then, people were anxious about the dangers competitive consumption might unleash. During China's

Ming Dynasty and in Renaissance Italy, the emergence of luxury markets and fast-changing fashions caused moral panics (in both places, affluent women took to wearing elaborate hair extensions, while some trendy Italians used napkins at table, the pinnacle of indulgence, and Chinese trendsetters pored over interior decorating guides). Long before "keeping up with the Joneses" was a phrase, governments tried to rein in the trend. Beijing magistrates fretted over expensive funerals; Venice passed regulations against "sumptuous" lifestyles; and European courts suppressed "Excesse in Apparayle" and fined "over-dressed" women for crimes like wearing a neck scarf too large for their station.[18]

The Scottish Enlightenment thinker Adam Smith helped to change all this, calming fears of gluttony and immoderation. Today, Smith is most famous for his metaphor of the "invisible hand" said to guide free markets; he was also the first person to use the term *consumption* in its modern sense, as the inverse of production. As he memorably remarked in his 1776 classic, *The Wealth of Nations*, people have long possessed the "propensity to truck, barter, and exchange"—the existence of markets in human society is nothing new. Commerce long precedes capitalism, and consumption, it's clear, is ancient. Capitalism's distinction lay in turning the possibility of commerce into the necessity of competitive production, a feat accomplished by imposing widespread insecurity, as the opening chapter discussed. In the eighteenth century, there were two further innovations. First, capitalism made the mass production of consumer goods possible. And second, it gave rise to a novel ideology that justified and encouraged their purchase and use—an ideology that Smith helped to articulate in his first and less well-known book, *The Theory of Moral Sentiments*. Smith formulated a theory of consumption that put insecurity, or what he sometimes called "anxiety," at the centre.[19] After Smith, governments would no longer see private consumption as a problem, nor would they try to rein in cycles of emulative spending: consumption was now a virtue, not a vice.

A sensitive and astute observer of emotions, Smith believed that the basic human desire for approval and admiration (in his words, "to be observed, to be attended to, to be taken notice of") is what makes people yearn for material things in the first place. Thus, consumption and capitalism have always been less about stuff and self-interest (let alone efficiency and innovation) than they are about insecurity and self-esteem. Those who envy others wish themselves to be envied in turn, thinking it will bring them happiness and security. It is this social aspiration, Smith thought, not solipsistic greed, that pushes people to truck and trade.

But there's a catch. The idea that the "attainment is well worth all the toil," Smith wrote, is a "deception"— a useful fallacy that propels capitalism forward. It is a ruse that "rouses and keeps in continual motion the industry of mankind," motivating farmers to plow bigger fields, entrepreneurs to open factories, colonizers to seize other people's territory, engineers to invent new gadgets, marketers to promote new products. Economic growth depends on this deception, and so it can never be dispelled.

To illustrate the depth of the deceit, Smith told a story about a poor man's son who, coveting the lavish lifestyle of his betters, relentlessly toils and joins their ranks. Finally, in the torpor of old age, he sees through the illusion, regretting his squandered youth in light of a newly apparent and discomfiting truth: "Power and riches appear then to be, what they are, enormous and operose machines contrived to produce a few trifling conveniencies to the body, consisting of springs the most nice and delicate, which must be kept in order with the most anxious attention, and which in spite of all our care are ready every moment to burst into pieces, and to crush in their ruins their unfortunate possessor."[20]

Wealth, Smith admits, is not a blessing but a curse. Instead of providing security, wealth coexists with insecurity: "always as much, and sometimes more exposed than before, to anxiety, to fear, and to sorrow; to diseases, to danger, and to death." By the time the poor man's son realizes that he could have been happy all along, it is too late. "Real happiness" and "real satisfaction" were at "all times in his power," Smith maintains, for they consist of "ease of body and peace of mind"— a state that can be accessed free of charge by anyone anywhere at any time. "The beggar, who suns himself by the side of the highway, possesses that security which kings are fighting for."[21]

With this, Smith, the father of modern economics and a man widely remembered as the patron saint of capitalism, anticipated the postmaterialist critique of consumer society by two hundred years—ironically at the very moment he was helping create that society. Yet Smith was no postmaterialist, as Inglehart would have it: he was simply clear-eyed and common-sensed. Money and things cannot buy happiness. Today many of us would agree with this statement, at least after a certain point—and research confirms that beyond a certain baseline of material security, increasing wealth does seem to have diminishing emotional returns. But it is Smith's view of human motivation under capitalism that concerns us here, for it remains the prevailing wisdom, though few people speak about it in such blunt terms. Our society assumes that we all need a promise to chase, some extrinsic incentive to drive us—an Instagrammable beach vacation, for example—lest we cause the wheels of commercial society to stop turning and economic growth to stall by lollygagging in the sun on the roadside. Sure, the system is based on a lie and makes even the winners miserable, but that's why, Smith thought, it works so well.

· · ·

PART OF THE PARADOX of postmaterialism is the fact it emerged from consumer abundance. Beginning in the late 1950s, as houses and apartments filled with those vacuum cleaners, Jell-O packets, and TVs, worries about emulative spending flared up once again. Like the poor man's son in Smith's fable, residents of the world's wealthiest democracies began to sense the market's deception at work.

In his 1958 bestseller, *The Affluent Society*, John Kenneth Galbraith painted the picture of a people gorging on private luxury while starved of public goods, thus lacking in overall well-being. Two years later, muckraking journalist Vance Packard's influential book *The Waste Makers* helped turn consumerism into a dirty word. Both authors sounded the alarm about the stimulation of artificial wants through the shadowy profession of public relations, otherwise known as advertising. "The modern corporation must manufacture not only goods but the desire for the goods it manufactures," Galbraith explained.[22] Packard quoted a leading businessman speaking at an apparel industry conference in 1950: "It is our job to make women unhappy with what they have," the executive said. "We must make them so unhappy that their husbands can find no happiness or peace in their excessive savings."[23] The challenge was persuading people to keep buying even though their closets and bellies were full.

To accomplish this, consumption's destructive attributes had to be brought to the fore—old things, even

yesterday's things, had to be made passé and disposable, tossed away and wasted to engender new longings.
Today this has reached its apogee in cellphones and lap-
tops designed to be upgraded or that break without the
possibility of repair. Dissatisfied and insecure customers, constantly churning through products, are best for
corporate bottom lines. Decades after Gaibraith and
Packard sounded their alarms, advertising remains one
of the primary means through which an endless array
of new wants, and the insecurities that spawn them,
are manufactured.

Like consumption, advertising has existed for a long
time. Ancient Rome, most famously the city of Pompeii,
was bedecked by billboard advertising, from signage
on storefronts to announcements of theatrical perfor-
mances and gladiatorial games, promotions boosting
new literary works, "for rent" notices, and election post-
ers galore.[24] For centuries, ads were refreshingly direct:
this bakery sells bread, this play will entertain, this clock
tells time, this deodorant helps you not stink. During the
Great Depression, under the guidance of a man named
Edward Bernays, who happened to be the nephew of the
famed psychoanalyst Sigmund Freud, marketing evolved
to tap into unconscious fears and aspirations; in other
words, our insecurities. In the post–World War II era,
the profession helped keep people buying even though
their homes were already stuffed full.

Bernays coined the term "public relations" for the
field he developed, which now employs hundreds of

thousands of people. By 2025, the global advertising industry is expected to hit one trillion dollars of annual revenue—more than enough to end world hunger multiple times over.[25] But instead of using those resources to fulfill people's basic material needs—an arrangement that would, according to Maslow's and Inglehart's predictions, free them to prioritize nonmaterial ones—corporations spend this money fuelling the deception Adam Smith identified and manufacturing insecurity to keep the treadmill of consumption running.

Advertising isn't just bigger and richer than ever—it has become automated, personalized, and fully integrated with the broader media ecosystem. Algorithms, embedded into the channels we depend on to access news and information, send us ads and content according to our consumer profiles and online habits, trapping each of us in what media critic Eli Pariser has dubbed a "filter bubble." The problem, here, is that advertising is incompatible with truth; public relations is, by definition, hype, which is how we distinguish it from journalism. When you have a communications architecture explicitly designed to bring readers' eyeballs to advertisers—as ours is structured to do—you have a communications architecture optimized for insecurity, whether it is the insecurity of body-shaming ads or the insecurity of truth-corroding disinformation. Both cases mess with our heads, making us feel bad about ourselves and about others.

Online, the ads you don't see are as important as the ads you do. Power differentials related to gender, class, race, and age are programmed into the algorithms that drive the systems of distribution. More affluent white audiences, for example, are more likely to be shown content about good jobs and safe housing than their Black counterparts, who are more apt to see their feeds crowded with solicitations for subprime lenders, overpriced insurance products, or political ads telling them to stay home on Election Day.[26] Older and isolated people are more liable to be targeted by and fall victim to scams, and to be funnelled down fear-inducing tunnels that trigger the authoritarian reflex, allowing unscrupulous politicians, shadowy billionaires, and malevolent foreign actors to incite fear, loathing, and insecurity for political and economic gain.[27]

Data brokers segment Internet users into categories that include "Established Elite," "Power Couples," and "Just Sailing Along" on the one side and "Rural and Barely Making It," "Probably Bipolar," "Gullible Elderly," and "Zero Mobility" on the other, enabling them to target the groups accordingly.[28] The aim is to know which vulnerabilities to target and the most effective time to do so. There are, in the ghastly words of one firm, "prime vulnerability moments" for brands to seize, for instance, when "women feel the most insecure about their bodies and overall appearance."[29] Or, in the no-nonsense summary of *Adweek Magazine*: "Women feel ugliest on Mondays and weekends."[30] Social media platforms are particularly damaging for teenagers, who are relentlessly fed content that pummels their self-esteem. A 2022 experiment conducted by the Center for Countering Digital Hate revealed that TikTok rapidly surfaced videos about body image, mental health, suicide, and eating disorders to accounts associated with thirteen-year-olds—they appeared, in some cases, every thirty-nine seconds.[31]

Insecurity has always been the currency of advertising, but today it is more explicit and extreme. We are, in a very real way, being bullied and abused by the algorithms that marketing firms have developed, as former Facebook product manager and whistleblower Frances Haugen revealed when she leaked tens of thousands of internal documents. Some clearly showed that company executives were well aware of Instagram's deleterious impact on young users' well-being; she also detailed the ways Facebook officials undermined efforts to fight hate speech and disinformation out of fear such efforts would dampen user growth and profits. Haugen stated it clearly in her testimony before the US Congress: "I believe that Facebook's products harm children, stoke division and weaken our democracy."[32]

Research by psychologist Tim Kasser shows that people who are more steeped in consumer culture feel physically worse: they report more headaches, back pain, sore throats, and other physical ailments than those less focused on money, image, and fame.[33] The harms done by commercial society to our self-esteem and health—not to mention the possibility of self-government—is, predictably, a bonanza for those who purport to sell cures. The global wellness industry—the "fitness mind-body market" in the jargon of financial analysts—is estimated to be worth well over $1.5 trillion and growing.[34] Postmaterialist values are repackaged to soothe the insecurities of daily life: eat superfoods, pop some supplements, breathe deeper, try journalling, practise gratitude, steam your yoni; click here to buy the correct kinds of supplements, journals, yoni-steamers! As sociologist Stephanie Alice Baker explains, the wellness movement emerged out of the California counterculture in the 1960s and 1970s, fusing postmaterialist ideas of freedom, experimentation, and self-realization. But where self-care in the 1960s was initially connected to bolder demands for equal access to health care, particularly for people who were discriminated against or underserved by the medical establishment due to their race, class, gender, and sexuality, the more recent iterations have been stripped of progressive and structural social critique.[35]

Take, for example, author and podcaster Brené Brown, one of the most popular self-help gurus of our age. She has built a media empire (books, podcasts, Oprah interviews, Netflix specials, and training modules) by empathetically describing the emotional harm meted out by what she calls our "culture of scarcity" and how it makes us feel awful about ourselves. Her advice, distilled to its essence, repackages postmaterialist precepts. Brown's recommendations include practising authenticity, engaging in creativity for its own sake, forsaking conventional measures of status and success, pursuing belonging over conformity, and embracing curiosity. Her enormous audience proves that her suggestions resonate: millions of people feel inadequate, belittled, and unable to measure up, and they desperately want to pursue more fulfilling, nonmaterial goals. Yet Brown never pauses to ask what forces might be colluding to create the feeling of scarcity she rightly condemns; nor does she consider the possibility that the insecurity and self-blame her followers feel is produced by the same Fortune 500 companies that frequently invite her to lecture. As with many of her successful peers, *capitalism* is a word she never utters. Instead, Brown counsels her suffering audience to embrace "enoughness" and become more vulnerable and courageous.[36]

Brown's advice appears to help her audience, which is certainly a good thing, but I think we deserve more than coping strategies: we need political ones. Trying to be less guarded, more resilient, and authentic does not preclude also trying, simultaneously, to change the structures that systematically assault our self-worth. The culture of scarcity Brown laments, and the striving and shame that attend it, calls out for collective action. We could, perhaps, begin by taking inspiration from those sixteenth-century officials who sought to inhibit excessive spending by the wealthy and impose a prohibition on private jets or a limitation on personal properties. We could also look to the European Union, which has made inroads toward outlawing business models that depend on disposability (or what is known as "planned obsolescence") to drive sales, and ensuring that all products are fixable (a so-called "right to repair").[37] The insidious insecurity-generating techniques deployed by advertising and social media also need to be seriously restrained. A more materially secure and less emotionally besieged society would go a long way toward achieving "enoughness" and creating conditions where Brown's purported values of openness, authenticity, and curiosity could actually flourish.

Such reforms might also reduce disinformation's reach and dampen the authoritarian reflex that is so easily activated online. At the start of the Covid-19 pandemic, social media platforms sucked frustrated and frightened wellness seekers down conspiratorial wormholes. The result has been an alarmingly robust "wellness-to-far-right-conspiracy pipeline."[38] Algorithms programmed to hijack people's insecurities direct audiences toward an army of self-appointed influencers who offer up faddish health advice, vaguely New Age platitudes, and a hefty dose of fear-mongering, racism, and lies—a toxic combination that spilled into the off-line world at the aforementioned Ottawa demonstrations and elsewhere.[39] (One *Rolling Stone* headline invited us to "Meet the 'Girl Boss Misinfo Types' Bringing Together Wellness Influencers and Canadian Trucker Convoy.")

This is postmaterialism through the looking glass: self-expression and individualism and free thinking, let loose in an insecure abyss.

As someone raised to respect self-education, I find it sad that I now shudder when people tell me they have done their "own research," a sure sign they've been sucked through a conspiratorial pipeline and come out the other side covered in hogwash. But I try not to forget that people have good reasons to feel beleaguered and afraid. We are, indeed, being manipulated by powerful forces, not least by the advertiser-beholden platforms that consumers of conspiracies use to find information. This process, to be clear, is not one that should be dignified by the word *research*, because the end results are known in advance, biases confirmed rather than challenged. The real point of conspiracies, like any article of dogmatic faith, is to avoid the discomfort and insecurity of not knowing by taking shelter in certitude. Conspiracists, then, do not actually question authority or expertise, as they often claim; they discount and reject it. Real questioning, in contrast, involves genuine curiosity and uncertainty and the acceptance of possibly being wrong. If my experience as an unschooler has taught me anything, it is that allowing people the freedom and security to question authority—rather than demanding unquestioning obedience—may be one of the best ways to ensure that meaningful respect for expertise and genuine curiosity ultimately prevail.

· · ·

THE WORDS *CURIOSITY, SECURITY,* AND *INSECURITY* all share a root. They stem from the Latin word *cura* — meaning worry, care, attention, and study. There is no learning without insecurity, without opening oneself up to experiences new and unknown. When we talk about something being secure, we typically mean that it is fixed in place; when we talk about being secure ourselves, we mean having the assurance of knowing what comes next. To be insecure, then, means being unfixed and unsure, to be in a place of possibility. Depending on the context, this kind of insecurity can be unpleasant or even terrifying, and it is especially awful when it is foisted on us by those looking to take advantage of our disorientation. But under the right conditions—when it is buttressed by a more fundamental kind of material security and self-confidence—it can also be generative and liberating. You cannot have real curiosity, or creativity, if everything is locked down and you know what comes next. Being open to new ideas means being open to your own limitations; being willing to experiment means being willing to possibly fail, and also willing to learn something that might change you.

The radical openness of curiosity makes it anathema to fundamentalists and dogmatists. It challenges the aggressive confidence of anti-vaccination conspiracists, climate change deniers, and the "woke"-bashing authoritarians who attack universities, free academic inquiry, and historical truth. The certainty these groups profess is curiosity's antithesis. Certainty is not security, it's a snapping shut and a cover-up—an attempt to escape from the insecurity of not knowing. Instead of showing strength, this kind of certainty makes us rigid, brittle, and closed-off.

Curiosity also poses a threat to neo-liberal doctrine, as Ronald Reagan made clear in 1967, when he served as governor of California. The state, he huffed at a press conference, should not be "subsidizing intellectual curiosity." Like his close ally Margaret Thatcher, Reagan aimed to increase the wealth of the few by reducing the security of the many—and shrinking higher education was a top priority. At the time Reagan made his remarks, he was busy waging a war on the state's colleges and universities, particularly the University of California at Berkeley, then the crown jewel of the American post-secondary education system. He could not stand how the students protested all the time—for free speech, for civil rights, and against the Vietnam war. He despised their dances, music, bad manners, and drugs. He denounced them as communists and bums. But most of all, he hated that they were able to learn for free. Shrinking the education commons, and imposing a higher price on university degree programs, was a way of limiting curiosity, which Reagan deemed a "luxury" the public could not afford.[40]

As Inglehart observed in *The Silent Revolution*, expanding access to post-secondary education was a major driver of 1960s postmaterialist values. Between 1950 and 1965, the rate of access to higher education doubled in the United States, more than doubled in West Germany, and more than tripled in France.[41] In Canada during this period, university participation rates more than doubled, with the percentage of women enrolling almost tripling.[42] Secondary and university-level education had never been so widely distributed across Western populations. What's more, tuition was generally nominal or non-existent, which meant that Reagan was right: governments were, in fact, subsidizing curiosity and helping people explore Maslow's higher, nonmaterial needs. When polls were conducted of incoming American freshman in the late sixties, a full 80 percent of respondents said it was essential to them to develop a meaningful philosophy of life; around 45 percent felt financial success was essential.[43] For the students surveyed, university was less about career training than self-actualization.

Two decades later, those values had basically traded places. Rising economic inequality and insecurity meant students felt more pressure to compete to get ahead, and ideas about school and learning shifted accordingly. Alternative approaches to education, the kinds of postmaterialist ideas my mother first encountered in Carcross, fell out of fashion. *Living and Learning*, the radical 1968 Ontario government report arguing for student-centred teaching methods, was deemed a risible relic. As one reporter put it in a feature story published in the *Globe and Mail*, "Now, it's the eighties and ... the [provincial government's new] goal is clear:

back-to-basics ... to structure."[44] The job precarity I discussed in the first chapter helped fuel a mad dash for
credentials; as incomes stagnated, the wage premium
of a college degree increased. At the same time, public
funding for post-secondary education declined precip-
itously. In Canada in the early eighties, government
funding accounted for around 83 percent of university operating revenue; by 2020,the figure was down
to 46 percent.[45] Today, the once fully public University
of California receives a little over 40 percent of its core
funding from state coffers.[46] As state subsidies shrink,
tuition grows to fill the gap. The escalating cost of post-
secondary education has had a corrupting effect on
learning, nudging students to think of themselves less
as citizens accessing a common good than as consumers purchasing a prestige commodity—often financed
by student debt.

Ostensibly about imparting knowledge, the modes
of education that dominate today manufacture insecurity as a spur to study. This approach to motivation
turns many kids off learning and numbs their natural,
intuitive curiosity. It's a phenomenon the trailblazing
cosmologist Carl Sagan noted in a 1995 TVO interview.
When he spoke to kindergartners, he said, they over-
flowed with enthusiasm and insightful questions. Why
is the moon round? What is the birthday of the world?
Why is grass green? Why do we have toes? "Profound,
important questions," Sagan says, "bubble right out of
them." But when he spoke to twelfth-grade classrooms,

the kids had become "leaden and incurious," unable or unwilling to engage. "Something terrible," he reflected, "has happened between kindergarten and twelfth grade and it's not just puberty."[47]

By the time I was a teenager in the nineties, the inequality and insecurity of the outside world was so palpable it motivated me to enrol in high school, despite my misgivings. I had never met an adult unschooler in my life, and if I kept educating myself, I feared I'd be labelled a dropout and a failure, forever barred from opportunity. Sadly, though, the teaching methods I encountered once I entered high school only heightened my sense of desperation, rather than assuaging it. In high school, I witnessed the phenomenon Sagan described, and began to feel its numbing effects. An institution ostensibly set up to facilitate education was effectively teaching students to despise the learning process. This aversion took a range of forms: the status-hungry striving of the high achievers, the bland disinterest of the tuned-out, and the overt anti-intellectualism that made *nerd* a favoured pejorative.

I was, of course, a nerd myself, but my fourth-grade experience of social ostracism was not repeated. I began my freshman year in the fall of 1993, and, on my first day, my home-cut hair and thrift store clothes were deemed not only acceptable, but the epitome of cool. It was the peak of the cultural phenomenon known as "grunge" and I was, undeniably, grungy. I could not believe my luck. As I wandered the school's halls, toting a backpack, stopping at my locker, taking tests, talking to friends, I felt like a strange simulacrum of the kids I had seen in movies and on TV. This, I thought, is what normal life is like! I was struck by how swiftly I came to identify with my high school peers, feeling just as disaffected and trapped as I imagined they must feel. Some days, I had to remind myself I was choosing to be there. For a short spell, I'll admit, there was a certain pleasure in handing over responsibility—in shifting from the ambiguity of unschooling, where there are no clear metrics for success and I had to be my own guide, to the autocratic structure of school, where I knew when I was doing well because the system told me so. My parents would have been supportive if I had stood up and left in the midst of a lesson but I never did. I stayed for three years and went on to university. But I stayed for the same reason I enrolled—fear of future unemployability.

Instead of being supported to follow my own curiosity, as I had been at home, at school I was driven by a combination of insecurity-inducing carrots and sticks. The sticks instilled fear and forced many of my fellow students to learn under duress—threats of time out, detention, suspension, a red pen, a failing grade. Education under these conditions became a defensive enterprise, one driven more by my peers' desire to avoid penalties than an authentic urge to comprehend, acclimating them to associate learning with punishment and shame. I, however, was more of a carrot chaser, motivated by praise. One day during my disastrous stint in fourth grade, the teacher let me know I'd received the lowest mark possible on my penmanship, "U" for unsatisfactory. Not caring one whit, I had responded that I knew how to write neatly but wrote swiftly and sloppily to get through dull assignments. But in high school, no mind-numbing bookwork, it seemed, was below me. I got kudos daily, not for my thinking, but for my diligence. Like all "good" students, I came to see myself reflected in the marks I received, a process that sours students on learning, too, though in less obvious ways. The "better" I did, the more I pleased others, the more insecure I felt—the insecurity produced by the pursuit of extrinsic rewards and a disconnection from my intrinsic motivations and interests. This is what psychologists call "contingent" as opposed to "secure" self-esteem.[48] In both cases, by carrot or by stick, the end result was the same. Insecurity made all of us retreat from risk, fearful of making mistakes, reluctant to get in trouble or to tarnish a glowing GPA. Reflecting back now, I can see that my cautious, self-protective approach was the death of authentic learning, which requires vulnerability and uncertainty—the kind of generative insecurity that opens us up to wanting to know more.

But something even deeper was amiss. Sticks and punishments affected some students more than others; insecurity was not fairly apportioned across the student body. In that first year, my diverse classrooms reflected the fact I attended a majority Black school. The second year, I was swept up into the "gifted" track. My classes

got smaller, and my classmates whiter and more affluent. We were being whizzed along on the equivalent of
an academic escalator, flanked by adults cheering us on
for being "talented," while our fellow students—overwhelmingly Black, Latino, Indigenous, and poor—were
told their comparatively stilted progress derived from
the fact they were "average" or "remedial." Our success
was predicated on keeping others down. Accolades,
good grades, and opportunities all seemed to be in short
supply, and as with all competitions for resources, there
were winners and losers. But in school this competition is particularly absurd: knowledge, unlike food or
water, can't be used up, and the desire to learn isn't a
need that evolved to be satiated. The boundlessness of
curiosity is what makes us learning animals; it is what
makes us human. Curiosity is something we can safely
be consumed by, since consuming knowledge enriches
us without creating waste.

Over the last decade, much of my organizing work
has focused on expanding access and funding for public education—and also on reimagining it. What would
public education look like if it relied more on the generative kind of insecurity—curiosity—to motivate
people, and less on manufacturing insecurity through
carrots and sticks? My work on this issue, I believe,
can be traced back to 1993—to the dramatic contrast
between my life as an unschooler and my disorienting
experience of public high school. In my view, subsidizing curiosity is precisely what the state, by funding

education, should be doing. But my ideal is very different from the form of public education I received. What we need, instead, is a system of education that is public, universal, reparative, and free. By *public* I mean funded by public dollars, not by tuition or by debt. By *universal*, I mean a space for everyone at every stage of life, where all subjects can be explored. By *reparative*, I mean an education system designed to acknowledge and actively redress past and ongoing social inequalities. By *free*, I mean in both price and purpose: education must be free in cost and aimed at freedom by unbinding curiosity. Should these conditions be met, education could actually be the motor of equality, opportunity, and learning so many of us want it to be. If we dedicate more public resources to cultivating curiosity, we can all be more secure.

BEFORE IT BECAME THE democratic free school that my mother attended in the 1970s, the main building of the Carcross Community Education Centre housed the Choutla Residential School. Founded in 1911, Choutla was run by the Anglican Church for half a century. In his book *The Fourth World*, George Manuel, the former Chief of the National Indian Brotherhood, describes residential schools as "the laboratory and the production line of the colonial system." What occurred across Canada, including at Choutla, was the manufacture of educational insecurity at its colonial, genocidal extreme.[49] In the property's earlier iteration, education was a tool of racist and religious indoctrination, colonization, and murder. (Choutla grounds, like similar sites, are now being searched for children's remains.) In its later phase, the one my mother knew, education became a forum for dialogue, personal development, and liberation. Prior to its demolition in 1993, the same building sheltered two conflicting approaches to education, to curiosity, and to conceptions of security.

Education, in any setting, entails a combination of curriculum and pedagogy, subject matter and teaching methods. In 1908, as part of an official assessment three years before Choutla Residential School opened, government inspectors warned that placing too much emphasis on academics at the school would only harm the future students, because excess learning would "unfit them for their condition in life."[50] Harsh methods of instruction were more important than the content of the lessons. Lakehead University political scientist Toby Rollo has shown that these attitudes and methods were only the latest development in a centuries-long project aimed at destroying Indigenous parenting and pedagogical practices, which French and English authorities deemed a threat to colonial settler security. For example, Paul Le Jeune, a seventeenth-century Jesuit who oversaw missionary projects in New France, complained that the Huron "will not tolerate the chastisement of their children, whatever they may do; they permit only

a simple reprimand." As Rollo notes, officials from various religious orders made similar observations of other
communities; the secure, loving, and respectful environment many Indigenous parents created for their
children was a barrier to cultural and religious assim-
ilation, and a threat to the brittle and defensive settler
security that colonialism instills—one they attempted
to demolish by removing Indigenous children from
their homes.[51]

In the 1960s, buoyed by the era's cresting wave
of movements demanding social change, Indigenous
activists mounted a new phase of resistance to settler
colonialism, including to its teaching methods. The
National Indian Brotherhood published an influential
policy paper, *Indian Control of Indian Education*, in 1971,
calling for school programs that emphasized Indigenous
principles of self-reliance, respect for personal freedom,
generosity, respect for nature, and wisdom. Two years
later, the Yukon Native Brotherhood released *Together
Today for Our Children Tomorrow*, which they delivered
to Prime Minister Pierre Elliott Trudeau, demanding a
recognition of Indigenous rights and land title, as well
as an overhaul of the education system.

Elijah Smith, the guiding force behind the Yukon
Native Brotherhood, spearheaded the *Together Today*
report. He was born in 1912, and his experience serving in World War II, and then being denied benefits
white veterans received, helped catalyze a lifetime of
activism, which included a commitment to uniting the

Yukon's Indigenous communities under one organizational roof to alchemize their shared experience of oppression and insecurity into solidarity.[52] The *Together Today* report demanded Indigenous control over curriculum, languages, teacher training and hiring, and teaching methods, citing the radical Brazilian educator Paulo Freire's 1968 classic *Pedagogy of the Oppressed* to criticize the colonial "banking" model of education, which treats knowledge like something to be deposited by an all-knowing teacher into children's heads.[53] Smith led the Yukon Brotherhood to a historic victory that took two decades to finalize: the successful negotiation of a land claim and modern-day treaty with the Canadian federal government.[54] Today, Whitehorse's Elijah Smith Elementary School bears the visionary organizer's name.

I learned about Smith and his efforts from Joseph Tisiga, a member of the Kaska Dena Nation who grew up in Whitehorse and knew my grandmother. Joseph's generation has benefited immensely from the efforts of Smith and his allies, but rates of poverty, housing insecurity, and food insecurity in the Yukon remain distressingly high, as do educational and professional disparities between Indigenous people and their white counterparts.[55] When we spoke most recently, Joseph, who was born in 1984 and has a thriving career as a visual artist, recalled attending what he described as a "dystopian" job fair aimed at Indigenous youth about a decade ago: there was nothing but military recruitment booths and offers of low-wage jobs at multinational corporations. "This is the best your mind can envision for us," he thought as he strolled the hall, "marginalized populations told to work at McDonald's or join the army?" To Joseph, the event epitomized capitalist and colonial systems of education, which, in little more than a century, helped devastate Indigenous communities that had lived on the land for at least fourteen thousand years.

Surviving and migrating across massive and often treacherous terrain, Tisiga told me, required deep knowledge, symbiosis, and skill passed from person to person, generation to generation, for millennia. "With the First Nation people living up in the north, relationship is at the core of everything. It's relationship to yourself, to your family, your community, and not to *your* land, but *the* land," Joseph explained. "There isn't coercion in that. It's relationship." The emphasis on storytelling in many Indigenous cultures, including his own, Joseph continued, is one example of a less coercive approach to education. Stories have multiple levels of meaning embedded in them—some accessible to children, others only revealed later in life. They combine information with entertainment to help make learning inviting, not fear-inspiring and insecurity-producing. They spark curiosity and a desire to know what happens next.

In her book *Dancing on Our Turtle's Back*, and in an essay entitled "Land as Pedagogy," Anishinaabe scholar and artist Leanne Betasamosake Simpson explores related themes, writing about the "fully consensual" and "learner-led" nature of Nishnaabeg education and conceptions of intelligence: "Like governance, leadership and every other aspect of reciprocated life, education comes from the roots up. It comes from being enveloped by land. An individual's intimate relationship with the spiritual and physical elements of creation is at the centre of a learning journey that is life-long."[56]

Where conventional Western education focuses on decontextualized knowledge and disembodied expertise, Nishnaabeg education, in Simpson's words, emerges out of a "compassionate web of interdependent relationships that are different and valuable because of that difference."[57] Children learn as they live, observing their surroundings and their elders, who answer questions and ask them in return. As Simpson describes it, the result is a mode of learning that is both deeply communal and highly individualistic—an individualism that is not selfish or competitive but secure and collaborative.

It's a mode of learning and teaching that makes each person a theorist, because everyone bears the responsibility to develop their own understandings and to share them according to the ethical precepts of the community.[58] Or as Simpson puts it, "Individuals carry the responsibility for generating meaning within their own lives—they carry the responsibility for engaging their minds, bodies and spirits in a practice of generating meaning." Even the most experienced and venerable teachers are careful to acknowledge that they are learners, too. These acknowledgements, Simpson explains, "position their ideas as their own understandings, and place their teachings within the context of their own lived experience." Not knowing everything, lacking information, is not shameful—it's a chance to gain insight.[59]

Today, the Yukon Archives holds the records of the Carcross Community Education Centre, which operated from 1972 to 1979. The school, the archive states, offered students "an opportunity to continue High School education while becoming part of a close-knit community" where "education was interpreted, in the broadest sense, to mean that all aspects of living were learning."[60] Though the founders knew the building had been a residential school, at the time they did not know, or perhaps did not want to know, the full details of what had transpired there. In a circuitous and tragic way, the people involved in that experiment in democratic education were groping toward the very thing the original residential school had sought to crush: a pedagogy rooted in land and relationships that aimed to help young people feel secure enough to be curious, to ask questions, to accept what they don't know, and to seek to know more.

· · ·

IN JANUARY OF 2021, my grandmother passed away at a hospital in Whitehorse. As a Buddhist, she understood death to involve not an ending but the passing into a new phase in the cycle of life, death, and rebirth. In Buddhist cosmology there are six realms that make up this cycle, which is known as samsara: the realms of gods, demi-gods, humans, animals, hell, and those insatiable hungry ghosts.

Each position on the wheel of life has its own meaning. The human realm is, in fact, a fortunate realm, for it is the one where awareness and action can take place. Hell, in contrast, is a land of misery and torment, while the animal realm is driven by basic needs. Demi-gods live in a state of constant warfare; the gods exist in peaceful oblivion. The realm of the hungry ghosts, meanwhile, is dominated by sentient beings who are starving and suffering. Their pinhole mouths and narrow necks can only consume tiny amounts of food or drink, leaving them forever wanting more. Their large bellies, emaciated and distended, illustrate their agony. The curse of the hungry ghost is to be tormented by cravings and desires that can never be satisfied.

For some Buddhists, the six realms are real places into which a person, depending on their karma, can be reborn after they die. For others, they represent primordial states of mind that we all, in one way or another, possess. According to this latter understanding, each of us has a little hungry ghost inside, one whose appetites can shrink or grow, possibly consuming our lives, or—should we all unleash our inner ghosts at once—the world. This 2,500-year-old tradition reminds us that desire is endemic to our species' condition as incomplete and interdependent beings. The question, as ever, is how we respond to this perpetual lack, this perpetual need for those things that make up Maslow's pyramid: sustenance, security, and self-actualization—and also, I would add, our need for solidarity, compassion, and care.

Within the tradition of Japanese Zen Buddhism, there is a ceremony called Segaki, the "Feeding of the Hungry Ghosts." It is a re-enactment of the ancient story of Moggallana, a disciple of the Buddha, who had a recurring dream about his deceased mother trapped and anguished in the hungry ghost realm and unable to eat or drink. Segaki entails an elaborate ceremony of making offerings to the ghosts in order to ease their suffering. Food and gifts are left far from any altars or statues of the Buddha, lest the ghosts choke; the sacrifice must be free of doctrine, so even those who do not accept the Dharma, the righteous way of life for Buddhists, can partake. All ghosts are invited to join, and to enter a space free of judgment. Segaki requires the acceptance of others, without expectation of repayment for one's kindness, while also presenting a chance to reflect on one's own cravings and compulsions.

When societies come together to ensure material security for everyone, they are, in a sense, engaging in a similar sort of ceremony—the collective establishment of social policies and rituals that can soothe our hungry ghosts.

We know this approach works. History shows that increased material security helps people be more open-minded, tolerant, and curious, whereas rising insecurity does the reverse, causing dogmatism, rigidity, and bigotry to spike. Today, young people report rising levels of sadness and distress; older people are getting lonelier and more depressed. Economic trends indicate that employment will remain unstable and that inequality will continue to climb. Climate disasters are only becoming more commonplace. Will all of this lead, inevitably, to an authoritarian revival? I don't believe that it has to—as long as we learn from the past. If we want to mitigate authoritarian threats, we cannot repeat the postmaterialist mistake of ignoring economic concerns, the pyramid's lower but all-important rungs. When people feel insecure, it is easier to convince them that immigrants are taking their jobs, that vaccines are a conspiracy, and that professors are indoctrinating students with "gender ideology." The far right knows this, which is why they have been so laser-focused on economic policies that promote insecurity. In response, we need to do more than chastise people for being closed-minded. We need to build both a ceiling and floor—to implement an upper limit on inequality's spiral and a baseline of support beneath which no one can fall.

In Buddhism, hungry ghosts are sometimes thought of as individuals who seek truth but cannot accept the insights that will help them break free. Part of the challenge we face today is creating conditions where people can let go of destructive beliefs. Material security can help, as can less coercive and more consensual forms of education—one of the lessons of Segaki. "I imagine that one of the reasons people cling to their hates so stubbornly is because they sense, once hate is gone, they will be forced to deal with pain," James Baldwin observed.[61] A sense of security can help people approach difficult things with a spirit of curiosity—both their own personal pain and the pain that comes from facing upsetting social truths—and potentially open them up to new and different ways of being. When we feed the ghosts, we feed ourselves, too.

CHAPTER 4

BEYOND HUMAN SECURITY

EVERY FOUR YEARS the US-based National Intelligence Council releases a report called *Global Trends* that attempts to forecast the threats and uncertainties that will shape the world for the next two decades. Authored by an association of professional spies with a name befitting an indie rock band—the Strategic Futures Group—the report is written to encourage the White House and its advisors to stretch their thinking toward a longer time horizon. As a result, the documents have a speculative quality and are typically declassified without much fanfare. That was certainly the case with the report released in 2017, which was mostly ignored by the public—until, seemingly out of the blue, the plague it envisioned arrived. The "global pandemic of 2023" did indeed halt international travel and wreak economic havoc precisely as predicted—only it did so three years ahead of schedule.[1]

Despite its predecessor's uncanny prescience, the next installment in the series garnered little public attention, perhaps because it focused on something both nebulous and omnipresent: rising insecurity. The 2021 edition of *Global Trends*, titled *A More Contested World*, focuses on the intersecting challenges facing humanity amid conditions of "expanding uncertainty." One of the report's main graphics features a box labelled "Eroding Human Security" surrounded by an array of menacing inputs or "drivers": extreme weather, water misuse, sea-level rise, geoengineering, societal and government change, unequal burdens, instability, conflict, and more. Inside that besieged box, the report argues, is the future we will all inhabit unless a miracle occurs.[2]

In the decades ahead, the report predicts, disequilibrium will become the new normal. "The ongoing Covid-19 pandemic marks the most significant, singular global disruption since World War II, with health, economic, political, and security implications that will ripple for years to come," the authors warn. "The effects of climate change and environmental degradation are likely to exacerbate food and water insecurity for poor countries, increase migration, precipitate new health challenges, and contribute to biodiversity losses." Soaring greenhouse gas emissions and concentrating wealth mean fragile social progress will stall. Members of the middle class will lose their precarious financial footing as gains made by vulnerable minorities and women crumble. Decreasing levels of social trust will contribute to a more "conflict-prone and volatile geo-political environment," while the "costs and challenges" of the coming upheaval will fall disproportionately on those who have the least—and are least responsible for the crisis—condemning over a billion people to the fate of climate refugee.

The report concludes by proffering five imagined scenarios, each envisioning a trajectory our uncertain future might take: a dystopian world where globalization has broken down; a fraught state of competitive coexistence dominated by Chinese and American hostilities; a revival of liberal democracy led by the United States and buoyed by technological innovation; a world broken into siloed blocs that leaves climate change unaddressed and poor countries collapsing. The fifth and final scenario strikes a hopeful note. Under the heading "Tragedy and Mobilization," it conjures a global revolution in human security.

In this possible future, a heating planet has led to extensive famine and strife, sparking bread riots in Philadelphia. Traumatized by their experiences of Covid-19 and hunger, young people launch a rebellious cross-border movement advocating for "bold systemic change," first for environmental policy and then public health and poverty. Green parties take power across Europe, the United Nations is revitalized, and China joins the alliance—followed by Australia, Canada, and even the United States after environmentalists sweep elections. The result? A new international organization, the Human Security Council. Under threat of backlash and boycott, wealthy countries and corporations fall in line. By 2038 a growing recognition of the unsustainability of past practices has transformed attitudes about food, health, and environmental security. The only disgruntled nations are the few remaining petrostates.

Reading this final scenario, I found myself nodding in agreement with American intelligence officials for the first time in my life—an unsettling experience in its own right. If we want to escape the little box labelled "Eroding Human Security," a massive and visionary social movement will indeed have to shift our social systems away from the fossil-fuel-guzzling status quo. As the authors of the 2021 *Global Trends* report rightly acknowledge, international institutions, domestic governments, economies, infrastructure, and incentives all must be remade. It reminded me of what the Intergovernmental Panel on Climate Change (IPCC), the world's climate science authority, had concluded three years before: "rapid, far-reaching and unprecedented changes in all aspects of society" are required to stave off catastrophe.[3]

At the same time, I wondered if a Human Security Council is really enough to set us on a stable course. If the challenges facing humanity are so enmeshed with a devastated planet, as both the National Intelligence Council and IPCC reports make clear they are, then shouldn't we also be asking what security means for the ecosystems, plants, and animals on which our own food, health, and environmental security depend?

One way of understanding our current predicament is that we are hurtling toward a future wrecked by our pursuit of human security alone. Many of the problems detailed in the *Global Trends* report stem from the fact that our political and social systems rarely, if ever, take other beings' survival or thriving into account. Instead of recognizing the earth as a commons we have a duty to care for and honouring the limits of ecosystems we need to protect, we treat the natural world as an inexhaustible resource we are entitled to exploit. But this human-centric approach now looks to be the source of our undoing; by attempting to conquer nature, we have brought ruin upon ourselves. What world views and ways of being have propelled this destructive and self-defeating spiral, and what other principles and practices might put us on a less solipsistic and more secure track? What other more holistic and inclusive visions of security might we aspire to?

INSECURITY AND SECURITY, AS I've argued thus far, have everything to do with time, and the same applies to climate change. The burning of carbon causes the past, present, and future to collide in disorienting and destructive ways. Fossil fuels are, in effect, the past condensed, every barrel of oil simultaneously a swath of land and an epoch of life—the product of photo-synthesis and the geological remains of once-living organisms—concentrated to a potent essence. Two and a half centuries after the first smokestacks blew exhaust into English skies, we are only beginning to come to grips with the consequences of combustion. The coal put to work in Manchester at the dawn of the Industrial Revolution shapes our environment today, just as the emissions from the burning of fuels from Saudi oil fields, American gas reserves, and Canadian tar sands will haunt life on earth for a long time to come.

As we incinerate our energy inheritance, nature's timekeeping methods become increasingly confused. April showers bring May flowers, or so they used to say, but this year I first spotted daffodils in February.[4] As the climate alters, delicately evolved biological clocks erratically speed up or slow down, causing plants and animals to fall out of sync. The majority of marine life, from seal to salmon, has adjusted its migration, breeding, and feeding patterns as a result of warming waters. As the permafrost melts, land animals across the Arctic are doing the same, forging new paths as formerly stable conditions change. Caribou travel further north and calve early, missing the sprouting of vital food sources on the tundra and pushing herds toward extinction's brink.[5]

Experts in phenology—the study of the timing of biological events such as plants flowering and insects laying eggs—call this a "mismatch."[6] Birds arrive late for spring, having timed their migration with the sun,

while plants are more attuned to temperature variation. A warming climate can mean leaves shoot early,
encouraging insects to emerge to feast, yet by the
time migrating flocks arrive to eat the insects in turn,
they are already gone. Flowers may bloom before—or
sometimes after—pollinating beetles, bees, or wasps
arrive, symbiotic partners misaligned. Spider orchids
and mining bees, puffins and herring, the red admiral
butterfly and the stinging nettle, caribou and lichen:
dependent but increasingly off-rhythm pairs abound,
co-evolved species failing to connect and endangering
both partners.

In a world this out of joint, how could we possibly
feel secure? No wonder climate anxiety, defined by the
New York Times as "anger, worry and insecurity stem-
ming from an awareness of a warming planet," now
affects people around the world. It's the eerie emotion I
felt as I gazed upon those unseasonably early blossoms,
one made eerier by the knowledge that such aberra-
tions will only become more frequent. Some who once
took security for granted are now grieving the loss of
a future previously believed to be guaranteed. Others
grieve a stable planet they never knew, with children,
especially Indigenous youth, showing particularly acute
symptoms of distress about what the future holds.[7] The
question, as always, is how we respond. Will we snap
shut with an authoritarian reflex, deny science, and
defend the unsustainable status quo? Build apocalypse-
proof bunkers or retreat to safer ground? Or can we

approach this crisis with curiosity, asking how we can work together to transform our relations to the more-than-human world?

Part of the insecurity many of us feel around climate change stems from the fact that no one knows what will happen next. But perhaps speculating about future scenarios is not the best use of our limited time. Not knowing can portend disaster or it can be a sign of possibility, and thus a spur to intervene. Fortunately, there are multiple ways to conceptualize and approach time. The first and more typical understanding emerges from the ancient Greek *chronos*, which means chronological time, a sequential unfolding. But the ancient Greeks had another concept, *kairos*, which refers to a propitious moment, the time for decision or action (and a term, coincidentally, that in modern Greek has come to mean weather).

Kairos, understood this way, is the time we seize. It is the time of those who turn their insecurity and anxiety into solidarity, knowing that every mote of mitigation matters, that every bit of carbon we don't release saves lives and buys time, and that without the sustained mobilizations of recent years, the catastrophe we face would be that much deadlier. Kairos says that time is of the essence and that it is not too late for the future to be changed in good and bad ways. The only way we risk a mismatch is by giving up and accepting our extinction as preordained. Kairos invites us to act now, whatever time it happens to be. It is the temporality of those who, even as they mourn, also organize—who vote, divest, strike, blockade, rewild, replenish, and sue.

IN 2018, ONTARIO'S CONSERVATIVE government, led by premier Doug Ford, dramatically reduced established greenhouse gas emissions targets, weakening the already inadequate policy set by the previous administration. In response, seven plaintiffs aged twelve to twenty-four filed a lawsuit, *Mathur v. Ontario*, channelling their insecurity and dread about the future into groundbreaking litigation. The lowering of standards, the plaintiffs contend, was both unscientific and unconstitutional, an infringement of their Section 7 rights to life, liberty, and the security of the person as defined by the Canadian Charter of Rights and Freedoms, as well as a breach of the rights of people not yet born. Their claims are bolstered by a growing chorus of scholars and activists who argue that the constitutional right to security of the person that Canadians possess must entail protection from environmental threats, lest the right be rendered meaningless. How can people ever be secure if government policies are actively undermining both personal and societal preservation?[8]

As Danielle Gallant, one of the lawyers representing the plaintiffs, explained to me, the constitutional right to security of the person entails both physical and psychological dimensions; in certain circumstances, emotional duress can be a sign of a rights violation. This means the insecurity and anxiety her clients feel is evidence that can be presented in court. Time, once again, has a role to play here—climate change hits differently depending on how much of the future you are likely to live to see. Younger generations and those not yet born will be the ones to suffer through the fires, floods, and crop failures that their law-making elders won't have to endure. This, Gallant told me, causes yet another layer of psychological harm. Knowing your government is exacerbating a crisis they should be mitigating only compounds the depression, post-traumatic stress, and suicidal ideation that many young people already feel.

Shelby Gagnon, one of the youth litigants, is an artist and organizer from Aroland First Nation who focuses on food security. She has lived most her life in Ontario's Thunder Bay. Now twenty-six, she sees the Canadian government's ongoing efforts to undermine people's security and self-preservation in the Indigenous communities she works with. Approximately 50 percent of Indigenous households are estimated to be food insecure, and they are also significantly more likely to experience extreme poverty than their white counterparts.[9] Despite being among the lowest contributors to greenhouse gas emissions in Canada, Indigenous people are disproportionately exposed to climate change's impacts.[10] The morning we spoke, Gagnon had to adjust her routine, heading up to the mountains at dawn to frost-scrape a bison hide before the sun made it too warm to do so. "We had to postpone our hide camp that was supposed to happen this weekend to next month, just because it's so mild right now," she told me. The Aroland First Nation are known as the blueberry people, but the year before last, after fires and a parched season, there were no berries to be picked. "That depletes food security," Gagnon said. "But you're also losing a part of your identity." What does it mean to be the blueberry people if no berries grow?

Sitting in front of a new painting she was working on, a portrait of Sabe, or Bigfoot, a symbol of honesty in Anishinaabe teachings, Gagnon told me she sees security and sovereignty as interconnected concepts, even one and the same. Her organizing work focuses on helping communities realize their own visions of food security given their limited economic resources and the unique ecology of a specific place, however strained that ecology may now be. There is no one-size-fits-all approach. Where food is concerned, sovereignty would mean the ability to eat a locally produced and culturally appropriate diet, a goal climate change undermines. Where governance is concerned, sovereignty would mean the power to say no to polluting and carbon-spewing projects and to pursue development on more equitable and sustainable terms—for example, by giving renewable energy infrastructure priority over crude-oil-transporting pipelines. This would require Canada paying real respect to Indigenous jurisdiction and giving Indigenous laws and conceptions of justice genuine weight.

Gagnon hopes the Mathur case will reinstate the previous stricter emissions standards and help establish a constitutional right for all Canadians to security that includes a healthy environment, though she knows that it is an uphill battle. In late 2022, the litigation broke ground by being the first of its kind to clear procedural hurdles and proceed to a full hearing. Seven months later, in April 2023, an Ontario Superior Court judge dismissed the case, but not before validating many of the plaintiff's arguments, including finding it "indisputable that, as a result of climate change, the Applicants and Ontarians in general are experiencing an increased risk of death and an increased risk to the security of the person." Moreover, by implementing a target that "falls severely short of the scientific consensus," Ontario is contributing to the problem, which means Section 7 rights are engaged. (Perhaps even more significantly, and related to the discussion of positive rights in Chapter 2, the judge found that the Applicants made "a compelling case that climate change and the existential threat that it poses to human life and security of the person present special circumstances that could justify the imposition of positive obligations under section 7 of the Charter.")[11] This leaves ample ground for an appeal, which means it may take many more years for a final decision to be handed down. Here we have a mismatch of potentially epic proportions: the grindingly slow procedures of the world's courts and the urgency of the climate crisis are alarmingly discordant.

The experience has reaffirmed Gagnon's sense that the Canadian legal system is not set up to protect people or the planet. "There should be more laws or a constitution for the land," she said. In the Anishinaabe tradition, she explained, land is regarded as a person and not as property to exploit or a resource to consume; people belong to the land more than the land belongs to them.[12] It follows that if the Mathur case were tried according to Anishinaabe principles, the environment would be represented very differently—with the respect and reciprocity a relative deserves. As Gagnon put it, "I think of a circle whenever I think about governance or law, no being higher or lower than who or what you are," no entity separate nor supreme. Being inside the circle as it hums around us, not outside it or above it, is where true security lies.

AROUND THE WORLD, ENVIRONMENTAL activists are creatively engaging with the law in order to defend the rights of children, future generations, and the more-than-human world—all entities that lack the traditional political rights enjoyed by most voting-age adults. From Sweden to the United States, young people have been filing lawsuits against their governments to force action on climate change on behalf of themselves

and those who haven't yet been born; in some places
this rights-based and forward-looking approach has
yielded remarkable victories. In 2015, the Dutch government was ordered to significantly and swiftly curb
emissions as a result of youth-led litigation, a then-
unprecedented decision that was upheld upon appeal.[13]
Three years later, Colombia's Supreme Court of Justice
found in favour of a group of youth plaintiffs seeking
to halt deforestation. The decision granted the Amazon
rainforest legal personhood—designating it as a rights-
bearing entity rather than a rightsless thing—and
enjoined the Colombian government to protect it, an
outcome that isn't that strange when you remember
that in some jurisdictions, corporations have the same
status. If Amazon the company can be a "legal person"
under the law, then why shouldn't the real Amazon be
one, too?

In 2008, Ecuador broke new ground when the
country enshrined the rights of Pachamama, Mother
Earth, in its newly adopted constitution. Two years
later, Bolivia followed suit, inspiring communities
around the world to begin to adapt the idea to their
own regions and struggles. Soon, laws reflective of the
culture of the Maori people granted legal personhood
to Te Urewera, an ancestral forest in New Zealand, and
later to the Whanganui River, recognizing it as a living whole spanning from the mountains to the sea.[14]
Citing those decisions, judges in India declared that the
Ganges and Yamuna Rivers and their tributaries would

be "legal and living entities having the status of a legal person with all corresponding rights, duties and liabilities."[15] In the United States, dozens of municipalities have passed local ordinances recognizing the rights of nature, including in Ohio, where voters bestowed legal rights on Lake Erie in an attempt to protect the nearly ten-thousand-square-mile body of water from runoff that causes toxic algae blooms—a move a federal judge struck down.[16] Although the US federal government has yet to grant rights to nature, in 2019, the Ojibwe White Earth Nation in Minnesota legally recognized the rights of manoomin, the wild rice that is a sacred and essential food within Anishinaabe culture, to flourish and exist.[17]

Canada joined this trend in 2021, when the three-hundred-kilometre Magpie River in Côte-Nord, Quebec—known to the Innu as the Muteshekau Shipu, "the river where water flows between square rocky cliffs"—became the country's first natural entity to be deemed a holder of rights. Parallel resolutions by the Innu Council of Ekuanitshit and the Minganie Regional County Municipality granted the waterway legal personhood as a way of protecting it from potential industrial development, which they hope will protect the people who live nearby in turn.[18] "We need to see that as humans we are not above the water or the animals," Uapukun Mestokosho, one of the river's advocates, told *National Geographic*. "We are part of a whole." Members of the Innu Council will serve as the river's guardians, tasked with protecting the nine rights the river now possesses—including the right to flow, to be free of pollution, to maintain biodiversity, and to sue.[19] Should Canadian ecosystems ever be recognized as legal persons at the federal level, perhaps they will be granted the constitutional right to "security of the person" that their human counterparts possess, too.

By placing humans and ecosystems in the same circle, the rights of nature movement poses a profound challenge to the conceptual underpinnings of Western legal systems. Indeed, it challenges one of the foundational tenets of Western thought, namely the elevation of human beings both above and apart from the rest of creation. When rendered into law, the dichotomy is clear. Humans and our proxies, corporations, are designated as legal persons with inalienable and justiciable rights, while everything else is just that—rightsless things.

It's a paradigm often traced back to the ancient Greeks, first Plato and then Aristotle, two philosophers who both saw man (yes, man) alone endowed with rational intellect, superseded in stature only by the gods. The idea that the organic world could be sorted into hierarchical categories was one of Aristotle's innovations. In the Middle Ages, the church adopted this motif and hammered it into what they called a Great Chain of Being, with minerals at the bottom, followed by plants, animals, humans, and then angels, all overseen by the Christian deity. In later centuries, the scheme was secularized and given a scientific sheen, a metaphysical chain replaced by an evolutionary tree, with *Homo sapiens* occupying the most distinguished branch as a higher organism looking down on the lower ones, part of the natural world but also better. Even if we don't go around gloating about our species' defining traits and talents—opposable thumbs, tool use, mastery of fire, language, and reason!—Western thinking, and the political structures we inhabit, are steeped in a paradigm that presumes human pre-eminence and dominion.

Whatever form it takes, the idea of creation as a hierarchy with our species sitting smugly at the summit always struck me as an image more illustrative of repressed insecurities than innate strengths. No doubt humans are wonderful, but we're also a bit absurd—gangly, furless, and extremely chatty. Only an insecure creature, or perhaps an insecure culture, would need to puff itself up with such a pompous self-image, an act of defensive narcissism taken to a society-wide extreme. A secure creature, I like to imagine, could celebrate its own unique abilities while also respecting other forms of intelligence and perception; a secure creature could marvel at its own amazing thumbs without denigrating the paws, hooves, claws, webbed feet, and fins that other beings possess. If that were the case, we would perhaps also be more inclined to recognize the ways our grasping hands have gotten us in trouble. The idea of human supremacy has lent credence to the idea that nature is a storehouse for our kind to own and exploit, an attitude my sister, the disability studies scholar Sunaura Taylor, calls "suicidal anthropocentrism."[20]

Endemic to Western thought, this self-aggrandizing and self-defeating view transcends eras and economic ideology. While it is a cornerstone of capitalism and colonialism, essential to the security of property and profits, communism has historically been just as capable of treating nature as a rightsless object to be hoarded, moulded, depleted, and destroyed. In the 1930s, aided by a scientist named Trofim Lysenko, Stalin rejected Darwinian natural selection in favour of a Lamarckian dogmatism, which insisted that plants and animals could be made to inherit traits gained over the course of an organism's lifetime. Just as a flower's stalk bends away from the shade as it grows, Stalin believed that all flora and fauna could be bent to serve his will. Attempts to re-educate crops, sometimes by dunking sprouts in freezing water or burying seeds in snow, combined with ill-conceived schemes to collectivize agricultural production, yielded little beyond mass death both for the plants and the people who depended on them.[21]

Two decades later, Mao Zedong rejected traditional Daoist precepts of intellectual humility and ecological harmony and adopted the slogan "Humans Must Conquer Nature." He launched his infamous "Four Pests" campaign, one prong of which was an all-out war against sparrows. The Chinese government commanded peasants to smash nests and eggs and to bang pots and pans to prevent the birds from landing in their fields. Sparrows flew and flew until they dropped dead from exhaustion; by some estimates, a hundred million perished. With their main predators gone, locust populations exploded, devouring everything in their wake. "Make the high mountain bow its head; make the river yield the way," Mao said in 1958, waging a war against the natural world that would prove impossible to win. The sparrow policy, along with other industrial-scale follies, contributed to a famine that killed tens of millions of people.[22]

Icarus-like fables of pride and its downfall, these stories speak of suffering both unfathomable and wholly avoidable. But our present situation is no less anguished or absurd. Long-standing attempts to achieve security by separating and elevating ourselves from the rest of the animal kingdom and trying to dominate nature are now backfiring on an unprecedented scale. One peer-reviewed and well-reported study released in 2021 estimated that climate change will cause 83 million cumulative excess human deaths—that is, deaths over and above what would naturally be expected—by the end of the century, a number the authors warned is likely a vast underestimation.[23] The same year, research published in the *Lancet Planetary Health* showed that extreme ambient temperatures have been responsible for nearly 10 percent of all fatalities globally between 2000 and 2019, or an estimated five million lives lost per year.[24] Should we stay the current course, nearly one in four children will live in extremely water insecure areas by 2040; over one billion people will be climate refugees by 2050; and approximately three billion people will live in hot zones, or areas outside of the narrow band of climatic conditions that shaped most of human civilization, by 2070.[25] In the decades ahead, a million animal and insect species are poised to disappear into the void—disrupting food chains and causing cascading consequences we can guess at but cannot accurately predict. The vanishing bugs are, of course, essential food for many birds, including sparrows; without these pollinators, many plants and food crops won't grow.

Granting legal rights to nature will not stop this doomed spiral, but it might help us slow it down—and speed matters. In an essay on not losing hope, one of the lead authors of the 2022 IPCC report wrote, "Every single metric ton of carbon dioxide we prevent from entering the atmosphere lessens the severity of the impacts we bake into the system."[26] The same goes for every day a fossil-fuel-transporting pipeline is blocked, every acre of natural habitat that is saved, every endangered creature that survives, and every gallon of water that remains safe to drink. These are fights in which the rights of nature are already being put to use.

Consider the battle that's been playing out in Western Pennsylvania, a region not known for its environmentalism and certainly not for its liberalism. It is deep Republican country but also a place where people recognized that their health and security were at risk. Grant Township is a tiny town of seven hundred residents with no stores, no traffic lights, no public sewage, few jobs, and little money. But it does have land and water, trees and animals, including the eastern hellbender, North America's largest aquatic salamander. In 2014 the community passed a resolution granting the local ecosystem the "right to exist, flourish, and naturally evolve" as a direct challenge to the Pennsylvania General Energy Company (PGE), which wanted to create a seven-thousand-foot injection well within the township's borders that would pump fracking waste into empty boreholes. Similar wells have been shown to produce toxic fluid that can seep through rock formations into local aquifers, tainting drinking water and ecosystems with hazardous chemicals and radioactive materials; injection sites have also been linked to small earthquakes. The company's plans jeopardized the security of the community by threatening residents' ability to drink local water without being poisoned and to trust in the stability of the ground beneath their homes.

When I reported on the story in 2016, Stacy Long, a town supervisor, told me that PGE mocked Grant Township residents for bestowing rights on nature— "What are you going to do," company officials said, "take a jar of creek water and put it on the stand and have it testify?"—while also taking the situation seriously enough to file suit. The Pennsylvania Department of Environmental Protection, determined to rubberstamp the project, also challenged the town's resolution in court. In response, the local ecosystem, the Little Mahoning Watershed, fought back. The 4.3-mile stretch of stream, which is home to fish, freshwater mussels, and aquatic insects, filed a motion to intervene, seeking to defend its legally enforceable rights. By granting the watershed rights, the town gained an important ally in a long and difficult campaign, one they have been winning against overwhelming odds.[27]

The gas company and the state eventually succeeded in stripping the local ecosystem of its entitlement to exist, but all was not lost. The strategy of recognizing the rights of nature bought the community valuable time and raised awareness of its plight. The question, according to Grant Township board member Jon Perry, is whose rights count: "Should a polluting corporation have the right to inject toxic waste, or should a community have the right to protect itself?"[28] Here, once again, the issue of security boils down to sovereignty. Across the US, conservative state legislatures have tried to deprive municipalities of the ability to say no to oil and gas projects. Long told me, "Rural areas like ours are the sacrifice zones for the gas industry." These are places where the security of corporate profits takes priority over the security of human and non-human life. Though litigation is ongoing, the community appears to have triumphed. In early 2023, the gas company announced its plans to plug and abandon the well. Security for ecosystems and security for people, Grant Township's inhabitants realized, are one and the same. Without this insight, the frackers would have won.

· · ·

IN 1516, THE PHILOSOPHER and statesman Thomas
More published his treatise *Utopia* and introduced a
new word into the English lexicon, a play on *ou-topos*,
meaning "no place" in Greek. In this tale within a tale, a
traveller describes his visit to a strange country where
the inhabitants hold all property in common. Viewing
themselves as cultivators of the land, not proprietors
of it, the Utopians, as they call themselves, are free of
the insecurity and tumult produced by competition,
acquisition, and loss. Men and women labour in essential trades such as farming, but only for six hours a day,
giving them plenty of time to study and enjoy their religious freedom. There are no alehouses and no lawyers
(notable, given that More was one himself), and couples get to see each other naked before they are wed.
If you inspect a horse before you buy it, the traveller
says to his astonished interlocutors, shouldn't you take
a good look at your future spouse before you commit?[29]

Combining speculative philosophy with a cutting
critique of the political status quo, More wrote *Utopia*
in the midst of the enclosure movement, that long
period when common fields and forests were fenced
and hedged for private gain. In an oft-quoted passage, *Utopia* denounces the wealthy nobility who have
seized common land to feed the growing and lucrative
wool trade, uprooting and impoverishing peasants to
make pasture for flocks of sheep and turning the "best
inhabited places into solitudes."[30] That the process of
enclosure commodified land and deprived commoners

of material security is something we already know. I quote More because he describes the ways humans conscripted domesticated animals to lead the charge. Sheep became four-footed agents of privatization, their wool the period's principal source of wealth. Those who enclose, More complained, "stop the course of agriculture, destroying houses and towns ... that they may lodge their sheep in them."[31] Sheep, More said, "devour men and unpeople" villages. (In the eighteenth century, large-scale sheep farming also devoured Scotland, the brutal Highland Clearances prompting the migration of thousands of displaced tenant farmers to Canada.) *Utopia* reminds us that hunger for profits, for land, and for animal products have been intertwined since capitalism's earliest days. It's a triad that has been shaping the modern world ever since.

Using sheep to propel enclosure adds a new dimension to the phenomenon I've been calling manufactured insecurity, expanding it beyond a limited human frame. The privatization of land and the birth of market society not only caused many human beings to lose their homes and their ability to sustain themselves, but it also affected non-humans. Farmed animals were forced to conform to industrializing modes of production, while wildlife habitats vanished, quickening the rush into what's known as the Sixth Extinction. When the radical Diggers led their spirited movement in defence of the commons amid the chaos of the English Civil War, they already recognized enclosure as a multi-species crisis. In the 1649 pamphlet that explained the aims of their resistance, Gerrard Winstanley described the earth as a "Common Treasury of relief for all, both Beasts and Men."[32] Diggers, like other radicals of the period, often greeted one another as "fellow creatures," a gesture of solidarity and identification with all poor and mistreated beings.

Generally speaking, though, such expressions of cross-species solidarity have always been exceedingly rare. More often than not, the central role animals have played in the evolution of our economic system has been obscured, despite the fact that their presence is contained within the word *capitalism* itself: the root Latin term *capitalis*, literally "of the head," originally referred to heads of cattle.[33] The etymology implies that capital is made of animals, which is at least partly true.[34] The drive to turn animals into commodities and thus into profits was central to the accumulation of North American wealth—wealth that was secured at the expense of animals and, of course, enslaved African people and Indigenous peoples, too.

The settlers who crossed the Atlantic did not travel alone. They brought plants and animals and also disease—disease that in many cases stemmed from their close habitation with livestock, jumping from cow or pig to human at some point in their distant evolution. Though there are no accounts describing what it was like for cows, goats, sheep, pigs, and chickens to cross the ocean while held in darkness below deck—records generally focus on the suffering of seasick humans—we know that a good portion perished en route. Those who survived followed in the footsteps of More's devouring sheep, put to work unpeopling New World land of its original inhabitants and stampeding over Indigenous territorial claims and hunting rights. In 1666, in a complaint to colonial authorities, an Indigenous leader named Mattagund, speaking for the Anacostin, Doeg, and Patuxent in the Maryland colony, pointed to livestock as the source of his community's insecurity and unhappiness: "Your cattle and hogs injure us you come too near to us to live and drive us from place to place. We can fly no further let us know where to live and how to be secured for the future from the hogs and cattle."[35]

The brewing conflict was both material and metaphysical, a question of controlling resources and, on a deeper level, conceptions of reality. Until settlers arrived, the idea that animals could be owned was alien to the Indigenous people of the Eastern Seaboard. Animals could be hunted but were not subservient to human beings.[36] Some cultures saw animals as members of their own autonomous Nations: Bear Nation, Deer Nation, Beaver Nation, and the like. Despite their differences, English, French, and Spanish colonists were united in their conviction that human beings were entitled to exercise dominion over nature, including animals, whether domesticated or not. The settlers' faith in the Great Chain of Being, which always put humans above beasts, was every bit as supernatural as those of the communities they encountered, but far more hierarchical. Domestic animals were private property, and wild ones were common property; in both cases, animals, like the rest of the natural world, were things God granted humans the right to own.

This metaphysical framework informed the settlers' shifting ideas of the commons. In England, as we've seen, the commons involved both rights and responsibilities, and the rules governing sharing could be strict. But in New England, the commons became a repository from which anyone could take, with no corresponding duty to reciprocate or replenish what was there. By the late seventeenth century in Massachusetts, one account tells us, the old "common-field system was gone, taking with it the common decisions and the frequent encounter of every farmer with his fellows which it entailed."[37] Allan Greer, a professor of history at McGill University, calls the new arrangement the "colonial commons," one that imagined the sprawling continent as an open and inexhaustible resource to be exploited and enclosed by settlers at will. The colonial commons, he explains, was made possible only by disregarding and undermining what he calls the Indigenous commons—the mosaic of distinct systems of government, each with unique rules for managing property and apportioning rights and responsibilities within clearly demarcated territories.[38]

The colonial commons found justification in the fervid insistence that Indigenous people had no systems at all; otherwise their land would not be free for settlers to commandeer. For settlers, the absence of fences and of domesticated animals provided ample and convenient proof of a lack of "civilization." John Winthrop, the second governor of the Massachusetts Bay Colony, reflected the standard settler perspective when he insisted that because Indigenous people "inclose noe land" nor "tame Cattle to improve the land," their abundant territory could be appropriated.[39] Colonists interpreted the lack of fencing as a sign of a lack of ownership, when in fact it was merely a sign of a lack of livestock and thus a lack of a need for fencing.

This view would find its quintessential expression in the writings of John Locke, the philosopher most associated with the development of modern ideas of liberty, democracy, private property, and security; the need for security, he believed, is why people get together to form a society in the first place. His *Two Treatises of Government* builds on the thinking of Winthrop and other early colonial theorists to explain why some people are entitled to take from others and to exclusively own what they take. God may have created the "Earth, and all inferior Creatures be common to all," Locke acknowledges, but it does not follow that this bounty must be fairly apportioned. Echoing upper-class proponents of enclosure in England, who justified the privatization of the commons on the grounds of "improvement," Locke argues that people are entitled to make land their sole possession by mixing their labour with the natural world, thereby "improving" and privatizing it. He contrasts these "industrious and Rational" people unfavourably with "commoners"—by which he meant both English peasants and the Indigenous people of the Americas—who he claimed let resources go to waste.

Locke's treatise was designed to prop up the ideology of the colonial commons—an ideology in which the esteemed philosopher had a direct financial stake. A former secretary for the Lords Proprietors of Carolina and later a member of the Board of Trade and Plantations, Locke used the imperialist fantasy of America as a vast open field to help steamroll the Indigenous commons and legal systems that stood in the way of the administrations in which he served.[40] In the early 1680s, the same period he was composing his disquisition on property, he was revising the *Fundamental Constitutions of Carolina,* a document that took a hard line against Indigenous property rights, prohibiting colonists from purchasing or receiving land as a gift directly from native people on the grounds that they did not actually own the land in question. The original Carolina land grant described the region as "hitherto untilled." It was *terra nullius,* nobody's land, and thus free for the taking.[41] Locke's argument upheld this classic justification for the English Crown's dominion over the continent, imagining bands of "wild Indians" who, lacking fences and unable to "subdue" the land, had no legitimate claim or "title" to their territory.[42]

The irony was that unlike in England, which was impeccably hedged, fences in seventeenth-century

New England were dodgy at best. Colonists, at least in the early period, generally let their animals fend for themselves, setting them loose to graze in the colonial commons. But no matter how far livestock wandered or how feral they became, they remained private property, invisible enclosures hanging over their heads wherever they went.[43] As Virginia DeJohn Anderson documents in her book *Creatures of Empire*, one of only a handful of works examining the role of livestock during the colonial period, the ecological consequences of settlers' rambling and ravenous menageries were evident as early as the seventeenth century. Free to forage for whatever they could find, cows and pigs consumed delicate grasses, seeds, and roots and quickly reduced the land's capacity to regenerate, spurring their owners to take them even further afield.[44] Hogs dug up clam beds, cattle spread weeds, erosion took its toll. From Canada to Mexico, in what scholars describe as an "ungulate irruption," the herds of hoofed mammals that arrived in colonization's wake radically changed the landscape and introduced a new biological regime that made it harder for Indigenous people and creatures to sustain themselves.[45] As the land became depleted, settlers pushed forward, moved elsewhere, enclosing and exhausting the land; the cycle repeated. It was the logical consequence of the colonial approach to the commons—one that undermines its own security by taking more and more instead of taking care.

· · ·

THE COLONIAL COMMONS WAS always about taking, including taking the lives of wild animals deemed common property. While many species were hunted, it was the beaver who would become the North American equivalent of gold. In medieval Europe, the animals' pelts were considered luxuries, their possession limited to elites through a series of sumptuary laws that allowed the nobility to dictate who could wear what, relegating commoners to lamb, rabbit, and cat skin. But as the merchant class rose in prominence, demand for fine fur increased. By the time *Utopia* was published at the start of the sixteenth century, Eurasian beavers had already been hunted to oblivion.[46] When vast beaver populations were discovered in North America, enterprising investors launched another deadly hunting spree.

Instead of constructing dams and wetland habitat, beavers built fortunes and nations, their lives sacrificed for the sake of high fashion. Canada's origins are synonymous, of course, with the beaver-pillaging Hudson's Bay Company (HBC); the first American millionaire, John Jacob Astor, owned the monopolistic American Fur Company, using fur trade wealth to fund real estate development in New York City. Felted beaver fur top hats epitomized the masculine style of the day, their waterproof surface practical in British fog and rain. Some wearers even believed the accessory made them more intelligent—an oblique acknowledgement of the astonishing ingenuity of the tens of millions of creatures who were transformed into headwear.[47]

However deadly it was for beavers, the fur trade was also brutal for humans, inciting bloody conflicts, including the explicitly named Beaver Wars, while Indigenous people fought bitterly over the right to trap and control beaver supply. Decimated by disease and displaced from their territories, they had few options but to help hunt their non-human relations nearly to extinction. For Indigenous communities, the exchange of pelts for guns and other European goods was a devil's bargain, with material insecurity the permanent condition of those who became dependent on markets designed to fleece them.[48] George Simpson, who helmed the Hudson's Bay Company at its height, became enraged when he thought trading posts were being too generous. "Interested motives" and a need for beaver, not "philanthropy" toward Indigenous people, he fumed in 1821, were the reason the company had set up shop in the northern regions.

Further south, the company took the exploitation of the colonial commons to a new extreme, aiming to make their business "more lucrative and secure," as one historian put it, through a campaign of total annihilation.[49] The ominously named "fur desert policy" sought to sabotage American rivals by creating an immense beaverless buffer across what was then called Oregon Country. As Simpson wrote in his journal in 1824, "If properly managed no question exists that it would yield handsome profits as we have convincing proof that the country is a rich preserve of Beaver and which for political reasons we should endeavor to destroy as fast as possible." Within a year, an HBC trader reported on the initiative's success: "This part of the Country tho' once abounding in Beaver is entirely ruined."[50] The landscape was indelibly altered, too. The frenzied massacre caused an estimated six thousand beaver ponds in the area to dry up, taking the riparian life they sustained with them. By the early twentieth century, where there had once been perhaps hundreds of millions of beavers across North America, only one hundred thousand remained, the fur desert spread far beyond its intended range.[51]

Today, thanks to coordinated efforts, beavers are a rare conservation success story. Their North American numbers now exceed ten million; in Europe they number more than one million, up from little more than a thousand at the beginning of the twentieth century. The benefits of their resurgence cascade like a spring-fed stream. Ecologists now recognize beavers as a "keystone species," one essential to maintaining an entire ecosystem's well-being. In the intermountain west, for example, beaver-filled wetlands make up just 2 percent of the overall environment while supporting 80 percent of the region's biodiversity.[52] Compared to the single-channel rivers and brooks we're now accustomed to, the marshy habitats beavers make can appear messy and chaotic, but that chaos is a sign of vibrancy and complexity. Beaver dams and channels create pools that feed waterfowl, shelter salmon, and attract surrounding wildlife. By slowing water's flow, they lessen flood-water damage while allowing sediment to settle and create conditions for surface and groundwater storage. The swampy vegetation filters out chemicals, ensuring water funnelled to parched landscapes is pollution-free.[53]

When beavers disappear, so do these vital wetlands and the ecological services they provide. When reintroduced to an area, beavers set in motion protective and reparative natural processes that can help fend off some of the dangers posed by a warming planet, from counteracting rising temperatures to combatting erosion and drought.[54] The presence of beaver dams has even been shown to fully offset the elevated levels of water contamination dryer seasons bring. As one researcher explains, "the outsized influence of beaver activity on water quality is a positive counter to climate change."[55]

Ecohydrologist Emily Fairfax calls the revitalized zones beavers create "refugia," areas where diverse groups of creatures can survive adverse conditions. Her research focuses on mega-fires, and how beaver-altered landscapes have the remarkable ability to withstand extreme heat and raging flames. Beaver refugia are a kind of utopia, only better because they are real. The antithesis of the colonial commons, they are places where plants and animals can find safety, rebound, and heal.[56] By cleansing water, fighting fires, and sheltering other species, beavers are model stewards of ecological security.

. . .

IN THE EARLY 1980S, when I was barely a toddler, my family decamped from Canada and headed south to the desert, trading Manitoba blizzards for scorched sand and open sky, towering saguaro cacti, and ten-foot succulents called elephant trees. As a kid, you learn fast that the fuzzy appearance and name of the teddy-bear cholla belies the harshness of its barbs. A jumping cactus, as they're also called—because they seem to reach out and attack you—will quickly teach you that nature is not a mere thing and certainly not something to be messed with. Arizona was where I got my first lesson in the importance of protecting the commons and the folly of Western conceptions of private property.

My father was a graduate student studying chemistry with a growing family to feed, and so we moved to Tucson's south side, where the rent was cheap. That was the house where Sunaura was born; she was named for the Sonoran Desert that surrounded us. Dad's parents lived a little more than an hour away, near the Mexican border and up a jagged driveway at the top of a dusty Patagonia mountain dotted with scraggly juniper trees and inhabited by squadrons of javelinas, the proper term for the bands of roaming and raucous creatures that resemble wild pigs but are, in fact, oversized rodents with hoofed feet. I loved the strange creatures, and my grandparents' strange house, with its wood-burning stove, cuckoo clocks, and hand-cranked coffee grinder. But most of all I was fascinated by my grandmother—fascinated by the ways in which we disagreed.

She baked big batches of sugar cookies, as grandmas are supposed to do, but with a gleam in her eye: she knew their sweet scent would fill the room and that I, a dedicated seven-year-old vegetarian, would refuse to eat them because they were fattened with bacon grease. My grandmother was as sharp as the prickly pears you could see from her porch. But I was just as obstinate.

Grandma's house was far from any stores and unconnected to most municipal services; resources were conserved out of necessity, not out of tender-hearted environmental concern. Rainwater was collected on the roof, toilets flushed sparingly, and all trash tossed into an abandoned mine shaft, a chore I initially cherished, heaving black bags into the void a satisfying test of my childish strength. Grandma was a diehard libertarian—emphasis on the word *hard*—and the land belonged to her. If she wanted to dispose of her garbage in a pit, that was her business, just as any veins of valuable metal would have been the previous owner's to exploit. My grandma had been a stay-at-home mother to six boys while Grandpa worked as an immigration officer. When he was stationed at the airport in Winnipeg, she discovered the work of Ayn Rand as part of a reading group. Rand and Milton Friedman were her gurus, capitalism was her gospel, and she saw any government regulation as an unforgivable imposition on individual freedom. The market, not the government, knew best. In my grandmother's imagination, private property was absolute, the line between what was hers and not hers watertight.

But land, of course, is never watertight, even in the desert, where water is scarce. As time went on, I'd lug the black garbage bags down the hill and throw them into the hole, watching them land with a thud atop the years of refuse piling up, and think of the other pits I had heard the grown-ups discussing. From the 1950s to the 1970s, not far from our first house on Tucson's poor and mostly Mexican-American south side, private military contractors had regularly dumped toxic waste into open-air holes in the desert floor, and this waste had filtered into parts of the city's public water supply. Thousands of people drank it, and many died, came down with rare illnesses, or, like my sister Sunaura, were born with disabilities. Like Grant Township in Pennsylvania, the south side of Tucson was an industrial sacrifice zone.

As a child, I didn't understand these dynamics fully, but the stories of water contamination shaped my sense of reality—and my sense of security, too. I became obsessed with pollution, recycling, the ozone hole, and extinction; I had climate anxiety long before the phenomenon had an official name. I knew that the garbage pit on my grandmother's mountain touched the valley below, that the boundaries between bodies and ecosystems, self and not self, were porous and blurred, that pollution did not just keep to a particular property because someone owned it.

My philosophical outlook was in some ways straightforward, an extension of the moral lessons children are regularly taught. By disposing of trash in the desert, a group of adults had polluted something that was not theirs to begin with, something we were all supposed to share. Earth, water, and air: these are things that every person and animal needs. They are commons that should not be cordoned off or corrupted. *Commons* was a word I did not yet know, of course, but I understood the concept nonetheless. I also understood that sharing had rules—rules being a basic tenet of any child's game. Something being common is not a licence to ruin or destroy it. My grandmother held a dimmer view: sharing, she thought, is destined to fail, because humans are selfish. She agreed with the economists and policy makers who argued that common resources will always be sullied and public goods taken advantage of. Because no single person or corporation owns the water or air or the welfare state, they will inevitably be overused and exploited by individuals seeking to maximize their own gain, dooming the commons to be even more poorly treated than the privately held ground bursting with her garbage.

My grandmother saw the colonial version of the commons as the only possibility—a pessimistic outlook that gained legitimacy from an influential article written by a biologist named Garrett Hardin in 1968. Published in the esteemed journal *Science*, "The Tragedy of the Commons" asks the reader to imagine a scene that would soon deteriorate: "Picture a pasture open to all." In a world of competitive individualism, a "rational herdsman," as Hardin called his protagonist, can be expected to put more and more animals out to graze on the land, precipitating environmental disaster. As he put it, "Individuals locked into the logic of the commons are free only to bring on universal ruin." In Hardin's fable, the overgrazed pasture is a metaphor for all of society, indeed the entire planet, one he believed was being wrecked by overpopulation. The commons—be they open fields and farmland, air and water, or the modern welfare state—need to be enclosed for their own security and preservation. Only private ownership can keep things from being wrecked.

Hardin's six-page article would become one of the most cited scientific papers of all time and part of the popular discourse.[57] But *scientific*, in this context, is a word that should be delivered in air quotes. "The Tragedy of the Commons" is more of a rant than a work of rigorous analysis, and more speculative than the final scenarios presented in the *Global Trends* report. There is no evidence or data to back up Hardin's sweeping generalizations. In 2009, at the age of seventy-five, political scientist Elinor Ostrom became the first woman ever to win the Nobel Prize in Economics for her work on the commons. She was honoured for a long career dedicated to debunking Hardin's exaggerated claims. And yet, despite her astonishing efforts, his article has retained its canonical status. Depending on the discipline, up to one half of college instructors still regard it as the "foremost thinking" on the issue.[58]

For Ostrom, exposing Hardin's fallacy was not some progressive crusade.[59] She was a capitalist— the kind who drew on neo-liberal economic theory, no less—but she was also an ardent empiricist, one curious to learn what real people actually do. To feed this curiosity, she spent decades meticulously collecting hundreds of examples of people sharing scarce resources: groundwater management near her native Los Angeles, cattle herding in Switzerland, lobster farming in Maine, communal forests in Japan, and fisheries in Nova Scotia and Sri Lanka. None functioned as the free-for-all open pasture Hardin had envisioned. Far from being tragic, commons have the potential to be maintained successfully and sustainably, in some cases for centuries on end. In the Spanish city of Valencia, for example, a vast and collectively run irrigation system established by Arab and Berber farmers over one thousand years ago still serves over ten thousand farmers today.[60] Security, under these arrangements, is the result of communally agreed-upon rules that cultivate trust, participation, and reciprocity—and that include systems for self-monitoring and resolving conflict, all geared toward a further time horizon, not immediate reward.[61] Ostrom was fond of saying that there are no panaceas, but there are possibilities. Private property or anti-democratic coercion (Hardin's other solution to avoid tragedy) are not the only options for managing scarce resources.[62] The destruction of the commons is not preordained.

When I was in my twenties, my grandmother asked where I got my "socialistic" ideas. She was as befuddled by my values as I was by her bacon cookies. Was it my Canadian mother's influence, some meddling professor I'd met in college, the intellectual crowd I'd fallen in with in New York? The libertarian comic strips and copies of Friedrich Hayek's *The Road to Serfdom* she had pressed into my hands had done me no good—in fact, they had only convinced me that making markets paramount was the wrong approach. If I could talk to her today, I'd say that my political commitments were born of observation—my own form of childhood empiricism. I saw that animals suffer, so I decided not to eat them; I understood the water streaming from our taps was connected to earth and industry, and I wanted it to be clean. It's always hard to trace why we evolve the way we do, but if there is a taproot for my world view, it reaches back to that trash-filled mine. I knew that I lived in a common world—one my grandmother's utopia of private property could neither properly value nor make secure.

WHEN THE NATIONAL INTELLIGENCE Council described a future of expanding insecurity, uncertainty, and contestation, they knew these terms would be unsettling to most readers. But uncertainty and insecurity are not always bad. If we want to prevent the worst consequences of the economic and ecological collapse their report warns of—and avoid living in some of the more foreboding future scenarios it portends—there are many entrenched systems and ingrained habits of thinking that need to be contested and made less certain and secure. Our world is becoming more unsettled in many troubling ways. In others, it is not nearly unsettled enough.

As the late Secwepemc leader and political strategist Arthur Manuel argues in his co-authored 2015 book *Unsettling Canada*, one thing that needs to be shaken up is the colonial claim to land itself. The recognition of Indigenous sovereignty would have profound implications for social justice and sustainability, for the economic security of Indigenous peoples, and for ecological stability more broadly.

It has taken generations of organizing and resistance by Indigenous people to get Canada to begin to accept the existence of what is officially called "Aboriginal title," Indigenous peoples' inherent right to their traditional territories—the very right Locke and his employers adamantly argued did not exist. In Manuel's account, ensuring that Indigenous rights were included in the Constitution Act of 1982 was a critical victory in the ongoing fight to unsettle the government's justification for Crown ownership of the vast majority of Canadian land. These justifications remain entangled with the incongruous sixteenth-century legal idea of *terra nullius*, which says that land people inhabited for tens of thousands of years was, in fact, empty and could be "discovered" by hungry and confused foreigners and magically made into a British possession.[63]

In a series of watershed legal decisions, the Canadian courts have slowly begun to chip away at this colonial absurdity, with *Delgamuukw v. British Columbia* marking a major turning point. In 1984, the Gitxsan and Wet'suwet'en Nations launched an unprecedented legal challenge to try to realize the Aboriginal rights recently enshrined by the new Constitution. The Nations sued for recognition of their Aboriginal title to more than 133 individual hereditary territories totalling fifty-eight thousand square kilometres of land that had never been ceded in a treaty, a claim that forced the Canadian government to reckon with the legal reality of the Indigenous commons and concepts of sovereignty, ownership, and property.[64]

As oral cultures, the Gitxsan and Wet'suwet'en Nations did not document land ownership through written contracts and deeds, and the plaintiffs set a precedent by using oral traditions, rather than written documentation, as legal proof. They affirmed their possession of the land through the Gitxsan *adaawk* and Wet'suwet'en *kungax*, verbal collections of legends, laws, rituals, and traditions elders presented as evidence, much to the judge's consternation.[65] On the first day of testimony, the hereditary Chiefs made statements explaining how their respective Nations approached the issue of property law. The Gitxsan Chief Delgamuukw Earl Muldoe, the case's named plaintiff, set the tone. "My power is carried in my House's histories, songs, dances, and crests," Delgamuukw said. "For us, the ownership of territory is a marriage of the Chief and the land. Each Chief has an ancestor who encountered and acknowledged the life and the land. From such encounters come power. The land, the plants, the animals, and the people all have spirit—they all must be shown respect. That is the basis of our law."[66] One of the elders invited to testify was Mary Johnson, who was asked to sing a song documenting territorial proprietorship—a dirge about two young girls saved from starvation by a bird after their brother has died. The judge objected. "To have witnesses singing songs in court is not the proper way to approach this problem," he said. Besides, he had a "tin ear," one incapable of hearing what a mournful song had to do with a specific place or history. How could property be secured by words that were sung?[67]

Following 318 days of evidence and 56 days of closing arguments, the judge delivered his verdict. Citing John Locke's intellectual precursor, the seventeenth-century philosopher Thomas Hobbes, the decision described life for the Gitxsan and Wet'suwet'en people before colonization as "nasty, brutish, and short" and ruled against the plaintiffs.[68] But when the Supreme Court of Canada heard the case on appeal a decade later, the justices were more inclined to listen. In 1997, the Supreme Court recognized the principle of Aboriginal title as a form of collective ownership, even as it declined to rule on the specific land

and title in question, advising the federal government to negotiate directly with First Nations and find a way to reconcile Aboriginal and Crown claims, which the government has so far refused to do. In the words of Toronto Metropolitan University professor Shiri Pasternak, "The Supreme Court agreed that Indigenous peoples held a unique property right to their land. It was a collective interest held by a nation" and by both present and future generations.[69] By affirming the validity of oral testimony, the decision was also an important step toward bridging Indigenous and Canadian legal traditions and making what is called common law more common, which is to say, more pluralistic and shared.

The verdict caused the private sector to panic. Government documents Pasternak obtained through a Freedom of Information request show lobbyists grasping for "certainty," by which they meant uncontested access to Indigenous property. The day after the ruling, Marlie Beets, then the vice-president of the B.C. Council of Forest Industries, complained that *Delgamuukw* "has only created more uncertainty and we are very concerned by how governments will react to the court's findings … The decision makes the need for certainty through surrender all the more clear." In emails and faxes, corporate lobbyists urged government officials to push First Nations to surrender their newly expanded rights to ensure the "certainty" of commercial interests. The director of the B.C. Cattlemen's Association vowed to put "great pressure on the provincial government

to commit to a cede, release and surrender approach."
A "certainty working group" meeting was arranged by
the B.C. Treaty Negotiations advisory committee lawyer, who counselled that a treaty process should seek
"an end of Aboriginal rights and title"—an approach the
United Nations has strongly opposed.[70]

Despite the Canadian Supreme Court's recognition
of Aboriginal title and the support of international
human rights law, the fight for Indigenous sovereignty
remains profoundly lopsided, with impoverished communities going up against multinational behemoths,
their powerful provincial lobbyists, and the government agencies that abet them.[71] Over the years,
various Supreme Court decisions have further bolstered Indigenous claims, but the Crown continues to
grant private companies permission to drill, mine, log,
and dam on unceded land, including approval of the
controversial 670-kilometre Coastal GasLink Pipeline
that would traffic fracked gas along what Pasternak
has described as a "coveted energy corridor" that runs
through traditional Wet'suwet'en territory.[72] Powered
by the fantasy of the colonial commons, Chevron,
TransCanada, and Enbridge are all determined to build
fossil-fuel economy infrastructure on Wet'suwet'en
land despite community opposition and an outpouring
of global solidarity.[73] When the hereditary leadership
who brought forward the *Delgamuukw* case asserted
their jurisdiction by defending unceded territory with
peaceful blockades, the government sent the police to

remove protesters from their own land at gunpoint. The RCMP's violent response revealed how threatening Aboriginal title is to the petroleum industry and the risk it poses to the security of their profits.

In *Unsettling Canada*, Manuel reminds us that the *Delgamuukw* decision not only confirmed and expanded Aboriginal rights but also affirmed the corresponding duties that come with them. The right to take from the earth is inseparable from the responsibility also to take care of and replenish it.[74] The Supreme Court ruled that the only situation in which Aboriginal title must be extinguished involves communities engaging in activities that destroy their land or are inconsistent with their connection to the land, thereby depriving future generations of its benefit (Manuel gives the example of building a parking lot on a sacred site). This condition, as Manuel explains, further obligates Indigenous peoples to protect their territories from irresponsible and unsustainable development—the kind of development the private sector wants a certain and secure right to pursue.[75] Here we have an example of just the kind of unsettling that our insecure age requires: the unsettling of a system of ownership that tramples on people's constitutional rights while injuring the planet.

IN 1974, GARRETT HARDIN published an article in *Psychology Today* in which he scoffed at the idea of returning land or making reparations to Indigenous communities, building on the arguments he put forth in "The Tragedy of the Commons." Titled "Lifeboat Ethics: The Case Against Helping the Poor," it once again invited the reader to picture a scene, this time an ocean instead of an open field. Small vessels full of wealthy passengers float perilously in a sea of drowning people who threaten to capsize the ships. The only way for the privileged few to protect themselves, Hardin argues, is to keep others out—out of the lifeboats, out of the rich countries, out of the commons—by hoarding resources, halting immigration, and ending international food aid in order to reduce the global population of the poor, who he acknowledges are overwhelmingly non-white. "For the foreseeable future," he writes, "our survival demands that we govern our actions by the ethics of a lifeboat, harsh though they may be." Hardin's ideas align with the current of thinking now called "eco-fascist," one on the rise in our uncertain times. It is based on the narrowest and meanest concept of security, of guarding one's privilege at the expense of others' lives. This is a vision, as one toxic and terrifying white supremacist slogan states, of "green futures for white babies."

Of course, there are the denialists, too. Rejecting the reality of climate change, they consider social change to be the true security threat—a threat to industry profits, consumer lifestyles, and established racial and gender hierarchies. Sociologist Cara Daggett has coined the term "petro-masculinity" to describe the way climate denial, gas-guzzling trucks, and slabs of red meat have become potent symbols of patriarchal virtue (hence the slur "soy boy," lobbed at men who are seen as soft or, worse, vegetarian). In this paradigm, contempt for the more-than-human world, and for anyone who tries to care for it, reinforces contempt for certain categories of people—for anyone who is not white, male, and able-bodied. Research by Queen's University political theorist Will Kymlicka found that faith in species hierarchy is "consistently associated with greater dehumanization of disadvantaged or marginalized human groups."[76] Or as the celebrated abolitionist Angela Davis recently told me, "The prioritizing of humans also leads to restrictive definitions of who counts as human, and the brutalization of animals is related to the brutalization of human animals." Here is yet another problem with the Great Chain of Being: its most passionate adherents inevitably believe that certain categories of humans are greater than others.

The scramble to subjugate other people and creatures has yielded a pyrrhic victory of mega-fires, heat domes, polar vortexes, superstorms, and droughts. Five hundred years after Thomas More wrote about the plague of sheep set loose on the English commons, livestock have devoured the earth. Domesticated and commodified animals, mainly cows and pigs, now make up more than 62 percent of all mammalian biomass, deforesting wide swaths of land and emitting huge amounts of carbon, while all wild animals have been reduced to a paltry 4 percent. The wilderness that remains is largely protected by Indigenous peoples, who make up around 5 percent of the world's population and protect 80 percent of global biodiversity. Proposals like those seeking to establish more Marine Protected Areas in partnership with First Nations on Canada's west coast are a promising sign of a growing recognition that environmental caretaking and repair needs investment and support. But ultimately, planetary stewardship is something everyone should be responsible for.[77]

My interest in rights for nature stems, in part, from my conviction that biodiversity has political as well as biological value. Each species we extinguish diminishes what we might call ecological democracy, underscoring the need to devise a political system that can effectively represent and protect the interests of other life forms.[78] The benefit to animals and insects, as well as the 40 percent of plant species now imperilled by climate change, should be more than enough to jolt us into fighting extinction. But we should also cultivate solidarity with the more-than-human world out of crass self-interest. Biodiversity is essential to our existence: to the security of the ecosystems we are embedded in, the food systems we rely on, and our ability to avoid future pandemics. When an ecosystem is healthy, biodiversity buffers the transmission of deadly pathogens; genetic variation dilutes and disrupts pathways of contagion. This means that the same shrinking and fragmenting of wild habitat that decreases biodiversity also increases opportunities for what scientists call "spillover," or human-animal contact and cross-species infection, the dynamic that likely led to recent Ebola outbreaks in Guinea.[79]

As a 2020 United Nations report on pandemic prevention explains, infectious diseases typically emerge as the result of human activity. They are yet another insecurity-producing symptom of human hubris, an outgrowth of long-standing attempts to conquer nature.[80] Land-use changes, above all the clearing of land for intensive animal agriculture, are responsible for one-third of all emerging diseases.[81] Like the hurricanes and droughts that result from a warming climate, novel and dangerous pathogens are connected to human activity, though not in the straightforwardly conspiratorial way some people like to imagine. The 1918 influenza, for example, likely began as a bird or swine flu on an industrial farm. Conditions are even more congenial to harmful microbes on modern feedlots, which crowd huge numbers of genetically similar animals together in cruel and unsanitary conditions. In the US and Canada, livestock are dosed with 80 percent of all medically important antibiotics the countries consume—a recipe for breeding drug-resistant superbugs.[82] As one medical journal recently put it, intensive animal agriculture gives viruses countless "spins at pandemic roulette."[83] The American Public Health Association, the largest organization of public health professionals in the United States, has repeatedly called for a moratorium on factory farming for this reason.[84]

Given these and countless other challenges, we can't limit our ambitions to the Human Security Council that the *Global Trends* report envisioned, though that would be an excellent start. Only More-Than-Human Security will suffice. We must work with the natural world rather than against it, co-operating with the sun and wind to harness renewable energy, with the oceans and forests to sequester carbon without choking and acidifying them, with biodiverse plants to cool our cities and feed the world, with animal allies like the water-protecting and firefighting beavers who provide refugia for other species. Yet despite the consensus from the United Nations and leading scientists and physicians that our future security requires paying attention to the interconnections between human, animal, and ecosystem well-being, a human-centric and profit-hungry attitude still dominates.[85] Instead of recognizing biodiversity as an essential component of biosecurity, Canada and the US have recently passed laws that paint environmentalists and animal rights activists as urgent security threats.[86]

In addition to working with nature, we also, of course, need to work with each other. This requires turning our climate anxiety and insecurity into solidarity—solidarity that is strong enough to respond to rising authoritarianism and to overcome the special interests championing the inadequate business-as-usual solutions that make up the standard menu of government climate policies today, including cap-and-trade.

This faulty scheme, which proponents claim can limit warming by creating property rights to greenhouse gas emissions, was first devised in the late 1960s by John Dales, a little-known economist at the University of Toronto. The Great Lakes were being overrun with algae as a result of laundry detergent runoff, and Dales proposed that governments create markets that sold rights to cause environmental harm, capping the overall amount of pollution allowed and then auctioning permits to pollute in tranches that firms could buy and sell.[87] According to historian Troy Vettese, Dales's proposal was ignored in Ontario but found an enthusiastic audience among economists working on British Columbia's fisheries before liberal environmentalists in the United States seized on it as a fiscally appealing fix, first to address acid rain before governments began promoting it to address climate change. In California, an early adopter of carbon cap-and-trade, oil and gas emissions have actually gone up.[88] If we want to effectively mitigate the climate crisis, we should look back to how the original laundry soap dilemma was actually solved. Canadian regulators banned high-phosphate detergents in 1973 and built additional sewage treatment plants that helped remove related contamination.[89] Instead of fiddling around with pollution pricing, the federal government stepped in to solve the problem at its source.

As the scientists behind the IPCC report and the spies of the National Intelligence Council have made abundantly clear, everything must change: our energy systems, our food systems, our transportation systems, and our welfare systems. Activist and author Naomi Klein has argued that ensuring a baseline of material security for people, especially a green jobs guarantee that could facilitate a just transition away from fossil fuels, is a critical part of coping with climate disruption. As she puts it, "the more secure people feel, knowing that their families will not want for food, medicine, and shelter, the less vulnerable they will be to the forces of racist demagoguery that will prey on the fears that invariably accompany times of great change." Material security, she argues, can help us "address the crisis of empathy in a warming world."[90]

As the opening chapter mentioned, the income supports provided by the US and Canadian governments in response to the Covid-19 pandemic were highly effective, improving material security in ways that hadn't been seen since the welfare state's creation in the wake of World War II. But as Klein and others rightly insist, we cannot simply revive the social policies of the New Deal or Covid eras. Instead of looking back nostalgically to the twentieth-century welfare state, which was predicated on assumptions of limitless economic growth and ecological extraction, and marred by racialized and gendered exclusions, we should aspire to a forward-looking vision of a state that provides security for all in a way that is sustainable, a state that is both decarbonized and democratic—what I like to call a solidarity state.[91] Rooted in the collaborative ethos of the commons, a solidarity state aspires to both political and economic equality and a recognition of our fundamental inter-dependence, including our interdependence with the more-than-human world.

As Anishinaabe linguist and lawyer Lindsay Borrows has said, nature needs rights, but humans need a "bill of obligations."[92] Above all, we need the obligation not to take anything from nature unless we also take care to replenish it, so that we honour eco-logical limits. Sometimes called a circular economy, this approach calls for systems that enable renewabil-ity, reuse, and regeneration, eliminating waste—a goal the Netherlands is the first country to commit to.[93] We now know where ignoring obligations and limits gets us: climate calamity and spiralling insecurity. But this is hardly a revelation. In the dialogue *Critias*, Plato laments land destroyed by mismanagement, describ-ing the barren soil, absence of trees, and abandoned shrines where fresh springs used to be as "the skeleton of a sick man, all the fat and soft earth having wasted away."[94] The Sumerians, Romans, Mayans, and other ancient societies pushed past ecological limits, spawn-ing instability and hastening civilizational collapse. To read accounts of the colonial era is to encounter set-tlers marvelling at their own destructive impact on the environment and sometimes planning the devastation outright. The difference today is that this destruction is now happening on a global scale.

Anthropocentric attempts to conquer the earth are always self-defeating. There is no way to conquer the world if we want to securely exist within it. We'll never be the confident all-powerful alpha wolves of the animal kingdom that petro-masculinists want us to be—which is fitting, because the idea of alpha wolves is a misconception that came from studying animals in captivity. In the wild, there are no wolf hierarchies that the animals fight to climb.[95]

Like the fallacy of the wolf pecking order, the myth of the Great Chain of Being needs to be demolished. The image of the natural world as an inclusive circle instead of an exclusive hierarchy is not rose-coloured romanticism; it is a more accurate reflection of the science that describes our reality, where we are embedded in an elaborate sustaining circle of life, non-life, and even semi-life. My father is a medicinal chemist whose research focuses on viruses, including the one that causes Covid-19. Viruses are microscopic sequences of DNA or RNA reliant on hijacking the energy of host cells to replicate; they inhabit a category-defying limbo, a strange grey zone between living and non-living, animate and not.[96] What I see in my father's work is less a drive for mastery than a sense of mystery. Viruses are hardly lovable, but my father has shown me they deserve our respect, and even awe. The fact that our lives depend on biological and physical processes we can barely categorize, and complex dynamics we certainly do not command, should occasion wonder—and a large dose of humility. This humility is the ethos I associate with the good and generative capacities of insecurity, the kind that can help us be curious, connect, evolve, and maybe survive in a radically changing world.

I don't have a blueprint for a society in which all of our problems are forever solved—no one does. As Ostrom said, there are no panaceas, only possibilities. I don't believe in utopia, but I can imagine a more hopeful future where our problems get more interesting and complex—a complexity befitting the tangled and unpredictable world we live in. Instead of the dull and demoralizing questions we are faced with today—should a handful of fossil-fuel executives have licence to incinerate the planet?—we could aim to build a secure and sustainable society that will force us to grapple with far more compelling philosophical and practical riddles. If nature has rights, should invasive species have equal protections? Where does a watershed end if all ecosystems are interconnected? How can we make decisions and exercise sovereignty when our actions have global repercussions? How can we ensure freedom and dignity for everyone while respecting ecological limits? These are the sorts of questions worth pondering, and the answers are not readily apparent. But for all that is uncertain and unsettled, there is one thing I know for sure: the illusion of human security at nature's expense cannot hold.

CHAPTER 5

ESCAPING THE BURROW

WE ALL KNOW FRANZ Kafka's most famous novels and stories, and even if we haven't read them, we at least know the term *Kafkaesque*. *The Metamorphosis* and *The Trial*, as well as his voluminous letters and diaries, have made him one of the world's most celebrated writers. But that's not all the prolific author wrote. For fourteen years, Kafka was employed at the Prague office of the Workers' Accident Insurance Institute of the Kingdom of Bohemia, a semi-government agency where he penned countless reports, briefs, and speeches. These less illustrious texts, published between 1908 and 1915, include "The Scope of Compulsory Insurance for the Building Trade," "Risk Classification and Accident Prevention in War Time," and "Fixed-Rate Insurance Premiums for Small Farms Using Machinery."

These documents are every bit as tedious as their titles imply. And yet they also make it clear how much Kafka's day job fed his incredible creativity: the

nightmarish bureaucracies and harrowed characters he
so memorably conjures were informed by his alienat-
ing and stifling professional milieu. By day, Kafka was
a diligent and dedicated functionary of a government
insurance agency (perhaps necessarily so, considering the
discrimination he faced—he was one of only two Jewish
employees among a staff of 263). By night, he wrote from
the perspective of outsiders trapped within inscrutable
systems, crushed by byzantine power structures, and
helpless to escape or even understand their fate.[1]

Kafka had talent, and he also had a conscience.
During his short life, he was known less as an artist
than as a devoted industrial reformer. While on the
clock, Kafka did his best to make the bureaucracy he
represented more responsive to ordinary people and
to make their lives less perilous.[2] The Prague Institute
insured more than 720,000 workers, or about one-third
of Austria's entire industrial workforce, and Kafka studied the conditions in which they toiled in minute and
technical detail.[3] One of his primary tasks involved
mediating conflicts between employers and employees
to determine liability in the event of workplace death
or injury.

Over the course of his career, Kafka championed
the "principle of mutuality," challenging employers'
insistence on worker culpability. Staff, bosses claimed,
deserved blame for any on-the-job accidents.[4] They saw
the workers as risks to their capital and often engaged
in fraud to deflect responsibility.[5] In a 1909 letter

to his friend and literary executor Max Brod, Kafka expressed his mounting frustration with hazardous industrial conditions: "In my four districts ... people fall off the scaffolds as if they were drunk, or fall into the machines, all the beams topple, all embankments give way, all ladders slide, whatever people carry up falls down, whatever they hand down they stumble over. And I have a headache from all these girls in porcelain factories who incessantly throw themselves down the stairs with mounds of dishware." Kafka wondered why workers did not rise up: "Instead of assaulting the company building and destroying everything, they submit petitions!"[6]

Despite incessant complaints that his job got in the way of his creative writing, Kafka also confessed that the "whole world of insurance" interested him "greatly."[7] He was right to be fascinated, not only because his job provided fodder for his fiction but because of its social and political implications. The insurance field grapples with profound and urgent challenges: how to prepare for an unpredictable future, how to cope with threats and vulnerability, and how to compensate for past harm. Insurance is often described as a technology for managing risk, which is another way of saying it is a technology for managing insecurity. We are all vulnerable—not only to aging and illness and bad luck but also to injustice, to systems designed to oppress and exploit us. The struggle, then, is over how risk is managed and apportioned. Who and what is exposed?

Who and what is covered? Is insurance a commercial product (like a standard auto policy) or a public good (think social security)? Who is deemed risky—whether a credit risk or a risk to someone else's security or property? Who is held responsible? Who evades liability?

Though it's hard to believe, given its current bland associations, the word *insurance* once had a radical ring. In the early twentieth century, the idea of sharing risk across an entire population was revolutionary. New forms of social insurance would provide millions of people with unprecedented material security—coverage against not only workplace accidents but also sickness, disability, and old age—creating the bedrock of the modern welfare state. Early proponents of these government programs believed they would help ordinary people to live as carefree as gods or kings. "One of the first and most salutary effects of insurance is to eliminate from human affairs the fear that paralyses all activity and numbs the soul," one French enthusiast extolled.[8] In 1913, Isaac Rubinow, America's leading authority on social insurance, called it "a new concept of the state as an instrument of organized collective action rather than of class oppression."[9]

With hindsight, we now know that the future refused to be so easily disciplined. Threatened by the prospect of a secure working class that might demand better wages and treatment, economic elites have relentlessly attacked the principles and policies of state-subsidized care, shifting risk and responsibility back onto individuals instead of sharing burdens across the whole society. The corporate sector's war on the welfare state has brought back conditions of generalized insecurity, including an explosion of personal debt and the criminalization of poverty—twin phenomena I will return to.

Today, the idea of worrying about workers dropping dishes or falling off ladders seems quaint; far greater anxieties now afflict us. In 1986, the influential German sociologist Ulrich Beck coined the term "risk society" to describe the world of compounding threats we currently inhabit: a broiling planet, diminishing biodiversity, infectious diseases, nuclear war, artificial intelligence, cyber attacks, deepening inequality, the erosion of democracy—the list goes on. He was clear, however, that the dangers we face are not simply the unintended consequences of industrial progress. They are not, in other words, mere accidents. For a well-positioned few, multiplying hazards are market opportunities. "As the risk society develops," Beck warned, "so does the antagonism between those afflicted by risks and those who profit from them."[10]

Everyone has to cope with the unknowability of the future. At its most capacious, this is what insurance is about: finding ways to protect ourselves and one another in the face of life's inevitable perils and uncertainties. Risk can be individualized and commodified or shared and treated as a kind of commons. We can approach risk reactively, covering past losses, or in ways that are preventive, reducing the chance that specific harms will happen. We can pursue defensive and fearful forms of security, or we can adopt an ethic of insecurity, creating systems of support and care that acknowledge our fundamental vulnerability.

As Kafka knew, managing risk is as much about economics as it is about morality; it speaks to questions of cost, blame, safety, justice, and solidarity. Most of us think of insurance as dull and tiresome, the province of policy wonks and maddening bureaucrats. In fact, when we're talking about insuring against future threats, we are talking about ourselves—about the kind of people we hope to be and what kind of world we want to live in. On a personal level, insurance forces us to reckon with our own frailty and mortality. Collectively, it presents us with a choice: Will we leave each other to sink or swim, or will we buoy strangers through life's rough waters, knowing that one day we might be the ones who need rescuing? Will we take the risk of counting on others, combining our fortunes to make more people more secure and more free, or instead subscribe to the doctrine of personal responsibility? These questions cut to the heart of this book's inquiry: How will we respond to the inevitable fact of life's insecurity?

AROUND A DECADE AGO, I found myself walking a small but spirited picket line, shouting at risk profiteers, our action part of a larger, chaotic demonstration marking the one-year anniversary of the Occupy Wall Street movement. It was a crisp September day, and we were doing tight loops near the entrance to the offices of the insurance giant American International Group Incorporated, more commonly known as AIG—a firm that helped trigger the 2008 financial crash by insuring vast tranches of overrated mortgage derivatives. When the bets went bad, the company was saved by a massive government bailout and the perpetrators let off the hook. "They're crooks! They're crooks! They cooked their fucking books!" we shouted. A man wearing a suit caught my eye as he walked toward the revolving door and licked his lips. "And they taste good, too," he sneered.

That day, bankers repeatedly shouted at protesters to "get a job," ignoring the fact that their profession was the reason so many of the demonstrators were unemployed. Millions of people across the country had lost their homes and livelihoods, while half of Black Americans' collective wealth evaporated. The penalties imposed on ordinary people for missing mortgage and credit card payments can be harsh, but Wall Street's bad behaviour was handsomely rewarded. After being rescued by the US government, seventy-three AIG employees received bonuses in excess of $1 million each, with the top bonus exceeding $6 million, high-handed perks to supplement already astronomical salaries.[11] The global financial crisis, and the imperious attitudes of the financiers who brought down the economy, informed my abiding interest in finance, risk, culpability, and security.

However grateful we might be for commercial insurance on occasion—when we total our car, say, or find our kitchen in flames—the commodification of risk too often comes at the expense of the common good, the mortgage fiasco being but one example. The insurance industry claims to provide protection from risk, but its actions and history tell a more complicated story.

Commercial insurance was born on the water. The word *risk* evolved from the Italian *risco*, originating in a Latin term for reefs. Used by sailors and traders navigating treacherous and uncharted routes, risco conveyed the prospects of a venture's success or failure and degree of danger.[12] While maritime insurance dates back thousands of years—early forms of coverage existed in ancient China and Babylonia—the industry as we know it took off as transatlantic trade boomed in the seventeenth and eighteenth centuries. The standard contracts of the period covered an impressive range of calamities, as one vintage agreement makes clear: "The seas, men of war, fire, enemies, pirates, rovers, assailing thieves, jettisons, letters of mart and counter-mart, surprisals, takings at sea, arrest, restraints, detainments of all kings, princes, or people ..."[13]

Not coincidentally, this was during one of the most lucrative of all businesses: the traffic in enslaved people. Lloyd's of London dominated the field, insuring vessels that transported merchandise, weapons, and captive human beings. During this period, the slave trade accounted for approximately 40 percent of the firm's business, with underwriters classifying enslaved people as "perishable goods."[14] Today Lloyd's is one of the world's leading insurance and reinsurance markets, a massively profitable business built on a foundation of contracts that insured people as property. In 2020, in response to increased public scrutiny following the police murder of George Floyd in Minneapolis, Lloyd's apologized for its "shameful" role in the slave trade and pledged to "invest in programmes to attract black and minority ethnic talent" and "support charities and organisations promoting opportunity for black and minority ethnic people" without making a specific monetary commitment—vague and inadequate compensation from a firm whose website has boasted of having over £36 billion in net resources on hand.[15]

Today, commercial insurance is one of the biggest industries in the world, with the US, where I live, by far and away the industry's largest national market. A significant portion of the business is private medical insurance, a sector that exists only because of ongoing efforts to undermine universal public health care—the model most Americans would like to see adopted.[16] As a result, private medical insurers consistently report record-breaking profits while their customers pay dearly. My husband and I hand over around $15,000 a year for coverage that comes with nearly $20,000 in deductibles. This dynamic of profiting from the absence of public provision—profiting, in other words, from people's insecurity—is widespread. The same thing is happening in Canada, where the insurance industry is lobbying hard against a universal single-payer pharmacare plan.[17] Or consider a 2023 report on the state of the global life-insurance market from the consulting firm McKinsey: the budget shortfalls associated with Japan's national pension system are one example of how the "uncertain availability of socially funded benefits" and a "growing awareness of personal risk" could be a boon to business.[18]

Climate change creates even more intense contradictions, with the sector engaged in practices that paradoxically threaten its own long-term solvency. As Ross Hammond of the Australian climate action group Sunrise Project explained to me, insurers underwrite all of the world's carbon-spewing coal mines, fracking sites, and oil and gas pipelines. Their coverage makes these projects possible; if they were not insured, they could not be built or operated. By some estimates, for example, Lloyd's of London provides approximately 40 percent of energy-market insurance globally, which means they are backing infrastructure that will cause more emergencies that will need to be insured against.[19] What's more, a large amount of the estimated $28 trillion in assets insurers collectively have under management— the pool of money that will pay claims now and into the future—is currently invested in fossil fuels, further escalating the odds of calamities and losses.[20] Just one perfect storm hitting only Florida, analysts warn, could decimate the industry and even crash the economy, with localized financial damage spreading internationally, not unlike the 2008 crisis.[21]

Extreme weather, as that unnerving possibility illustrates, puts insurers on the hook for hundreds of billions, even trillions, of dollars in potential liabilities. This is why insurers seek reinsurance—which is essentially insurance for insurers, or a way of transferring some of the risk they hold—though the recent spike in weather disasters makes this additional coverage increasingly expensive. Reinsurers go on to hedge the offloaded risk, trading it among themselves on what is called the "retrocession" market. As Matt Davison, co-author of a 2016 Bank of Canada paper on systemic risk in reinsurance, told a journalist in 2019, "Sometimes risks are traded, and then traded again, and then traded again in complicated layers and even the people trading them are no longer quite exactly sure which risk they're buying."[22] Reinsurers have also developed new forms of insurance-linked securities, including so-called catastrophe bonds. These debt instruments, which package and repackage ecological uncertainties to provide another layer of financial protection, have been likened by people in the business to the now-notorious economy-sinking mortgage-backed securities.[23] There may well be scenarios similar to 2008 in which the government has to pick up the tab to prevent cascading failures.

Insurers are already suffering some of the highest losses on record, sending them scrambling for reliable data to make better assessments. Climate risk modellers and risk management firms are experiencing a "gold rush," making climate change, to quote Greg Case, CEO of the reinsurance and catastrophe modelling company Aon, a "tremendous opportunity."[24] These firms, which critics warn vastly oversell the accuracy of their predictions, have a vested interest in hoarding information and licensing proprietary risk assessment tools. Academics and activists, in contrast, argue that climate data should be treated as a global commons, available to everyone and subject to robust peer review.

By now, it should hardly surprise us that an industry hawking security increases overall insecurity; commercial insurers make the world more perilous, and then sell insurance to guard against the problems they help spawn. In the US, for example, insurance companies now offer concierge service to protect the homes of high-end customers from the wildfires climate change is making more frequent, a market dominated by none other than AIG.[25] As a capitalist business model, it's brilliant; as a way of managing risk, it's horrific. This is the dynamic that Ulrich Beck was getting at when he described risk as the inexhaustible engine of demand that economists have long dreamed of unleashing. "Hunger can be sated, needs can be satisfied," Beck writes, but risks are "unsatisfiable" and "infinite."[26]

Because risks can be infinite—which means insurance premiums can be, too—we need to push for security for the many, not just for the wealthy few. Activists like

Hammond, for example, are organizing for more egalitarian and sensible ways of evaluating and responding to ecological perils. "We're trying to find leverage points where we can create some sort of risk for the financial sector, such that they start to reduce their support for expanded fossil-fuel production," Hammond told me. In effect, organizers aim to shift the industry's risk calculus, limiting the upsides of fossil-fuel production. In Canada, an alliance of Indigenous organizers and civil society groups has been pressuring insurers to keep their distance from the controversial Trans Mountain Pipeline. In 2021, Trans Mountain asked regulators for permission to keep its insurers anonymous, lest "targeting and pressure" result in a "material loss" to the company and "prejudice the competitive position of its insurers"—a right to secrecy that was swiftly granted despite the fact that government contractors are usually subject to public disclosure.[27] Undeterred, activists keep pushing insurers to cut ties (including AIG after the firm was revealed to have signed on), foregrounding the project's high economic and environmental costs and the danger posed to nearby communities.

Trans Mountain's plea for secrecy showed that the protesters are on to something. The company *was* scared, and for good reason. At least eighteen insurers have ruled out working on the pipeline.[28] In this way, organizing can be thought of as a kind of social insurance program. By bringing people together to challenge and transform the energy and financial sectors, it safeguards the future.

· · ·

TODAY, WE UNDERSTAND THE future in terms of probabilities: there are odds we might slip and fall, wreck our car, be struck by lightning, or maybe win the lottery. According to the Canadian philosopher of science Ian Hacking, this mode of thinking was a conceptual breakthrough that swept the world in the seventeenth century.[29] Humans have been fascinated by chance since time immemorial, as evidenced by the existence of dice dating back thousands of years before Christ. But randomness is not the same as probability. Probability developed when people began trying to figure out how the dice might roll.

The French mathematician Blaise Pascal, a child prodigy born in 1623, laid the groundwork for modern probability by helping to solve the so-called problem of points, which asked how to divvy up the stakes of an unfinished game where one player was slightly ahead of the other. Not long after his breakthrough, some biographers tell us, Pascal nearly died when the horses pulling his carriage plunged into the Seine, an accident he believed was not random but rather an angry message from God. As a youth, Pascal had been as pious as he was precocious, and the crash renewed his spiritual fervour. His posthumously published *Pensées* describes the tragic and horrible aspects of human existence before laying out the terms of what is now known as "Pascal's wager." If God exists, then believing in Him will lead to infinite happiness in heaven; the potential rewards, Pascal argued, were more than worth risking a meagre and pain-filled mortal life on. Betting on God, it follows, is the only sensible bet to make. With that, Pascal turned his back on science and reason—and also gambling—even as he likened religious faith to a speculator's coin toss: "A game is being played at the extremity of this infinite distance where heads or tails will turn up."[30] Pascal kept his eye on infinity, leaving it to others to use his discoveries to improve conditions on earth.

Later thinkers built on Pascal's innovation by applying the methods used to study natural phenomena to a social world undergoing epochal transformation. Amid the ferment of industrialization, new frameworks for thinking about causality and responsibility, fortune and fault, slowly took hold. Dangerous factories, collapsing mines, and faulty railroad tracks brought a broader political and material context into view. To lose a limb or an eye, or even your life, at work, as so many did, was no longer thought to be a sign of God's wrath but rather of an unsafe job or a bout of bad luck. This new paradigm paved the way for what we now know as social insurance, overcoming the objections of those who, like the nineteenth-century Calvinists, believed such risk-hedging revealed an impudent lack of faith.[31]

In order for social insurance to become possible, what historian John Fabian Witt calls the "nonnegligent victim of nonfaulty harm" first had to be conceived.[32] The idea of the accident had to be invented; put differently, we had to embrace the possibility that shit happens. Accidents were secularized and subjected to statistical analysis. They were no longer preordained nor completely random but predictable, made calculable with the help of the law of averages. A combination of math and public policy promised to turn individual misfortunes and mistakes into common problems to be collectively solved, the risk shared among the many so that personal adversity could be rendered more bearable. In addition to displacing old ideas of divine providence, this new approach also challenged presumptions of individual fault and so conflicted with liberal economic doctrine—the worker-blaming view that Kafka spent his career combatting.

Germany, a hub of data collection and classification, was the first to adopt this new approach to risk-sharing as a matter of public policy. Beginning in 1883, Otto von Bismarck, the "Iron Chancellor," implemented a triad of novel social insurance policies that provided security in sickness and old age, and in the event of workplace accidents. Bismarck's programs marked the first time a modern state enlisted the government to pool and spread risk across huge populations, protecting citizens from insecurity, in Bismarck's words, "as a right," not as charity. At Bismarck's behest, Germany's emperor, William the First, wrote a letter to the parliament justifying the programs: "those who are disabled from work, by age, and invalidity have a well-grounded claim to care from the state."[33]

In the late nineteenth century, this was a radical

proposal, particularly the possibility of retirement in an era when most people laboured until they died— as a growing number of us fear we will have to do today.[34] (The catch with Bismarck's plan was that benefits only kicked in at the age of seventy, which very few people lived to attain.) Bismarck was no liberal, and he cared little for easing suffering: a ruthless autocrat, he adopted his insurance programs as a strategy to undercut the socialists, who were calling for even more radical reforms. His political manoeuvre failed: the Social Democratic Party kept gaining members and winning votes. No matter his intentions, though, Bismarck's programs changed the course of history by shifting our understanding of accidents and establishing insurance as a state-subsidized collective entitlement, laying a foundation for the modern welfare state that other countries would go on to emulate.

In North America, at the dawn of the twentieth century, socialist and labour radicals also pushed to make social insurance a viable political possibility. One fight focused on overturning the assumption of worker culpability then etched into law.[35] The common-law doctrine of "assumption of risk" stipulated that workers accepted any and all hazards when they began a job, making what were called "death contracts" standard practice; if you died, you did so having agreed to the lethal risks your occupation entailed. The corresponding doctrine of "contributory negligence"—which the *Manitoba Free Press* blasted in 1909 as the "most one-sided law that had ever been enacted"—stated that if a worker played even a trivial role in an accident, no matter how dangerous the tasks they performed or deadly the machinery they operated, employers could not be held liable.[36]

In 1910, Canada's Royal Commission on the Relations of Labour and Capital appointed Justice William Meredith to study workers' compensation throughout the world. His report laid out the principles that would form the basis of Canada's no-fault system, which requires benefits to be paid no matter who is to blame for an accident.[37] The same year, a remarkable twenty-nine-year-old New Yorker named Crystal Eastman, a rare woman lawyer and an iconoclastic feminist and socialist, published *Work-Accidents and the Law*, a 350-page tome that was the product of intensive fieldwork in the industrial capital of Pittsburgh, Pennsylvania. Realizing no one was keeping track of workplace fatalities, Eastman interviewed workers and widows and hung out at morgues to compile her data. She tallied the men who fell from beams as they constructed skyscrapers, got electrocuted while hanging power lines, or were crushed by the heavy earth they quarried. Elevators, she found, offered "a peculiar temptation to recklessness," repeatedly falling on people's heads or plunging to the ground to kill their riders.[38]

After returning to New York, Eastman helped craft a mandatory workers' compensation program for the state, the first of its kind in the country.[39] Challenged in court by employers, the law was struck down by a judge the day before the infamous Triangle Shirtwaist Factory fire in Manhattan killed 146 workers who had been locked in the building to keep them productive. Many of them, mostly young women, leapt to their deaths, their bodies piling up on the sidewalk as people looked on in horror. In response, Eastman and others redoubled their organizing efforts. "When the dead bodies of girls are found piled up against locked doors leading to the exits after a factory fire," Eastman said, "who wants to hear about a great relief fund? What we want is to start a revolution."[40] In 1913, the state constitution was amended and a more robust workers' compensation law eventually adopted.

One of the people standing on the street, watching as Triangle Shirtwaist workers perished, was an activist named Frances Perkins. When President Roosevelt asked her to serve as his secretary of labour a little over two decades later, Perkins agreed on the condition that he commit to a range of social insurance policies: workers' compensation; unemployment relief; minimum-wage laws; disability, old age, and health insurance; and a federal jobs program. Soon she was chairwoman of the Committee on Economic Security.[41] The programs she helped enact would protect millions of people from what Roosevelt called the "hazards and vicissitudes of life" and "one of the most fearsome evils of our economic system—insecurity." At the height of the Great Depression, when most Americans were apprehensive and desperate, Roosevelt insisted that treating risk as a commons, instead of privatizing it, would make everyone safer and better off in the end. "There can be no security for the individual," he said, "in the midst of general insecurity."[42]

THE SAME DAY WE walked the picket line outside the offices of AIG, my friends and I passed out pamphlets to protesters and passersby. We had spent the previous three months researching and writing *The Debt Resisters' Operations Manual*, a financial literacy handbook with a radical edge. In a little over one hundred pages, we tried to provide our fellow debtors with everything they needed to know to stay afloat. Short, pithy chapters explained the basic operations of student debt, credit cards, payday loans, medical bills, mortgages, municipal debt, bankruptcy law, debt collection, and credit scores—those ubiquitous numbers that assess the credit risk posed by a person, town, state, province, or country. These topics sound about as exciting as the memos Kafka wrote on the intricacies of insurance over one hundred years ago. But they have a profound effect on most people's lives, which is why the five thousand copies we had printed on cheap newsprint were soon gone and the online version was downloaded more than one hundred thousand times in the weeks after its release.

Our project was not unlike Crystal Eastman's survey

of Pittsburgh's working class if it had been conducted by the workers themselves. By examining and exposing how financial systems are designed to perpetuate and profit from people's insecurity, we aimed to challenge the idea that debtors are solely at fault for their financial woes. Perhaps more importantly, we wanted to encourage collective action. The text paid homage to the massive 2012 protests in Quebec that had begun over university tuition hikes and that had popularized the symbol of a red square, signifying being "squarely in the red," or in debt. We adopted the red square in hopes of sparking a similar uprising in the United States. A few years later, a group of us would go on to found the Debt Collective, the organization that would put debt cancellation on the political map. Wherever our members gather, red squares still abound.

It was an endeavour at once political and personal. Our research and writing project began, in part, as a rejoinder to the American media's initial explanation for the financial crisis and its causes. According to conservative pundits and politicians, the trouble began not with Wall Street but with fiscally irresponsible poor and mostly Black homeowners who had taken out mortgages they could not afford. In reality, these were the communities aggressively targeted with predatory subprime loans. Wells Fargo loan officers in Baltimore, for example, pushed so-called "ghetto loans" on clients they called "mud people," leading vulnerable families to lose their homes in foreclosure. "We just went right after them," a bank employee told the *New York Times*.[43] Similar subprime loans were peddled across the nation before being sliced, bundled, securitized, and then insured by entities like AIG, tanking the global economy.

Though the repercussions I felt were not particularly severe, the bankers' bad behaviour changed the course of my life. Like millions of others, I became strapped for cash when the economy crashed; I couldn't keep up with my student loan payments and defaulted. As punishment for my inability to pay, my principal ballooned by 19 percent, and my credit score was shot, too. I cried tears of hot shame as I confessed the depth of my predicament to my partner. I was $42,000 in the hole, I told him, but over the next decade or two, I'd likely have to pay over six figures before I was free. I was standing on the equivalent of economic quicksand—the more I paid, the more I owed. It was only when I got swept up in Occupy Wall Street that I realized my situation was not unique. Almost everyone who gathered in Manhattan's Zuccotti Park was in the same insecure and sinking boat. We had all taken on debt for necessities—to get an education, see a doctor, buy a home, or even have food to eat—only to realize that what had been sold as a lifeline was, in fac,t an anchor, dragging us down with compounding interest and fees.

The political scientist Jacob Hacker calls this phenomenon the "great risk shift."[44] Over the past fifty years, indebtedness and insecurity have exploded as a direct consequence of systematic and well-funded attacks on the systems of social insurance and welfare I've just discussed. Beginning in the 1970s, the corporate sector mobilized to undermine working-class gains: slashing taxes, crushing organized labour, deregulating the financial sector, and shrinking and privatizing essential social services. This shift of risk, Hacker argues, has coincided with a revival of the old discourse of personal responsibility. An individual should strive for success—but if they fail, it is their fault. Today, both the US and Canada rank low on the list of overall social spending among wealthy industrialized nations.[45] Ordinary Americans and Canadians are more exposed to the hazards of unemployment, disability, and old age than they were a few decades ago.

This leaves growing numbers of people no choice but to rely on what is sometimes called the "plastic safety net." Debt today functions as a kind of makeshift insurance scheme for people without recourse to adequate wages or social assistance, pushing household borrowing to record highs—Canadian households now have the worst debt ratio of any G7 country, outpacing the US.[46] In both countries, the number of seniors struggling with debt, including non-mortgage debt, has been steadily climbing.[47] The growth of student debt, meanwhile, puts financial security further out of reach for younger generations, who have to pay back school loans instead of saving for retirement or a down payment on a home. Today the average American borrower graduates with

US$30,000 in loans while their Canadian counterparts owe C$28,000 for a bachelor's degree.[48] Our monthly interest payments, meanwhile, enrich the investors who hold our debts as assets, a wealth transfer that fuels inequality, corrodes democracy, and further destabilizes the economy.

Rising inflation and interest rates only make it harder for ordinary people to make ends meet. As a result, credit card debt and delinquencies are surging, and a significant number of Canadian homeowners' monthly payments no longer cover the interest portion of their loans, their balances growing even as they keep paying—the same economic quicksand that once held me in its grip. To cover exorbitant mortgage costs, people are getting second jobs, cancelling family vacations, and cashing in their investments. [49] Before Covid-19 hit, one poll found that nearly half of Canadians were at best $200 away from insolvency, while 29 percent could not meet their monthly debt obligations.[50] An early 2023 poll signals where things are heading, with over 70 percent of respondents "concerned about their ability to pay off their debts as interest rates spike." The same year, financial analysts described Canada's overall mortgage debt as "a ticking time bomb" set to detonate in "a couple of years," while the Bank of Canada expressed growing concern about "the ability of households to service their debt," warning that some payments will swell by 40 percent.[51] The individualization of risk and responsibility ensures indebtedness and insecurity will continue to spread unless struggling debtors come together and demand relief. It's worth noting, for example, that student debt loads are lowest in Quebec, where public investment in education is more robust, thanks in good part to protests like the ones my friends and I found so inspiring years ago.

IN 2022, AFTER YEARS of organizing led by the Debt Collective—including research, street protests, lawsuits, and multiple student loan strikes—the Biden administration finally announced a plan to wipe out $10,000 to $20,000 in student debt per borrower. Republicans and their billionaire backers immediately filed multiple lawsuits seeking to block the measure. Their reasoning? Erasing debt would make it harder for employers to retain indebted employees and would discourage young people from joining the military. Opponents of Biden's plan took to Twitter and TV to denounce the idea of handouts for "slacker baristas," overeducated Ivy League lawyers, and impractical "lesbian dance theory" majors. Immune to accusations of hypocrisy, members of Congress who had recently received hundreds of thousands (in some cases millions) of dollars in pandemic loan forgiveness lambasted the proposal.[52] It was all incredibly upsetting, but I also knew it was coming. The powerful have long put debt to use as a source of profit and tool of domination, including racial domination.[53] The fight over student debt relief is just the latest chapter of a much longer story.

Today we tend to see being in debt not only as a financial failure but also as a moral one. The German word for debt, *schuld*, also means guilt and blame. For millennia, however, it was creditors, not debtors, who were regarded as immoral. In *Politics*, for example, Aristotle describes usury as "hated" and "unnatural," for "money was intended to be used in exchange, but not to increase at interest."[54] The Christian church saw charging interest as sinful, associating usury with avarice and sloth. The Bible, after all, commands debts be forgiven, and making money on interest without lifting a finger was thought to be an insult to the Lord, who said, "By the sweat of your face shall you get bread to eat." Economists have described these long-standing prohibitions as a "kind of social insurance" and a check on inequality. Poor people had access to emergency funds on terms they could afford, while the ability of the rich to grow their fortunes was constrained.[55]

In the modern world, however, usury is not only legal but arguably the foundation of our highly financialized economic system. This understanding developed over several centuries, as the rise of modern industry and capitalism ushered in new theories of risk that challenged time-honoured religious restrictions on lending at interest.[56] Born to aid the rising merchant class, these new theories did not see risk as something to be managed collectively, but rather as a mechanism for amassing wealth and exercising social control.

As trade expanded in the Middle Ages, the argument for legalizing interest-charging loans in situations where lenders shared in the risk of a venture won a steady stream of converts.[57] In 1390, the Lord Mayor of London argued that the term *usury* only applied on gains made on loans "without risk," and by the late sixteenth century, the Church was largely in agreement.[58] This handy theological loophole facilitated the rise of merchant capitalism across Europe, a system that quickly flipped the long-standing moral polarity that had framed lenders as miscreants and debtors as victims. As market society developed, debtors became the transgressors.

But as the historian Bruce Mann has argued, this conception evolved to contain a crucial double standard—one that shapes our world to this day.[59] In the eighteenth century, as commerce boomed and lending proliferated, insolvency (much like workplace accidents) came to be seen as inevitable, but in this case, only for the well-to-do. Where corporations and their elite backers were concerned, the occasional default was reframed as the cost of doing business, an unfortunate but unavoidable consequence of entrepreneurial risk-taking. For the poor, in contrast, default was taken as a sign of moral failure, with debtors imprisoned or publicly humiliated. And so it continues today. Banks and corporations routinely receive government bailouts or engage in "strategic" defaults, while debt relief for ordinary people remains as rare as it is controversial. This double standard serves as a form of security or insurance for the privileged: poor debtors are pushed to pay off their loans to avoid harsh penalties, while the affluent are shielded from risk and responsibility.

Consider the critical role predatory debt contracts played in the development of the British colonies.[60] In Canada, the Hudson's Bay Company kept Indigenous communities in hock to the company by paying Innu and Cree traders not in pounds sterling but "beaver tokens," a proprietary currency that limited traders' ability to take their business elsewhere. Indigenous trappers travelled to trading posts in the late summer and purchased the various provisions required to carry out the winter hunt, the bounty of which they would return to sell in hopes of settling their debt. In practice, trappers were rarely able to break even, compelling them to keep working year after year—debt effectively trapping the trappers.[61] Such price-gouging and freedom-limiting practices continued well into the twentieth century, as revealed by *The Other Side of the Ledger*, a 1972 documentary directed by Martin Defalco and Willie Dunn that presents an Indigenous perspective on HBC's history. In the words of narrator George Manuel, "perpetual debt binds us firmly to the store."[62]

In the United States, colonization progressed by deploying debt to similarly manipulative ends. Before mortgages became the cornerstone of middle-class home ownership that they are today, they were used to steal Indigenous territory. In England, laws ensured that land could not be seized to settle mortgage obligations, a practice that afforded families who fell upon hard times a measure of protection. A creditor could demand a debtor's personal possessions or the "rents and fruits" of land to clear a debt, or even assume tenancy on half the land (which must have resulted in some rather awkward situations), but they could not permanently take the land itself.[63] As legal scholar K-Sue Park has shown, this changed in the seventeenth century, when American colonists developed new and easy practices of foreclosure, which were initially used exclusively to expropriate land from indebted Indigenous people.[64] In 1615, for example, John Rolfe, a man most famous for marrying Pocahontas, noted the tendency of local Chiefs to mortgage "all their lands to the colony in exchange for wheat."[65] Foreclosure, Park explains, turned land into what is literally called a security, the thing that secures a debt or line of credit. This development not only facilitated the dispossession of Indigenous people, it also helped transform land into something abstracted and alienable, a speculative and easily tradeable asset.

Thomas Jefferson, the American statesman who epitomized the elite view of "debt relief for me, but not for thee," was an enthusiast of this new technique. Where propertied white men were concerned, he argued that any balance unpaid after "natural limits," which he took to be the span of a generation, should be eliminated.[66] At the same time, he counselled his peers to wield debt as a weapon to overcome Indigenous resistance, writing in 1803 to the governor of Indiana, "We shall push our trading houses, and be glad to see the good & influential individuals among them run in debt, because we observe that when these debts get beyond what the individuals can pay, they become willing to lop them off by a cession of lands."[67] (Jefferson, tellingly, spent most of his life racking up massive personal debts; upon his death the enslaved people on his estate were sold to pay the enormous sum he owed.[68])

A little over two hundred years later, this same dynamic of financial insecurity and indebtedness is driving predominantly white farmers on the Canadian prairies to sell their land to corporate investors. In 2022, Katherine Aske, a young farmer and researcher originally from Nova Scotia, published an insightful report on farm economics and the perils of treating farmland as a speculative asset, its purchase price disconnected from its productive use, meaning how much income can be earned by growing food. "It is also a model," she writes, "that has indebted and pushed out a great many farmers, and hollowed out rural communities."[69] For investors, however, farmer hardship is a boon. "Any farmer with enough debt is going to be tempted to cave to an investor group," Aske told me. "High levels of debt lead people into the hands of investors, even though they otherwise would like things to be different." Banks also benefit, issuing big loans to cover artificially inflated prices.

When we spoke, Aske gave me a history lesson. The trouble began in the 1980s, when policies designed to empower farmers and share risk—collective marketing mechanisms, co-operative control of grain elevators, and subsidized grain freight rates, for example— were dismantled in favour of more market-friendly approaches. Canadian agricultural policy became increasingly focused on encouraging large-scale pro- duction for export, at the expense of other social and ecological metrics. Farmer income plummeted to a mere 2 percent of gross revenue as transnational agribusi- ness increased its profits, leaving farmers little choice but to take on more and more debt to keep their opera- tions running or else to leave the industry altogether.[70] Today, Canadian farmers collectively owe $129 billion, four times what was due in the 1990s.[71] "In places like the prairies, where agriculture is really dominant," Aske said, "it's a community-level burden. Everybody collec- tively feels this crushing weight of debt." The Canadian public shares the burden, too. Between 1986 and 2018, Canadian farmers paid a total of $93 billion in interest on their debt—approximately $10 billion less than they received in public subsidies during the same period. In other words, the public effectively paid for the banks' handsome profits on the farmers' loans.[72]

Predictably, the 2008 global financial crash deepened the crisis, in this case by sending investors scrambling for secure places to store their money. Rich individuals, real estate investment firms, pension funds, hedge funds, sovereign wealth funds, and other entities began buying up farmland and haven't stopped, further concentrating

ownership, inflating prices, and betting on future insecurity. "When stock prices are slumping and inflation
is soaring, farmland looks to be an appealing investment," a 2022 *Barron's* article advises, not least because
"farmland prices stand to benefit from growing concerns
about food and land scarcity."[73] (Investors are also buying
farmland for the water rights, anticipating a payoff as dry
seasons become more extreme due to climate change, or
what one asset manager has called "a trillion-dollar market opportunity."[74]) While this means some farmers can
sell their property at a tidy profit, pay off their mortgage,
and retire in comfort, things are often more complicated.
After all, selling means you lose your land, which you
might want to keep working or pass on to your kids or
to other aspiring farmers. Many farmers sell their land
only to rent the same property back from the buyers.
And for most new farmers, renting farmland is the only
financially viable option.

This turn toward tenant farming, Aske told me, creates ecological risks we all bear. Whether under pressure
from banks or investor-landlords, farmers are driven to
maximize production. High debt loads and costly rental
contracts inhibit the transition to the life-sustaining
practices that our planet needs. (It takes three years to
go organic, for example, which is longer than most lease
terms, putting farmers at risk of losing all their efforts to
transition.) One farmer told Aske that the shift to tenant
farming is "a dead end" as far as climate change is concerned, because renting "doesn't allow the methods that

are going to be necessary." Economically, the safest thing is to stick to conventional practices, no matter how hazardous they are ecologically.

Aske believes that transforming the agricultural system to mitigate climate change will require many more farmers working in very different, more agroecological and socially sustainable ways. But for decades the number of family farmers has been diminishing as the business becomes more consolidated; the high cost of land and prospect of a lifetime of debt blocks young people who want to become farmers from entering the profession. "Every aspiring farmer gone to pursue another career, every farmer who sinks into debt, every quarter bought by an investor, every bidding war lost by a smaller farmer to a larger one diminishes our capacity to enact alternative production systems and land relations," Aske writes. Like the student debtors cornered by employers and army recruiters, farmers are limited in their freedom and sovereignty by the threat of insolvency. This is yet another example of debt's utility as a tool of social control, echoing recent research showing that rising household indebtedness has led to declining labour action and strike activity around the world.[75]

Shame is a key ingredient of debt's oppressive power. While conducting her research, Aske learned that farmers were happy to talk about their neighbours' financial struggles but were far more tight-lipped about their own—a stoicism that only serves the status quo by keeping people isolated and unable to recognize their common struggles. Across the country, smaller-scale growers and their allies are organizing for change at the local level, creating community land trusts and running businesses co-operatively. But the scale of the problems farmers face requires government intervention: for example, reviving the land bank policies enacted in Saskatchewan and Prince Edward Island in the 1970s, which enabled young farmers to lease land at fair prices directly from the state, or providing public pensions that allow farmers to retire in dignity without having to sell their land to the highest bidder.[76] To build the power required to win these kinds of changes, indebted farmers will need to draw on the rich tradition of agrarian risk-sharing and collectivism, rejecting shame and challenging the doctrine of personal responsibility. The fault lies not with struggling individuals but with an economy structured to profit from indebtedness, treat land as a speculative asset, and keep us overwhelmed, isolated, and insecure.

IN LATE 2021, MY Debt Collective collaborators and I mailed letters to more than twenty thousand people in Mississippi and Florida who were on probation, a court-mandated and often costly period of supervision following a crime. The letters began as follows: "Jubilant Greetings! We are writing to you with good news: We just got rid of some of your private probation debt! ...

You no longer owe the balance of this particular debt. It is gone, a gift with no strings attached."

Before we wiped out the $270 he owed, thirty-one-year-old Douglas Harper of Quitman, Mississippi, was on probation due to unpaid traffic fines. "It'll scare you to the point you don't know what to do," he told the local paper. "You have to choose between paying your light bill or paying your supervision fee that you could get locked up for." Despite his best efforts, Harper couldn't settle the account and still feed his family, especially after he was laid off at the start of the pandemic.[77] "I was so happy to get the letter, it was great, it was a blessing," he said. "Now I can get my license back and go back to my job."[78]

All told, we erased over $3 million of probation debt, after purchasing it for around $90,000, or three cents on the dollar. (Few people realize that most personal debts are sold on shady secondary markets. The debt collector who calls you demanding payment is typically a speculator who bought your account as part of a larger portfolio for far less than they are hoping you will pay them.) Over the course of a decade, we have abolished hundreds of millions of dollars of medical, tuition, and payday loan debt, belonging to tens of thousands of people across the United States. We erase the debts of strangers to provide them some relief and solidarity—and to shine a light on the mechanics of financial speculation and ignite a movement for systemic change.[79]

The Debt Collective now organizes around financial obligations of all kinds. Our members owe student loans, back rent, medical bills, credit card debt, and also the myriad fines and fees, including for parole and probation, associated with the criminal legal system. Though Jacob Hacker does not include policing in his account of the great risk shift, the attacks on the social welfare state that gained steam in the 1970s dovetailed not only with the explosion of household indebtedness but also the rise of mass incarceration.

Though the slogan "defund the police" has become a political lightning rod, the sentiment is utterly sensible: activists simply want to restore balance by investing in social services instead of punishment—or as the activist slogan puts it, in "care, not cops." We can't police and imprison our way out of poverty, mental health disorders, and addiction, or a lack of secure housing and opportunity. A carceral approach to social problems doesn't solve them, it only deepens insecurity.

It's revealing that the people who are locked up are said to owe a "debt to society," rather than rich individuals who have benefited from a vastly unequal economy. While the affluent rely on police to protect their wealth and property, the people most likely to be portrayed as a security threat and to be heavily policed are also those most likely to be deemed a credit risk: individuals who are Black, brown, Indigenous, and poor. For many formerly incarcerated people, even small debts can feel monumental, like Harper's $270 bill. In the US, however, people are released owing an average of $13,000 in court fines and fees, not including bail debt.[80] In many cases the state contracts with private probation companies that gouge people for services and often collect what's due through ethically and legally suspect means. In California, for example, probationers who owe money can be forced to work under conditions experts have likened to "involuntary servitude."[81]

Though few people realize it, the problem of carceral debt helped galvanize the movement against police violence we now know as Black Lives Matter, which began when police killed eighteen-year-old Michael Brown in Ferguson, Missouri. In 2013, the year before Brown's death, Ferguson officials had issued over thirty-three thousand arrest warrants for a city of just over twenty-one thousand people. Many of these warrants were issued because people could not pay their municipal fines and fees, often charges for trivial offences: a broken tail light, for example, or leaving a trash can on the street. Failure to pay could lead to jail. The criminal legal system in Ferguson effectively merged an elaborate and punitive mechanism of regressive taxation with a modern-day debtors' prison.

Across North America, poverty is criminalized, with debt used as a tool of coercion. Most court-related interactions produce fees that weigh heaviest on the most insecure and vulnerable: people who are indigent, unhoused, and struggling with mental illness and addiction. Failure to pay can lead to serious consequences, including a suspended driver's licence or, in some cases, incarceration, which, of course, jeopardizes people's ability to find work and stay employed—in other words, to earn money to make their debt payments.[82] Insecurity begets insecurity, intensifying economic and racial disparities.

One recent study of municipal records in Montreal found that unhoused people receive 40 percent of all tickets for bylaw infractions, though they make up less than 1 percent of the city's total population.[83] Since First Nations, Inuit, and Métis people are disproportionately represented among the unhoused, they bear the brunt of these fines. The penalty for sleeping on a park bench, for example, can be $100; individuals can receive multiple citations in a single day or even for the same infraction.[84] Research shows that the number of tickets being issued is rising "exponentially," with devastating consequences.[85] Emily Jean Knox, a volunteer at a Montreal legal clinic, told me that she has assisted individuals with debts ranging from hundreds to tens of thousands of dollars, all incurred as a result of living in the streets—one man owed the city $40,000, a balance that ballooned while he was unhoused during the Covid-19 pandemic. Providing "secure, dignified housing for all residents," Knox wrote in an essay for the CBC, "would be far more effective at maintaining public safety than ticketing people" who have nowhere to go.[86]

Huge amounts of precious public resources are spent burying penniless people in debt and then attempting to shake them down for payment, though the exact financial details of these schemes are alarmingly foggy.

There's a striking lack of research and clarity around the scope, scale, and costs of municipal ticketing programs, by which I mean both the social costs—the damage to vulnerable people's lives and self-esteem—and the economic costs. We can extrapolate from analyses of Ontario's Safe Streets Act, which was adopted to curb panhandling: one 2011 report found that in the span of a decade, the Toronto Police Service spent close to $1 million issuing tickets and reaped a paltry $8,000 in fines paid.[87] A 2019 *Toronto Star* editorial calling for the act's repeal described a disabled man named Donald Dunbar: "The province has spent a small fortune jailing him for missing court dates and probation appointments related to the $45,000 in fines he has accumulated," when what he and others need is social assistance, "not persecution and punishment."[88]

On both sides of the border, it often costs upward of six figures to incarcerate a single individual for a year, significantly more than the amount required to provide mental health and related supports to those in need.[89] This sort of fiscal irrationality helps explain why police budgets are so often astronomical, consuming between one-tenth to nearly a third of municipal expenditures in Canada and up to 40 percent in the US.[90] Montreal's Defund the Police Coalition, an alliance of sixty-five community organizations, has proposed reallocating half of the city's police budget to "support the security and wellbeing of communities most targeted by the police"; they suggest investing in health, housing, and education, as well as a universal basic income.[91] But despite community opposition, police budgets across the US and Canada have continued to swell. In 2023, Montreal's police budget was set at nearly $800 million, $63 million more than the previous year—money that could have been spent providing shelter, improving schools and public transit, coping with climate change, or helping people make ends meet as costs rise and economic insecurity deepens.[92]

Mariame Kaba and Andrea Ritchie, two prominent advocates of transformative justice, have compared defunding the police to the revitalization of the commons, the communally managed fields and forests that once ensured the peasantry's collective survival. As Kaba and Ritchie understand it, the act of commoning is antithetical to policing: "It is about affirming humanity, eliminating inequality and social hierarchies, and promoting shared well-being and greater safety." Like the community groups that make up the Montreal Coalition, Kaba and Ritchie want to see systems of social insurance and welfare based not on fear and punishment but care and solidarity.[93] Many communities have already developed effective and non-violent programs to support public safety, from the Bear Clan Patrol in Winnipeg, Manitoba to the CAHOOTS mobile crisis team in Eugene, Oregon.[94] Expanding such efforts is hardly the radical proposition it is often made out to be. None of us is safer when men like Douglas Harper are threatened with arrest because they lack money, or when poor or ill people are ticketed, harassed, or hauled off to jail. The most secure communities do not have the most police. They are the ones with the resources to meet people's needs.

THE STRUGGLE AGAINST POLICE violence today is, fundamentally, a struggle over how we understand security. Its roots trace back to the seventeenth and eighteenth centuries, when philosophers debated what originally motivated people to come together and create society. Thomas Hobbes, Jean-Jacques Rousseau, and John Locke were unanimous in their answer: security. In varying ways, each imagined a group of men (only men) in a perilous "state of nature" mutually agreeing to a social contract that would protect their lives and possessions from violence and larceny. In Locke's words, this state of nature was "very unsafe, very insecure" and "full of fears and continual dangers," prompting people to "unite for the mutual Preservation of their Lives, Liberties and Estates."[95]

The equation of security with the defensive protection of life and property was widespread. In 1765, the famed English jurist William Blackstone averred that a citizen's fundamental rights "consist, primarily, in the free enjoyment of personal security, of personal liberty, and of private property."[96] A short time later, Adam Smith concurred in his influential *Wealth of Nations*:

"It is only under the shelter of the civil magistrate that the owner of that valuable property … can sleep a single night in security."[97] For these prominent men, providing insurance against theft through policing was the single most important function of the state.

In 1842, Karl Marx criticized this view, denouncing the liberal obsession with a possessive and defensive notion of security, one he argued only served to buttress the wealthy's commitment to maintaining inequality. As a young journalist, Marx was radicalized by reporting on conflicts over peasants' customary rights to the commons. The expansion of the railroads and the market for commercial goods had increased the price of German lumber, prompting a ban on gathering firewood from local forests and leading to the persecution of poor people who were now threatened with fines and forced labour as they foraged for fuel to heat their homes. As Marx learned about their plight, he began to think critically about economics and power relations. "The wood thief has robbed the forest owner of wood," Marx wrote, "but the forest owner has made use of the wood thief to purloin the state itself."[98]

As we now know, the centuries-long process of enclosure displaced peasants from common lands that once sustained them, turning old traditions of subsistence into offences punishable by death. Recall Thomas More's 1516 book *Utopia*, published as this process was just beginning in Britain. More blasted the nobility not only for seizing land for the wool industry and creating poverty, but also for criminalizing it. Peasants had no choice, More wrote, but to beg and steal, "and so to be hanged."[99] A popular folk poem composed soon after called attention to this grave injustice:

> The law locks up the man or woman
> Who steals the goose off the common
> But leaves the greater villain loose
> Who steals the common from the goose.

> The law demands that we atone
> When we take things we do not own
> But leaves the lords and ladies fine
> Who takes things that are yours and mine.[100]

Wealthy proponents of enclosure rationalized their misdeeds by insisting that increasing poverty had public benefits. The material security of the commons, they thought, made people lazy, and the threat of destitution and punishment would spur them to work diligently. Economic elites have been busy manufacturing insecurity ever since, prodding us along while claiming it is for our own good. Consider what the chief actuary of Prudential Life Insurance Company said in 1919, voicing common critiques of the early social insurance programs that his industry saw as direct competition. He called the threat of poverty and hunger in old age "the most powerful incentive which makes for character and growth in a democracy" and

said "gratuitous governmental pensions" would undermine "character-building."[101] As we saw in Chapter 1,
today's purveyors of insecurity speak in the idioms of
inflation, efficiency, and economic growth rather than
invoking the health of democracy, but the message is
the same: broadly shared material security must be
avoided, lest society crumble.

Time and again we are told that caring for other people poses unacceptable risks, or what economists call
"moral hazard," a concept borrowed from the field of
commercial insurance. If we are too lenient with people, this line of thinking goes, they will be tempted
to commit more crimes; if we give our fellow citizens
an inch, they will take a mile. Providing robust systems of social insurance and public welfare, this logic
says, creates perverse incentives, encouraging people
to shirk on the job, visit a doctor more than is needed,
spend money instead of saving for old age, or study
something impractical like foreign languages, history, or—the horror—painting and poetry. In the early
days of workers' compensation and unemployment
insurance, opponents imagined armies of employees
scamming the system to collect benefits. In the 1980s
and 1990s, panic over a "culture" of welfare "depen-
dency" justified paring back social services across the
US and Canada.[102] More recently, a bipartisan coalition
killed the American child tax credit, the Covid-era policy that dramatically reduced child poverty, out of fears
some parents might slack off or use drugs—better to risk

letting kids going hungry.[103] It's the same argument now invoked to crush student debt relief; the conservative Heritage Foundation recently warned that "the moral hazard" of cancelling student debt "is massive."[104] Should their financial burdens be lifted, young people might make different career choices—and then join a labour union. Or, god forbid, they might just enjoy a much-needed vacation. The hazard, in other words, comes from the possibility that millions of people might be less stressed-out and more free.

IF WE TRULY WANT to be liberated from insecurity, we need to redefine security for ourselves. The real threat comes not from caring for our fellow citizens but from the systems and entities that undermine the public good for private gain: the unregulated financial sector creating derivatives markets capable of crashing the economy, lenders willing to destroy people's lives to collect a debt, employers colluding to cheapen the price of labour, fossil-fuel companies profiting from the atmosphere's destruction, privatizers who want to enclose the welfare commons. Commercial insurance and policing, mass consumption and the military, capitalism and human supremacy—like the mythical symbol of the ouroboros, these systems eat their own tails, devouring the future as we race to escape the insecurity they generate.[105]

Just as urgently, we need to reject the idea that ordinary people's security is something to fear—an idea that flies in the face of both morality and evidence. In *The Affluent Society*, John Kenneth Galbraith argues that the impact of losses from "shirking" and other such supposed moral hazards is trivial compared to the overall economic and social costs of promoting generalized insecurity. Highlighting the hypocrisy of conservative economic dogma, he notes that the powerful always push insecurity on others, not themselves, claiming it will spur productivity and innovation. But the data tells a different story. "The most impressive increases in output in the history of both the United States and other western countries," Galbraith writes, "have occurred since men began to concern themselves with reducing the risks of the competitive system."[106] Labour productivity and material security, in other words, are not at odds—they have a reciprocal relationship. This means, he continues, that eliminating uncertainty in economic life is possible if we can muster the political will to do so.[107]

But the benefits of material security are not merely economic; they are also social and psychological. Consider a universal basic income, or UBI, which is enjoying something of a resurgence. The idea was first proposed in the United States in 1966 by the Black Panther Party in their Ten-Point Program and then picked up by Martin Luther King Jr. and the National Welfare Rights Union before finding an unlikely champion in Republican president Richard Nixon. After his plan to provide an income floor died in the US Senate, Nixon opted for another understanding of security, abandoning social provision for beefed-up policing.

During this same period, the Canadian federal government also flirted with a UBI, calling it an idea "whose time had come."[108] Yet public officials were predictably worried about moral hazard. What if people stopped working? To figure out what would happen, they funded an enormous social experiment. Beginning in 1974, every resident of Dauphin, a small agricultural town in western Manitoba, was eligible for a minimum annual income—a little over $23,000 for a family of four, adjusted for inflation. In 1979, as Progressive Conservative governments came to power, the project's funding dried up. As a result, the data wasn't analyzed until thirty years later, when Evelyn Forget, a professor at the University of Manitoba, visited the archives and found 1,800 boxes of records.[109] She began crunching the numbers and contacting people who had been part of the program—and learned that it had left a remarkably positive impression. MINCOME, as the project was known, transformed people's lives, changing their economic circumstances while also relieving mountains of anxiety. Part of MINCOME's power stemmed from the fact it was free of the stigma so often associated with public welfare: if you met the income threshold, you were eligible, no questions asked and no blame or judgment passed.[110]

A MINCOME handbook from the period describes a UBI as an efficient way of ensuring that "Canadians have a reasonable and secure income." Residents of Dauphin told Forget that "the money acted as an insurance policy."[111] Dropout rates waned, hospitalizations fell, and people's mental health improved. Kids went to the dentist for the first time, and their moms took longer maternity leaves or pursued higher education.[112] People still worked, but they worked a little bit less, in order to spend time with their families or to study. When teenage boys turned down jobs, it wasn't because they were slacking; it was because they were staying in school. More people turned down employment that underpaid or humiliated them, and some started their own businesses. According to a 2020 analysis, both property crime and violent crime significantly decreased. Improving financial security, it turns out, is an effective way to improve public safety— and a way to do so peacefully.[113]

In her article "The Town with No Poverty," Forget shows how everyone in the community benefited from what she calls "the reduction of risk," including those who did not receive payments directly. Even when an individual or family's earnings exceeded the program's financial cut-off, the existence of an economic safety net provided them peace of mind, the benefits redounding through the entire town. What's known as a "social multiplier" effect took hold: the ability of some teenagers to stay in school, for example, influenced their classmates to do the same.[114] "I'm a huge advocate of basic income to this day," a former Dauphin resident recently told the BBC. "Knowing that extra money was coming in made life that bit easier. You no longer needed to be afraid."[115] But this salutary effect is precisely why the program ended. As was the case with the income supports provided at the start of the Covid-19 pandemic, politicians and business leaders saw the absence of fear as a threat to their own security.[116]

ONE OF THE LAST stories Kafka wrote takes place in an elaborate underground fortress. "The Burrow" is narrated by a creature—maybe a mole—who spends his days fortifying his home, pacing the maze of tunnels, inspecting his abundant food supplies, and warding off potential threats. There are thieves, or maybe predators, to thwart; it is never clear exactly what kind of danger lurks. The reader is in the den and in the narrator's head, the burrow a space at once physical and psychological. "Any wound to it hurts me as if I myself were hit," the restless protagonist proclaims, constantly monitoring, assessing, and fretting.[117] Yet no matter how desperate his efforts to escape "uncertain fate," a sense of safety eludes him. Even in his own burrow within the burrow, or what he calls his "Castle Keep"—"my castle which can never belong to anyone else"—the mole feels ill at ease.

The story becomes increasingly claustrophobic, as Kafka's stories tend to do. The mole fixates on a sound, a distant whistling that he can neither identify nor find the source of but believes must portend a threat, a hungry beast or perhaps a dangerous enemy. He sets about redesigning his stronghold, working ever more obsessively. "I have no right to complain that I am alone and have nobody that I can trust," the mole laments; now even his home cannot be trusted. "The burrow does provide a considerable security," he acknowledges, "but by no means enough." The creature's luxurious accommodations become a kind of cell, a holding pen for his mounting anxiety.

Kafka supposedly found his own writings very amusing. I can picture him chuckling to his friends as he read this story aloud, recounting the mole's frantic, fruitless labours. But what gives the tale its unsettling power—what makes it a parable and not just a parody—is the fact that it is, on some level, relatable. "The Burrow" offers a warning about the risks posed by the quest for individual security. It portrays the perils of accumulation—how wealth and possessions become things we need to jealously guard—while also inviting us to question our own feelings. What makes us insecure and anxious? Are our fears real or imagined?

No doubt, our fears and insecurities can have much to teach us, but we should approach our emotions with discernment. In my liberal city, many of my neighbours feel scared of unhoused people and public drug use and call for more aggressive policing. This heated reaction ignores the fact that police are not equipped to address the root cause of homelessness or addiction, and that people on the streets are far more likely to be the ones facing mortal danger, rather than my safely housed neighbours. That said, the explosion of homeless encampments *should* spark feelings of insecurity—not because the unhoused are threats to us, but because we live in a rich society that refuses to provide struggling people basic shelter and dignity. In this sort of society, how can any of us feel secure?

What I've called existential insecurity, along with its companion fear, are, of course, core components of the human condition. In Chapter 1, I called this Cura's gift and suggested that our fundamental fragility also bonds us: to care for another is to contribute to a world in which someone will, someday, care for you, too. Of course, our species' existential insecurity has long been the focus of nearly every venerable spiritual and philosophical tradition. Buddhism, for example, recognizes that life is suffering and counsels compassion, for how can attachment to a fixed state of being provide security in a world of impermanence? The Stoics of antiquity sought tranquility, or *securitas*, by letting the future be what it will be. As Seneca proclaimed, quoting Hecato of Rhodes, "Cease to hope and you will cease to fear."[118]

I find these and other approaches to our existential dilemmas interesting, and useful to varying degrees; at different points, I've found solace in Buddhist empathy and Stoic equanimity. But the organizer in me always returns to something more grounded and engaged—an ethic of insecurity that channels our shared vulnerability into a force for social change. Aspiring not to worry about the future may have made sense for the opulently wealthy Seneca, who spent his days hobnobbing with mercurial emperors and lending money at steep interest rates. (Legend has it he prompted a revolt by British debtors when he attempted to collect on a loan equivalent to the combined annual salaries of over forty-four thousand Roman troops.) But today few of us, no matter how rich or poor we happen to be, can afford to simply kick back and accept whatever comes our way. Given the risks we face—economic meltdowns, cyber warfare, pandemics, and a burning planet—worrying about the future seems wise and pragmatic. We must find a way to live on what Ulrich Beck called the "volcano of civilization" without suffocating from fear or the poisonous vapours it emits.[119]

Kafka's own approach to security offers one route to a more humane and appealing alternative. His response to employers who sought to deflect responsibility for workplace accidents was to try to stop accidents from happening at all. He conducted an in-depth study of the conditions at quarries, analyzing blasting practices and the process of "erratic" boulder extraction and proposing remedies to keep workers alive—including an end to bosses' cost-saving measure of paying wages in brandy, which he sensibly noted made blowing up massive rocks a lot more dangerous. His study "Measures for Preventing Accidents on Wood-Planing Machines" contained diagrams of both tools and workers' finger-less hands, offering plans for saws that would merely cause "lacerations."[120] With these contributions and others, Kafka insisted that insurance need not only be retrospective but that it could also be preventive and protective. Why compensate workers or their widows for lost appendages or lives when you could spare them suffering in the first place? His efforts, scholars agree, averted untold injuries and unnecessary deaths.

While health and safety standards on work sites have certainly improved since Kafka's time—at least in some countries—his basic proposal of prevention remains a worthy lodestar. Why not house people instead of fining them for sleeping on the street? Why cancel student debt when education could be free? Why let corporations and billionaires exploit us instead of prioritizing equality and democracy? Why endure environmental catastrophes when we can pursue sustainability?

To effectively exercise precaution, we need to identify potential risks while also reassessing questions of blame and responsibility. In the early twentieth century, the adoption of no-fault worker's accident insurance was an important measure of social progress. Employees were no longer culpable for mishaps, and employers were shielded from lawsuits. But as journalist Jessie Singer convincingly argues in *There Are No Accidents*, we have taken this good idea too far.[121] We need more nuanced frameworks to help us hold wrongdoers to account for our current predicaments. As Pascal taught us, accidents are probabilistic, not random. But in a just society, Singer points out, they would also be evenly distributed. When we examine the data today, misfortune clusters in troubling and predictable patterns: for example, poor and marginalized people are more likely to die in house fires, drink polluted water, drown in debt, get ticketed by the police, and be displaced by climate change. These outcomes are not "accidents." They are the products of arrangements that distribute risks unevenly: racism, inequality, unchecked corporate power, and bad public policy. They are the outcomes, in other words, of a system that manufactures material insecurity.

This is why—rather than acceptance or equanimity—manufactured insecurity demands solidarity and political engagement. These are actions that require placing faith in other people and embracing the unknown. Where Pascal maintained that we gamble our lives on the existence or non-existence of God, I would emphasize a different choice before us: Do we or do we not take collective action? We can place our bet on the status quo and watch as instability spirals or we can cast our lot with intentional efforts to improve life on earth, however uncertain the outcomes of such efforts may be.

Where some insist that the real risk lies in taking care of others, I see a moral and political opportunity. As the Dauphin experiment illustrates, having a baseline of material security is about more than money—it increases people's dignity and autonomy. The fact is, most of us do not want to be spurred to work and scramble to earn until we die. Even Americans, steeped in a culture of competition and striving, wish they could stop the chase. When the Pew Charitable Trusts conducted a poll asking if people would prefer financial stability to upward mobility, more than nine out of ten respondents said they would eagerly abandon the pursuit of wealth for security.[122]

Yet as Kafka's story reminds us, perfect security is an impossibility. More robust social insurance programs can cushion us from shocks and setbacks, but they cannot eliminate risk entirely. When Kafka was a young man, his sympathy for workers was sparked by his experience managing the small industrial factory his family owned. Though he bristled at the indignities employees suffered, he had no way of knowing the true scope of the danger they faced—danger now obvious from the business's name: the Prague Asbestos Works. As we unleash new technologies, we are more like the poorly paid women unknowingly spinning toxic yarn than we might care to admit. Acknowledging our ignorance and being inquisitive about the unknown can help us navigate inevitable perils.

The concept of insurance is rooted in a recognition that we all need protection from life's hazards and vicissitudes, whether natural or human-made. At its best, insurance pools risk to provide everyone with protection, leaving no one out, no matter how poor or vulnerable. It can partly do so, as Kafka made clear, by working to prevent injury and disaster. But as anyone who has filed a claim knows, insurance also looks to the past, providing fair compensation for bad things that have already happened. This reparative principle is essential if we want to create an equitable and secure society. Rehabilitating damaged ecosystems, paying reparations for slavery, returning land to Indigenous peoples, closing the wealth gap, cancelling unjust debts, and honestly recounting our tangled and troubling histories—these reparative acts will help our ecology and social divisions begin to heal by addressing, at last, the root causes of what makes each of our lives so full of stress and desperation. Though often tarred as unrealistic or threatening, reparation, in fact, ensures our own salvation. These are not acts of charity but rather acts of solidarity and self-preservation.

At the same time, an ethic of insecurity encourages us to approach the future with humility—with a sense of curiosity rooted in uncertainty and the kind of caution implied by the phrase "taking care." Yet however unknowable the future may be, there is no doubt our fortunes will remain interlinked. Risks proliferate, time passes, and things fall apart. But even amid the rubble, we can always reimagine, repair, and rebuild. Accepting our fundamental insecurity—the gift we all share—is the first step toward escaping our fear-filled burrows and ensuring our collective freedom, safety, and well-being.

CODA

ACCEPTING CURA'S GIFT

THE GODDESS CURA, who opens this book, is a mysterious character. What inspires her to stop by a river to mould a human figure from clay? In a spontaneous and generous act of creativity, she conjures our species into being, calling on Earth, Saturn, and Jupiter to provide crucial assistance. Cura gives us the gift of life, which is also, at the same time, the gift of finitude and fragility. As long as we breathe, there is the inescapable fact of our mortality, our existential insecurity. She fates us to need care and to care in turn.

To be vulnerable and dependent on others is not a burden to escape but the essence of human existence, as well as the basis of what I have called, throughout this book, an ethic of insecurity—a potentially powerful source of connection, solidarity, and transformation. We are, as the philosopher Cornel West once told me, channelling philosophers past, "beings-toward-death …

featherless, two-legged, linguistically conscious creatures born between urine and feces whose body will one
day be the culinary delight of terrestrial worms." Cura's
gift invites us to face and embrace this rather than flee
from it unnerved. When we accept our vulnerability,
we can begin to rethink conventional ideas about what
security is and how we might attain it, while unlock-
ing a powerful catalyst for social change.

ACCEPTING CURA'S GIFT IS not easy to do. This is especially true when insecurity envelops us, a feeling
captured poignantly in "The Second Coming," the poem
echoed in this book's subtitle:

> *Turning and turning in the widening gyre*
> *The falcon cannot hear the falconer;*
> *Things fall apart; the centre cannot hold;*
> *Mere anarchy is loosed upon the world,*
> *The blood-dimmed tide is loosed, and everywhere*
> *The ceremony of innocence is drowned;*
> *The best lack all conviction, while the worst*
> *Are full of passionate intensity.*[1]

The Irish poet William Butler Yeats composed these
memorable lines in 1919, a period of heightened tension
and upheaval, both political and personal: the aftershocks of the Russian revolution, the recent strife of

the First World War, and the Spanish flu pandemic that had left the writer's pregnant wife close to death. Traumatized and spiralling, Yeats hammered the events overwhelming him into potent verse that has provided a century of companionship to readers who feel marooned by chaos, a composition for people beset by forces they neither comprehend nor control but fear and grieve. It is a poem steeped in the terror that insecurity can bring, and one that yearns for an impossible solidity, for a centre fixed and stable. Yeats longed for order and permanence, for the falcon to once again hear the falconer's command.

In my own way, I wrote this book in what felt like a vortex, amid the myriad social and political crises these chapters address as well as troubles that hit closer to home. Not long after I started writing, my husband received an unexpected diagnosis. A visit to the doctor revealed he had cancer. While drafting the first chapter, I had briefly mentioned cancer as a common source of insecurity, an example of the ways our lives can be suddenly derailed. I had imagined it as the kind of misfortune that strikes other people, not something in my family's imminent future.

We waited for test results and surgery while I wrote Chapter 3, my subject matter now unsettlingly real. As I sat at the keyboard to formulate intellectual arguments about insecurity as a systemic phenomenon, worst-case scenarios played out in my mind, my anxiety manifesting as room-spinning vertigo. We were fortunate to have health insurance and the ability to pay the bills it didn't cover; unlike many of the people I organize with, we didn't have to go into debt to receive life-saving treatment, which spared us the added strain of financial hardship. Friends offered support, helping me think through material that, once clear, was now swirling. Thanks to good luck and the prompt and capable care of doctors and nurses, my husband was cured. The episode resolved nearly as quickly as it started, leaving us stunned and grateful. My equilibrium returned, now tinged with a deeper appreciation of life's tenuousness and unpredictability—and a renewed commitment to transforming how our society relates to vulnerability.

NONE OF US ARE strangers to insecurity, whether it's the kind of panic inspired by my husband's illness, the pang of self-doubt felt at school or on the job, or apprehension about the state of the world. But insecurity, as we have seen, is more than just a subjective state of mind. It also describes objective material circumstances: lack of access to health care, unstable income or employment, precarious housing, extreme weather patterns, and the like. Insecurity thus spans the psychological and physical, emotional and economic, and in doing so reminds us that these seemingly distinct registers are, in fact, entwined and inseparable—an entanglement Yeats's poem movingly conveys. Insecurity is not only in our heads, even if it is a core aspect of the human condition: it can also be imposed upon us in ways that amplify rather than tend to our fragility. It is, to borrow a phrase from feminism, personal as well as political.

Throughout these chapters I have tried to show how our economic system depends on manufacturing insecurity to create more pliable workers and insatiable consumers. Economists have long commented on capitalism's tendency toward crisis and instability, a feature Karl Marx and Friedrich Engels identified in the nineteenth century. Market society, they wrote, is defined by the "constant revolutionising of production, uninterrupted disturbance of all social conditions, everlasting uncertainty and agitation." Capitalism generates change and rupture; it's a system in which "all fixed, fast-frozen relations ... are swept away, all new-formed ones become antiquated before they can ossify."[2] For centuries now, insecurity has kept us scrambling, serving as an engine of striving, buying, and endless expansion—a motor propelling us toward the cliff of ecological calamity.

But amid this incessant turbulence, some things remain remarkably consistent. It is inevitably the most vulnerable who bear the brunt of volatility. The privileged find ways to shield themselves from risk, turning periodic shocks to their advantage, while claiming that material insecurity is required to keep everyone else toiling and productive. And yet they've rigged a game that can't be won, one that keeps them stressed and miserable. They, too, have much to gain from adopting an ethic of insecurity, one that, instead of fuelling inequality and feeding feelings of inadequacy, asserts a universal human right to security—a right that, as we saw in Chapter 2, we possess in principle but that too often languishes unheeded on the page.

This right has been undermined, in part, by our culture's denial of Cura's gift. Instead of understanding the desire to give and receive care as an essential human motivation, we rely on coercion and punishment to keep society moving. Instead of creating systems that prioritize care, we stigmatize it, while also undervaluing the labour caretaking entails: just compare the income of a hedge fund manager or tech executive to a teacher, custodian, or home health worker. We valorize "production" (the paid work performed in offices or factories, for example) while ignoring "social reproduction" (think child-rearing and homemaking, which fall disproportionately, though not exclusively, on women). Capitalism tells us that security flows from physical health and financial success, from able-bodiedness and wealth, and we consider people who possess these traits to be secure and self-sufficient. In contrast, those who obviously rely on others, and especially on assistance from the state, are denigrated as weak, dependent, and deficient. This is a lesson I first learned from disability movements: we all need care throughout our lives, from birth to death, not only when we are struck by illness.

What the writer Rebecca Solnit has called capitalism's "ideology of isolation" encourages us to ignore all

of the ways we are, in fact, mutually dependent.[3] When
we are shamed into denying the gift of care that we all
need, we turn inward and put up defences, which only
makes the world seem more inhospitable and hostile
and ourselves more adrift and lost. In reality, other people are our best and most reliable form of security—the
security of working with others to create a more caring society.

YEATS'S POEM ENDS WITH an image of caretaking, but
an ambiguous one—a cradle rocked by social disinte-
gration, upheaval, and, perhaps, renewal.

> *The darkness drops again; but now I know*
> *That twenty centuries of stony sleep*
> *Were vexed to nightmare by a rocking cradle,*
> *And what rough beast,*
> *its hour come round at last,*
> *Slouches towards Bethlehem to be born?*[4]

At once prophetic and open-ended, the poem
evokes both despair and redemptive possibility. It condemns the ruinous and deadly forces that modernity
has unleashed, and the complacency of those "best"
positioned to resist. But who has loosed anarchy and
violence upon the world, and what is the nature of the
rough beast who will be born to confront it? Yeats's

personal views, however, were far from equivocal, for he was quite politically engaged, serving for six years as one of the first senators of the Irish Free State. For a time, at least, he was convinced that nationalism and authoritarianism could slow or halt the widening of the gyre and force the centre to hold. Faced with the tumult and uncertainty of life, Yeats rejected Cura's gift, preferring the promise of security offered by the strongmen he admired, including Benito Mussolini, over what he considered the instability of equality and democracy.[5]

Unlike Yeats, I fear business as usual more than anarchy. I do not want the centre to hold, and certainly not the centre the esteemed poet longed for. Sometimes we need to decentralize and encourage other centres to proliferate. Things falling apart can portend doom, but it can also presage regeneration, allowing new possibilities to emerge amid the ruins. Many of the most inspiring chapters in modern history consist of marginalized people accepting Cura's gift, finding power in their shared experience of insecurity to challenge an entrenched and oppressive status quo.

We have the right to vote, weekends and minimum wage, laws against sexual harassment and racial discrimination, and basic (though inadequate) environmental regulations because ordinary people caused what the powerful took to be mayhem—like the disabled activists who stopped traffic with their wheelchairs to demand accessibility, or the Indigenous organizers who blockade pipelines to protect their territories. We've followed this tradition at the Debt Collective, which has won tens of billions of dollars of financial relief for hundreds of thousands of people, not by asking nicely but by waging campaigns of militant non-payment. Time and again, history shows that falcons have to defy the falconer's authority if they want to be free.

This process can be profoundly rewarding, and intimidating. It involves exposing one's personal struggles and hopes to public judgment and scrutiny; it involves taking risks and, also, responsibility. At the Debt Collective, for example, we host gatherings we call debtors' assemblies, inspired by the feminist consciousness-raising circles of the 1970s. These are forums where people share their stories, often confessing financial struggles they have never spoken aloud, let alone aired publicly. Without fail, people cry. They also find life-changing strength and camaraderie. In these sessions, insecurity becomes a kind of gateway. Movements can facilitate what some have called post-traumatic growth—the kind of transformation that stems from vulnerability and solidarity.

Though I always wanted to be an activist, I spent a long time on the sidelines. It took years before I found the confidence to begin organizing seriously. Partly I was shy, but I also didn't know where to begin. It felt risky to throw my lot in with causes other people dismissed as impossible or naive, and that some insisted would reduce my journalistic and intellectual credibility. (As if objecting to injustice signals a

lack of objectivity!) But while organizing can benefit from certain skills, like being able to phone-bank
or run a tight meeting, I quickly learned that mostly
it requires embracing insecurity. The best organizers
are not the most knowledgeable, self-righteous, or even
charismatic, but rather those most able to empathize,
experiment, and navigate uncertainty. Real organizing involves reaching out to people who don't already
agree with you in order to expand your base and build
a formidable coalition, which means that discomfort
and rejection is always a possibility. It involves coming
together with others to take a leap into the unknown,
to attempt to change the future without knowing you'll
succeed or what that future might hold. Challenging the
centre takes power and strategy. It also takes a willingness to improvise and a large dose of humility.

IN HIS 1844 BOOK *The Concept of Anxiety*, the philosopher Søren Kierkegaard writes that our ability to
shape the future is a cause of both dread and exhilara-
tion. It is, in effect, a source of existential insecurity.
"Anxiety is the dizziness of freedom," he writes, offering an insight that philosophers have pondered ever
since.[6] The German theorist Martin Heidegger followed
in his footsteps, grappling with the concepts of care,
anxiety, and freedom. It was Heidegger who initially
called humans "beings toward death," and he is the only

canonical Western thinker to contemplate the myth of Cura, a story he thought was significant because it presented humanity "as having its 'origin' in care."[7] And yet Heidegger also recoiled from the goddess's gift, choosing dogma and genocide over care and ambiguity when, in 1933, he joined the Nazi Party.

A little over a decade later, the recent horrors of World War II weighing heavy on her mind, the French feminist and existentialist Simone de Beauvoir argued that because we are free to choose, we can choose to live ethically or unethically. "One does not offer an ethics to a God," she wrote in 1947. It is only mortal and conflicted human beings who need help discerning moral principles.[8] For Beauvoir, however, the choice was clear: we can confront the things that discomfit us, including our own freedom and vulnerability, or try vainly and destructively to evade them.

Today, many people respond to insecurity by donning masks of superiority and invincibility. They denounce "snowflakes" who need "safe spaces" while taking shelter behind bigotry, clinging to a centre that oppresses the periphery. An ethic of insecurity seeks to mitigate this tendency, knowing that history shows that more materially secure and egalitarian conditions make people less reactive and more tolerant. When we shrink the welfare state because we expect the worst from people, we end up hurting ourselves and those we care about, creating a vicious cycle that stokes desperation and division. When we extend trust and support to others, we improve everyone's security—moving from a culture of fear and scarcity toward one of abundance, generosity, and stability. For de Beauvoir, this interconnected approach is the path of true liberation: "freedom can be achieved only through the freedom of others."[9]

Unlike the predatory, rigid, and nostalgic conceptions of security that grip us today, this future-oriented and collaborative vision of security adapts the freedom of the commons for the twenty-first century. It ensures the autonomy that flows from knowing you won't become destitute in old age, unhoused if you lose your job, or buried in debt if you pursue higher education or get sick—and also from knowing that business models that perpetuate and profit from insecurity will no longer pummel your self-esteem or endanger your life. Finally realizing our right to security will enable more people to face the future with confidence and curiosity, bracing them to adapt to change instead of recoiling from risk and uncertainty. This is the kind of strength that comes from flexibility, like the massive trees that stay standing because they are both rooted in the ground and have the ability to sway. Sometimes their roots intertwine with other trees' for mutual reinforcement, and as the Canadian scientist Suzanne Simard discovered, they also share nutrients through underground networks.[10] This is not the competitive capitalist freedom of the "self-made" individual, but the kind of freedom that is enabled by community. It is the security that helps us to pursue what Albert Maslow called higher needs: beauty, self-expression, and creativity.

This creativity can be cultural and political. Our social systems are human creations, which means that we can change them. It reminds me of the words of my late friend David Graeber, the ingenious and mischievous anthropologist who helped us launch the debt resistance movement. "The ultimate, hidden truth of the world," David said, "is that it is something that we make, and could just as easily make differently."[11] Like Cura fashioning a figure from mud, we can work to refashion our societies. And like Cura, we will need to call on others to assist us in this monumental task.

For decades, progressive organizers have been working to advance a different paradigm, one that resists the ideology of isolation by acknowledging the fact of our interdependence. There are nurses, teachers, and domestic workers mobilizing for better wages, and environmentalists fighting to decarbonize our societies. The essential and life-sustaining labour of caring for people and the planet, they argue, cannot be automated or outsourced, which means that care work has the potential to be the meaningful, well-compensated, and secure work of the future. Caring for communities, institutions, and ecosystems could be the foundation of an expanded version of what is often described as a "care economy."

An expansive and inclusive care economy is one possible expression of an ethic of insecurity, and one that would require dismantling systems that produce and exploit vulnerability. Instead of profit-hungry recklessness, a care economy would proceed cautiously, taking care of people and the planet by doing less harm, and by seeking to repair the damage that has already been done.

Viewed in this light, *taking care* is a revealing phrase. It implies forethought and vigilance while also reminding us that by providing care for others, we are, at the same time, receiving something in return. When we say we are "taking care," we can mean we are being careful or, alternatively, that we are giving care; to take care of a person, animal, plant, or place is to protect or nurture something beyond ourselves. But as we all know from experience, this is not an entirely selfless enterprise. Taking care of others rewards and replenishes us, and helps ensure we are cared for in return. By giving the gift of care, we take care of ourselves, too. We are all endowed with Cura's gift and also with Cura's power. By tending to each other, we can crack the centre, widen the gyre, and create the world anew.

ACKNOWLEDGEMENTS

IT'S A TREMENDOUS HONOUR to be invited to give the Massey Lectures, a series that I have long admired and one that I have known primarily in book form. Books are, of course, always collaborative enterprises, building on other people's work and ideas while incorporating feedback from early readers and editors. But the unique nature of this specific undertaking, in combination with unexpected factors that made life unusually harried, prompted me to lean more heavily on others than I have during previous writing projects. Many people shared their expertise, read drafts, and helped with fact checking. Needless to say, all errors and omissions remain mine.

My first thanks go to the fantastic and always erudite CBC *Ideas* team: Philip Coulter and Pauline Holdsworth, as well as to Greg Kelly and Nahlah Ayed. I'm very grateful to editor Leigh Nash for the dedication, thoughtfulness, and skill she brought to the project. I also want to acknowledge the team at House of Anansi Press, including Michelle MacAleese, designer and typesetter

Greg Tabor, proofreader Stuart Ross, publicists Emma Rhodes and Debby de Groot, and my stellar copy editor Peter Norman. I owe a massive debt to my friend and comrade Jessie Kindig for her deft and incisive editorial interventions. Thanks, too, to my friend Sarah Fan for her trenchant engagement with key chapters. Mel Flashman is the best agent a nerdy writer could have. And enormous appreciation is due to Patricia Boushel, whose big brain and heart marked this endeavour, not least by directing me to the myth of Cura.

Thank you to the people who shared their knowledge with me and who shaped my thinking even if they are not directly quoted: Shiri Pasternak, Jennifer Welsh, Payam Akhavan, Pearl Eliadis, Colleen Flood, David Hulchanski, Mari Ruti, Ted Rutland, Nathan Tankus, David Boyd, Deborah Cowen, Todd McGowan, Ryan Engley, Tarek Loubani, Katherine Aske, Carla Bergman, Joseph Tisiga, Peter Linebaugh, Daniel Aldana Cohen, Troy Vettese, Martin Lukacs, and especially Martha Jackman. Though we have never met, I want to express my appreciation of Mark Neocleous and his critical, thought-provoking work on the theme of security. Will Tavlin provided invaluable research reinforcement, and I'm grateful to Maddie Ritts for her topical briefs and brainstorming and dialogue, too. The multi-talented Ian Beacock signed up to help with research and became a thought partner on a challenging chapter, while also lending his discerning editorial eye at formative junctures. David L. Clark provided fortifying feedback. Avi Lewis was a true friend, reading select drafts and sharing his formidable political knowledge and insight. Huge thanks to Eleni Schirmer, a real one, for her sagacious commentary and encouragement. The inimitable Rebecca Solnit gave me a big boost at the end, just as I was flagging.

Profound thanks to Ben Tarnoff, founding editor of *Logic Magazine*, where I published "The Insecurity Machine," the essay that set the stage for this book. In addition to building on ideas I explored there, I also drew on an article about unschooling that I long ago published in *n+1*, an exploration of the rights of nature I wrote for *The Baffler* magazine, and a piece on ecology and time in *Lapham's Quarterly*. My thinking on debt and finance is indelibly shaped by my collaborators at the Debt Collective, the smartest and most committed rabblerousers I know.

Thanks to my parents, as ever, for their support and inspiration. My beloved Jeff put up with three solid months of unrelenting, monkish focus as I cranked this text out and he never stopped cheering me on. My sister Sunaura Taylor, my co-conspirator on all things ecological and animal, was a razor-sharp reader, taking time away from her own writing obligations to help me and to commiserate. My brother Alexander helped me understand some basic features of tort law. And last but not least, boundless gratitude to my brilliant sister Nye, to whom this book is dedicated. Her wisdom, critical sensibilities, and moral and aesthetic judgements all informed this project. It was a gift and a pleasure to engage these ideas together.

NOTES

Chapter 1: Cura's Gift

1. Seneca, *Moral Epistles* (c. 65 AD), trans. Richard M. Gummere, letter 85.

2. Cicero, De Officiis, Bk. I, Para 69, quoted in Mark Neocleous, *"Securitati perpetuae*: Death, Fear and the History of Insecurity," *Radical Philosophy* 206 (winter 2019), 19–33. As Neocleous notes, he has altered the standard translation by rendering securitas as "security" instead of "freedom from care." See Cicero, De Officiis, trans. Walter Miller (London: Heinemann, 1913).

3. The myth of Cura is fruitfully analyzed in J. T. Hamilton, *Security: Politics, Humanity, and the Philology of Care* (United Kingdom: Princeton University Press, 2016), and most famously by the philosopher Martin Heidegger in *Being and Time: A Revised Edition of the Stambaugh Translation* (United Kingdom: State University of New York Press, 2010), 198–201.

4. Quoted in Stuart Ewen, *Captains of Consciousness: Advertising and the Social Roots of the Consumer Culture* (New York: McGraw Hill, 1976), 39.

5. Moya Lothian-McLean, "I'm the Perfect Target for Buccal Fat Removal—This Is How I've Resisted It," *Guardian*, January 11, 2023, https://www.theguardian.com/commentisfree/2023/jan/11/buccal-fat-removal-self-esteem-beauty-ideal.

6. Oxfam International, "Ten Richest Men Double Their Fortunes in Pandemic While Incomes of 99 Percent of Humanity Fall," January 17, 2022, https://www.oxfam.org/en/press-releases/ten-richest-men-double-their-fortunes-pandemic-while-incomes-99-percent-humanity.

7. Barbara Ehrenreich, *Fear of Falling* (New York: Pantheon, 1989).

8. Richard Wilkinson and Kate Pickett, *The Spirit Level: Why Equality Is Better for Everyone* (London: Allen Lane, 1989); Michael Marmot, *The Status Syndrome: How Social Standing Affects Our Health and Longevity* (London: Henry Holt and Company, 2005).

9. Cody R. Melcher, "Economic Self-Interest and Americans' Redistributive, Class, and Racial Attitudes: The Case of Economic Insecurity," *Political Behavior*, March 7, 2021, https://link.springer.com/article/10.1007/s11109-021-09694-x.

10. George S. Rigakos, *Security/Capital: A General Theory of Pacification* (Edinburgh: Edinburgh University Press, 2016), 49–54.

11. John Kenneth Galbraith, *The Affluent Society* (1958; pbk. repr., Boston: Houghton Mifflin, 1998), 65.

12. Peter Linebaugh and Marcus Rediker, *The Many-Headed Hydra: Sailors, Slaves, Commoners, and the Hidden History of the Revolutionary Atlantic* (Boston: Beacon Press, 2000), 106.

13. Gerrard Winstanley, *The True Levellers Standard Advanced* (London, 1649), https://quod.lib.umich.edu/e/eebo2/A95059.0001.001, 7.

14. Winstanley, *True Levellers*, 15. Also see Astra Taylor, *Democracy May Not Exist, But We'll Miss It When It's Gone* (United States: Henry Holt and Company, 2019), 263 and 273.

15. Gerrard Winstanley, G. and T. Benn, *A Common Treasury* (United Kingdom: Verso Books, 2011), 6.

16. E. P. Thompson, *Customs in Common: Studies in Traditional Popular Culture* (Germany: New Press, 2015), 156.

17. J. M. Neeson, *Commoners: Common Right, Enclosure and Social Change in England, 1700–1820* (Cambridge: Cambridge University Press, 1993), 28–29, 45.

18. Peter Linebaugh, *Stop, Thief! The Commons, Enclosures, and Resistance* (Binghamton, NY: PM Press, 2012), 44.

19. Neeson, *Commoners*, 28.

20. Neeson, *Commoners*, 28, 32.

21. Thomas Rudge, *General View of the Agriculture of the County of Gloucester* (1807), quoted in Neeson, 29; Richard Mabey, *Flora Britannica* (London: Chatto & Windus, 1996), 209.

22. John Clare, "The Moors," in *"I Am": The Selected Poetry of John Clare*, ed. Jonathan Bate (New York: Farrar, Straus & Giroux, 2003), 89.

23. Neeson, *Commoners*, 41.

24. Michael Denning, "Wageless Life," *New Left Review* 66 (2010), https://newleftreview.org/issues/ii66/articles/michael-denning-wageless-life.

25. The Regina Manifesto (1933), Article 7, https://artsonline.uwaterloo.ca/rneedham/sites/ca.rneedham/files/needhdata/Regina_Manifesto.html.

26. George Soule, "Security for Americas VII: Can We Provide Security?" *New Republic*, January 16, 1935.

27. Franklin D. Roosevelt, Presidential Statement Signing the Social Security Act, August 14, 1935, https://www.ssa.gov/history/fdrstmts.html.

28. Nicholas Sokic, "Unemployment Is at Record Low, So Why Are Canadians So Worried about Job Insecurity, Recession, and Cost of Living?" *Financial Post*, June 11, 2019, https://financialpost.com/news/economy/unemployment-is-at-record-low-but-canadians-worry-about-job-insecurity-recession-and-cost-of-living-survey.

29. Statistics Canada, Labour Force Survey, December 2022, https://www150.statcan.gc.ca/n1/daily-quotidien/230106/dq230106a-eng.htm?HPA=1.

30. Kari Paul, "The Uber Drivers Forced to Sleep in Parking Lots to Make a Decent Living," *Guardian*, May 8, 2019, https://www.theguardian.com/technology/2019/may/07/the-uber-drivers-forced-to-sleep-in-parking-lots-to-make-a-decent-living.

31. Il-ho Kim et al., "Is Job Insecurity Worse for Mental Health than Having a Part-Time Job in Canada?" *Journal of Preventative Medicine & Public Health* 54, no. 2 (2021), 110–18; Daniel Sullivan and Till von Wachter, "Job Displacement and Mortality: An Analysis Using Administrative Data," *Quarterly Journal of Economics* 124, no. 3 (August 2009), 1265–1306; Dupre ME, George LK, Liu G, Peterson ED, "The Cumulative Effect of Unemployment on Risks for Acute Myocardial Infarction." Arch Intern Med. 2012 Dec 10;172(22):1731-7. doi: 10.1001/2013.jamainternmed.447. PMID: 23401888.

32. Congressman Don Beyer, "JEC Analysis Finds Opioid Epidemic Cost US Nearly $1.5 Trillion in 2020," press release, September 28, 2022, https://beyer.house.gov/news/documentsingle.aspx?DocumentID=5684#; Canadian Substance Use Costs and Harms, "Costs of Substance Use: National Landscape," https://beyer.house.gov/news/documentsingle.aspx?DocumentID=5684#. It's also important to note, as Maddie Ritts of the York University School of Social Work pointed out to me, that a major driver of death is governmental neglect and failure to tend to the safety of drug users, particularly regarding the toxic supply of street drugs that account for a significant proportion of overdose-related deaths; see also Mark Tyndall, "A Safer Drug Supply: A Pragmatic and Ethical Response to the Overdose Crisis," *Canadian Medical Association Journal* 192, no. 34 (August 2020), E986–87.

33. Jennifer Lavalley et al., "Reconciliation and Canada's Overdose Crisis: Responding to the Needs of Indigenous Peoples," *Canadian Medical Association Journal* 190, no. 50 (December 2018), E1466–67.

34. Alexandra Mae Jones, "Canada's Construction Industry Uniquely Vulnerable to Opioid-Related Deaths, New Study Reveals," CTV News, July 28, 2022, https://www.ctvnews.ca/health/ontario-s-construction-industry-uniquely-vulnerable-to-opioid-related-deaths-new-study-reveals-1.6006501.

35. Alina Dizik, "Can a Fear of Getting Fired Make You Work Harder?" BBC, May 23, 2017, https://www.bbc.com/worklife/article/20170524-can-a-fear-of-getting-fired-make-you-work-harder; John Hassard and Jonathan Morris, "Contrived Competition and Manufactured Uncertainty: Understanding Managerial Job Insecurity Narratives in Large Corporations," *Work, Employment and Society* 32, no. 3 (2018), 564–80.

36. Sophie Mellor, "Mark Zuckerberg Warns Staff Facebook Will Be "Turning Up the Heat to Weed Out Underperformers," *Fortune*, July 1, 2022, https://fortune.com/2022/07/01/facebook-warns-staff-not-expect-big-budgets-new-hires-be-prepared-to-work-harder/.

37. Trish Hennessy and Ricardo Tranjan, *No Safe Harbour: Precarious Work and Economic Insecurity Among Skilled Professionals in Canada*, Canadian Centre for Policy Alternatives, August 21, 2018, https://policyalternatives.ca/publications/reports/no-safe-harbour.

38. Bank of Canada, "Our Renewed Monetary Policy Framework," https://www.bankofcanada.ca/core-functions/monetary-policy/monetary-policy-framework-renewal/.

39. Louis Uchitelle, "Job Insecurity of Workers Is a Big Factor in Fed Policy," *New York Times,* February 27, 1997, https://www.nytimes.com/1997/02/27/business/job-insecurity-of-workers-is-a-big-factor-in-fed-policy.html.

40. Janet Yellen, "Job Insecurity, the Natural Rate of Unemployment, and the Phillips Curve," memo to Chairman Greenspan, Board of Governors of the Federal Reserve System, June 10, 1996, https://ourtime.substack.com/api/v1/file/ca14e08f-387e-4425-ac23-ab343c846be4.pdf.

41. Jessica Mundie, "Quiet Quitting: What the Workplace Trend Sweeping Social Media Actually Means," *National Post*, August 19, 2022, https://nationalpost.com/news/world/what-does-quiet-quitting-mean.

42. Chris Webb, "Pandemic Lessons for Rebuilding Canada's Welfare State," November 23, 2022, *Canadian Dimension*, https://canadiandimension.com/articles/view/pandemic-lessons-for-rebuilding-canadas-welfare-state; Nicolas Vega, "Federal Stimulus Measures Reduced Poverty in 2020, Census Bureau Reports," CNBC, September 15, 2021, https://www.cnbc.com/2021/09/15/stimulus-measures-reduced-poverty-in-2020-census-bureau-reports.html; Kalee Burns, Liana Fox, and Danielle Wilson, "Child Poverty Fell to Record Low 5.2% in 2021," United States Census Bureau, September 13, 2022, https://www.census.gov/library/stories/2022/09/record-drop-in-child-poverty.html. The 40 percent statistic is from "Pandemic Lessons: Ending Family and Child Poverty Is Possible," Campaign 2000, February 14, 2023, https://campaign2000.ca/pandemic-lessons-ending-child-and-family-poverty-is-possible/.

43.   Kim Parker and Juliana Menasce Horowitz, "Majority of Workers Who Quit a Job in 2021 Cite Low Pay, No Opportunities for Advancement, Feeling Disrespected," Pew Research Center, March 9, 2022, https://www.pewresearch.org/fact-tank/2022/03/09/majority-of-workers-who-quit-a-job-in-2021-cite-low-pay-no-opportunities-for-advancement-feeling-disrespected/.

44.   Victoria Wells, "Quiet Quitting Is Picking Up Speed as Workers Tune Out from Their Jobs," *Financial Post,* November 8, 2022, https://financialpost.com/fp-work/quiet-quitting-gaining-disengaged-workers.

45.   Teresa Ghilarducci, "Why Does the Federal Reserve Go to War with Workers?" *Forbes*, June 15, 2022, https://www.forbes.com/sites/teresaghilarducci/2022/06/15/why-does-the-federal-reserve-go-to-war-with-workers/?sh=70fe7391e0c9.

46.   Victoria Guida, "Powell's Tense Moment with Elizabeth Warren," *Politico*, March 7, 2023, https://www.politico.com/news/2023/03/07/powell-fed-employment-congress-00085899.

47.   Craig Torres and Catarina Saraiva, "Fed's Inflation Battle to Strip Workers of Rare Bargaining Power," *Bloomberg*, June 19, 2022, https://www.bloomberg.com/news/articles/2022-06-19/fed-s-inflation-battle-to-strip-workers-of-rare-bargaining-power.

48.   Bank of Canada, *Monetary Policy Report—July 2022*, https://www.bankofcanada.ca/wp-content/uploads/2022/07/mpr-2022-07-13.pdf.

49.   Tiff Macklem, remarks at Governor of the Bank of Canada Public Policy Forum, November 10, 2022, Toronto, https://www.bankofcanada.ca/wp-content/uploads/2022/11/remarks-2022-11-10.pdf.

50.   Jim Stanford, "15 Super-Profitable Industries Fuel Canada's Inflation," Centre for Future Work, November 2022, https://centreforfuturework.ca/wp-content/uploads/2022/12/Fifteen-SuperProfitable-Industries.pdf; Breach Media, "Inflation: Canada's Elite Are Making Workers Pick Up the Bill," *The Breach*, February 28, 2023, https://www.youtube.com/watch?v=Sbo9cAyhFMA; Federica Cocco and Keith Fray, "Unchecked Corporate Pricing Power Is a Factor in US Inflation," *Financial Times*, March 19, 2023; Justin Ho, "Corporate Profits Are Up 10% Over the Same Quarter Last Year," *Marketplace,* December 22, 2022, https://www.marketplace.org/2022/12/22/corporate-profits-are-up-10-over-the-same-quarter-last-year/.

51.   Robert Burton, *The Anatomy of Melancholia* (1621–51), quoted in Mark Neocleous, "*Securitati perpetuae*: Death, Fear and the History of Insecurity," *Radical Philosophy* 206 (winter 2019), 19–33.

52.   Galbraith, 93. As Galbraith noted in 1958, large corporations have

mostly managed to minimize their insecurity and exposure to risk, a point that still holds. Just think about the bank bailouts of the 2008 global financial crisis, and generous government subsidies made to large corporations at the onset of the coronavirus pandemic.

53.   Jeremy Bentham, *The Theory of Legislation* (Boston, 1840).

54.   Rachel Sherman, *Uneasy Street: The Anxieties of Influence* (Princeton: Princeton University Press, 2017).

55.   Chuck Collins, *The Wealth Hoarders: How Billionaires Pay Millions to Hide Trillions* (New York: Polity, 2021).

56.   *Herakleitos and Diogenes*, trans. Guy Davenport (Eugene, OR: Wipf and Stock, 1979), 42.

57.   David Goldman, *Elon Musk Has Lost a Bigger Fortune than Anyone in History*, CNN, January 3, 2023, https://www.cnn.com/2023/01/02/investing/elon-musk-wealth/index.html.

58.   Alexandria Ocasio-Cortez (@AOC), "Also my twitter mentions/notifications conveniently aren't working tonight …" Twitter, November 3, 2022.

59.   Jon Clifton, "The Global Rise of Unhappiness," *Gallup Blog*, September 15, 2022, https://news.gallup.com/opinion/gallup/401216/global-rise-unhappiness.aspx.

60.   Alexandria White, "77% of Americans Are Anxious about Their Financial Situation—Here's How to Take Control," CNBC, April 18, 2023, https://news.gallup.com/opinion/gallup/401216/global-rise-unhappiness.aspx; Meagan Gill, "Financial Woes to Blame for Half of Canadians Losing Sleep: Poll." CTV News, November 25, 2022, https://bc.ctvnews.ca/financial-woes-to-blame-for-half-of-canadians-losing-sleep-poll-1.6169182.

61.   "Global Prevalence and Burden of Depressive and Anxiety Issues in 204 Countries and Territories Due to the COVID-19 Pandemic," *Lancet* 398, no. 10312, October 8, 2021, https://doi.org/10.1016/S0140-6736(21)02143-7.

62.   "Climate Anxiety in Children and Young People and Their Beliefs about Government Responses to Climate Change: A Global Survey," *Lancet Planetary Health* 5, no. 12 (December 2021), https://doi.org/10.1016/S2542-5196(21)00278-3.

63.   "People in Homes with Handguns More Likely to Be Shot Dead, Major Study Finds," *Guardian*, April 7, 2022, https://www.theguardian.com/us-news/2022/apr/07/guns-handguns-safety-homicide-killing-study.

64.   Beth Duff-Brown, "Handgun Ownership Associated with Much Higher Suicide Risk," Stanford Medicine News Center, June 3, 2020,

https://med.stanford.edu/news/all-news/2020/06/handgun-owner-ship-associated-with-much-higher-suicide-risk.html.

65.   Elizabeth Weise, "Doomsday Clock 2023 Says the World Is Closer than Ever to Global Catastrophe," *USA Today*, January 24, 2023, https://www.usatoday.com/in-depth/news/nation/2023/01/24/dooms-day-clock-2023-time-announced/11026446002/.

66.   Oliver Kessler and Christopher Daase, "From Insecurity to Uncertainty: Risk and the Paradox of Security Politics," *Alternatives* 33 (2008), 211–32.

67.   Brown University, "Costs of the 20-Year War on Terror: $8 Trillion and 900,000 Deaths," September 1, 2021, https://www.brown.edu/news/2021-09-01/costsofwar.

68.   Thomas Hobbes, *On the Citizen* (1642; Cambridge: Cambridge University Press, 1998), 25–26.

69.   The Universal Declaration of Human Rights can be read online at https://www.un.org/en/about-us/universal-declaration-of-human-rights.

70.   The International Covenant on Economic, Social and Cultural Rights can be read online at https://www.ohchr.org/en/instruments-mecha-nisms/instruments/international-covenant-economic-social-and-cul-tural-rights; the Declaration on the Rights of Indigenous Peoples can be read online at https://social.desa.un.org/issues/indigenous-peoples/united-nations-declaration-on-the-rights-of-indigenous-peoples.

71.   The Canadian Charter of Rights and Freedoms can be read online at https://laws-lois.justice.gc.ca/eng/const/page-12.html.

72.   Gabor Maté and Daniel Maté, *The Myth of Normal* (New York: Avery, 2022), 187.

Chapter 2: Barons or Commoners?

1.   Papal Bull Annulling Magna Carta, 1215, British Library, https://www.bl.uk/collection-items/the-papal-bull-annulling-magna-carta.

2.   Reference re Secession of Quebec, [1998] 2 SCR 217, https://scc-csc.lexum.com/scc-csc/scc-csc/en/item/1643/index.do.

3.   Caroline Wilson, "Why Magna Carter Remains a Foundation of Our Common Law Inheritance," UK Foreign & Commonwealth Office, November 9, 2015, https://www.gov.uk/government/speeches/why-magna-carta-remains-a-foundation-of-our-common-law-inheritance.

4.   English Translation of Magna Carta, 1215, British Library, https://

www.bl.uk/magna-carta/articles/magna-carta-english-translation.

5. P. T. Babie, "Magna Carta and the Forest Charter: Two Stories of Property—What Will You Be Doing in 2017?" *North Carolina Law Review* 94 (2016), University of Adelaide Law Research Paper no. 2016-40, https://papers.ssrn.com/sol3/papers.cfm?abstract_id=2848008.

6. Charter of the Forest, 1225, UK National Archives, https://www.nationalarchives.gov.uk/education/resources/magna-carta/charter-forest-1225-westminster/.

7. My thinking on the commons and on the specific early history in this chapter owe a huge debt to Peter's work, including his books *The Magna Carta Manifesto: Liberties and Commons for All* (Berkeley: University of California Press, 2009) and *Stop, Thief! The Commons, Enclosures, and Resistance* (Binghamton, NY: PM Press, 2012).

8. UN General Assembly, Guidelines for the Implementation of the Right to Adequate Housing, A/HRC/43/43 (December 26, 2019), https://documents-dds-ny.un.org/doc/UNDOC/GEN/G19/353/90/PDF/G1935390.pdf?OpenElement, 3.

9. Jeremy Bentham, *Principles of the Civil Code* (Boston, 1843).

10. Laura Payton, "Supreme Court Says Yes to Doctor-Assisted Suicide in Specific Cases," CBC, February 6, 2015, https://www.cbc.ca/news/politics/supreme-court-says-yes-to-doctor-assisted-suicide-in-specific-cases-1.2947487.

11. Tanudjaja v. Attorney General (Canada) (Application), 2013 ONSC 5410; further information about this and other recent Canadian social rights cases can be found at https://socialrights.ca/.

12. Brennan Leffler and Marianne Dimain, "How Poverty, Not Pain, Is Driving Canadians with Disabilities to Consider Medically-Assisted Death," Global News, October 8, 2022. The goal of MAiD is to enable death with dignity. But when people are driven to choose state-assisted death because state-assisted life is not an option, dignity is being denied.

13. See Martha Jackman, "The Protection of Welfare Rights Under the Charter," *Ottawa Law Review* 20 (1988), 257–338, and also Louise Arbour and Fannie Lafontaine, "Beyond Self-Congratulations: The Charter at 25 in an International Perspective," *Osgoode Hall Law Journal*, vol. 45, no. 2 (Summer 2007), 239–75.

14. Peter André Globensky, "The Life of a Canadian Internationalist: Dr. John Peters Humphrey and the Universal Declaration of Human Rights," *University of New Brunswick Law Journal* 47 (1998), 5–17.

15. As historian Johannes Morsink puts it, "Someone else with a different background and of a different philosophical persuasion than Humphrey

might well have prepared a first draft without including any of the social and economic provisions." Johannes also details the profound influence the socialist and left-leaning constitutions of Latin American countries had on Humphrey's contribution. Johannes Morsink, *The Universal Declaration of Human Rights: Origins, Drafting, and Intent.* (United States: University of Pennsylvania Press, 1999), 113.

16.   Erin C. Roth, "John Peters Humphrey: Canadian Nationalist and World Government Advocate," *Canadian Yearbook of International Law* 45 (2008), 305–46, https://doi.org/10.1017/S0069005800009358.

17.   See the league's manifesto at http://www.canadahistory.ca/sections/ documents/news/1932%20Social%20Reform.html. Also see the influential 1943 government-commissioned *Report on Social Security for Canada,* by two-term league president Leonard Marsh, which is widely regarded as the "blueprint" for the Canadian welfare state.

18.   For a detailed account of the Declaration drafting process, and a sense of the multi-faceted and multi-polar messiness it entailed, including some of the conflicts between Eleanor Roosevelt and John Humphrey, see Alfred William Brian Simpson, *Human Rights and the End of Empire: Britain and the Genesis of the European Convention* (United Kingdom: Oxford University Press, 2004).

19.   Michael Ignatieff, *The Rights Revolution* (Toronto: House of Anansi, 2000), 10.

20.   Samuel Moyn, *Human Rights and the Uses of History* (London: Verso, 2014), 87.

21.   A. J. Hobbins, "Eleanor Roosevelt, John Humphrey and Canadian Opposition to the Universal Declaration of Human Rights: Looking Back on the 50th Anniversary of UNDHR," *International Journal* 53, no. 2 (1998), 325–42.

22.   I owe much of my account of this history to Martha Jackman and to her path-breaking and critically important work on economic and social rights and Canadian constitutional law, including *Advancing Social Rights in Canada*, edited by Jackman and Bruce Porter (Toronto: Irwin Law, 2014).

23.   Gosselin v. Quebec (Attorney General), [2002] 4 SCR 429, https://scc-csc.lexum.com/scc-csc/scc-csc/en/item/2027/index.do; Michael Da Silva, "When Can We Open the 'Door'?" Osgoode Legal Studies Research Paper, May 23, 2021, https://dx.doi.org/10.2139/ssrn.3853161; Martha Jackman, "One Step Forward and Two Steps Back: Poverty, the Charter and the Legacy of Gosselin," *National Journal of Constitutional Law* 39, No. 1 (2019), 85–121.

24. Louise Arbour, "'Freedom from Want'—From Charity to Entitlement," LaFontaine-Baldwin Lecture, Quebec City, March 3, 2005, https://www.ohchr.org/en/statements/2009/10/lafontaine-baldwin-lecture-2005-freedom-want-charity-entitlement-liberer-du.

25. Bruce Porter, "Some Reflections on Nell Toussaint: The Person Behind the Historic Human Rights Case," Bruce Porter, Maytree, January 26, 2023, https://maytree.com/publications/some-reflections-on-nell-toussaint-the-person-behind-the-historic-human-rights-case/.

26. Nicholas Keung, "She Went from Undocumented to Undeniable," *Toronto Star*, January 21, 2023, https://www.thestar.com/news/canada/2023/01/21/she-went-from-undocumented-to-undeniable-advocate-whose-fight-against-canadian-government-reached-the-unremembered-as-an-inspiration.html.

27. Nicholas Keung, "After Canada Denied Her Health Care, She Lost a Leg, Her Sight, and Her Kidneys," *Toronto Star*, August 19, 2022, https://www.thestar.com/news/canada/2022/08/19/after-canada-denied-her-health-care-she-lost-a-leg-her-sight-and-her-kidneys-a-court-just-ruled-she-can-sue.html.

28. Chaoulli v. Quebec (Attorney General), [2005] 1 S.C.R. 791, 2005 SCC 35

29. "Ontario Expanding Number and Range of Surgeries Offered at For-Profit Clinics," CBC, January 16, 2023, https://www.cbc.ca/news/canada/toronto/ford-jones-health-surgeries-private-clinics-1.6715117; Hannah Kost, "Alberta Government to Contract More Private Surgical Facilities," CBC, September 7, 2022, https://www.cbc.ca/news/canada/calgary/kenney-alberta-surgical-initiative-calgary-1.6574589; Jason Herring, "'Deeply Concerning': Smith Suggests Privatizing Major Alberta Hospitals in 2021 Video," *Calgary Herald*, May 10, 2023, https://calgaryherald.com/news/politics/smith-suggests-privatizing-major-alberta-hospitals-in-2021-video; Ian Froese, "More Private-Sector Involvement in Health Care Promised in Manitoba Throne Speech," CBC, November 15, 2022, https://www.cbc.ca/news/canada/manitoba/throne-speech-stefanson-2022-1.6652101.

30. Nadeem Esmail and Bacchus Barua, "Court Ruling Locks Patients into Government-Run Health Care," Fraser Institute (first published in *Calgary Sun*, September 17, 2020), https://www.fraserinstitute.org/article/court-ruling-locks-patients-into-government-run-health-care; Susan Delacourt, "Justin Trudeau Calls Doug Ford's For-Profit Health Plans 'Innovation,'" *Toronto Star*, January 19, 2023, https://www.thestar.com/politics/political-opinion/2023/01/19/justin-trudeau-calls-doug-fords-for-profit-health-plans-innovation.html.

31. Taylor Wirtz and Matthew Seaver, "ER Wait Times Are Increasing

Despite Decline in COVID-19 Cases," WINK News, February 22, 2022, https://www.winknews.com/2022/02/22/er-wait-times-are-increasing-despite-decline-in-covid-19-cases/.

32.   Peter W. Hogg, "Is There a Constitutional Right to Health Care?" website of Dr. Brian Day, October 23, 2005, https://www.brianday.ca/news/is-there-a-constitutional-right-to-health-care/; Jason Herring, "Health Care Advocates Worry Wave of Privatization Coming in Budget 2022," *Calgary Herald*, February 22, 2022, https://calgaryherald.com/news/politics/public-health-advocates-worry-wave-of-privatization-incoming-in-budget-2022; Brian Day, "After Decades of Broken Health Care Promises, Canada's Governments Need to Prove Themselves," *Globe and Mail*, November 18, 2022, https://www.theglobeandmail.com/opinion/article-after-decades-of-broken-health-care-promises-canadas-governments-need/.

33.   Kevin Bliss, "Growing Concerns Over Medical Debt Leading to Jail Time," *Prison Legal News*, February 2020, 43.

34.   Sarah O'Brien, "100 Million Adults Have Health-Care Debt—and 12% of Them Owe $10,000 or More," CNBC, June 22, 2022, https://www.cnbc.com/2022/06/22/100-million-adults-have-health-care-debt-and-some-owe-10000-or-more.html; CareCredit is a well-known problem among consumer rights advocates but it is not well-reported on. "CFPB Orders GE CareCredit to Refund $34.1 Million for Deceptive Health-Care Credit Card Enrollment," December 10, 2013, https://www.consumerfinance.gov/about-us/newsroom/cfpb-orders-ge-carecredit-to-refund-34-1-million-for-deceptive-health-care-credit-card-enrollment/; https://ag.ny.gov/press-release/2010/attorney-general-cuomo-launches-industry-wide-investigation-predatory-health-care

35.   Sarah Kliff, "Covid Killed His Father. Then Came $1 Million in Medical Bills," *New York Times*, May 21, 2021, https://www.nytimes.com/2021/05/21/upshot/covid-bills-financial-long-haulers.html.

36.   *The Ontario Hospital Capacity Crisis: Eastern Ontario: Overcapacity and Under Threat*, Ontario Council of Hospital Unions and CUPE, April 2021, 8. Paris Marx, "PM Trudeau, There's Nothing 'Innovative' about Privatized Health Care," *Breach*, February 21, 2023.

37.   "Residents 'Overwhelmed' after Judge Rules They Can Stay in CRAB Park Encampment," CBC, January 14, 2022, https://www.cbc.ca/news/canada/british-columbia/crab-park-residents-vancouver-1.6315762.

38.   United Nations Special Rapporteur on the right to adequate housing, "The Human Right to Adequate Housing," Office of the United Nations High Commissioner for Human Rights, https://www.ohchr.org/en/special-procedures/sr-housing/human-right-adequate-housing.

39.   Canadian Centre for Housing Rights, "The National Housing Strategy

Act—A Primer," March 9, 2021, https://housingrightscanada.com/re-sources/the-national-housing-strategy-act-a-primer/.

40. Statistics Canada, "Housing Challenges Remain for Vulnerable Populations in 2021," July 21, 2022, https://www150.statcan.gc.ca/n1/daily-quotidien/220721/dq220721b-eng.htm.

41. Peter Dreier, "Why America Needs More Social Housing," *The American Prospect*, April 16, 2018, https://prospect.org/infrastructure/america-needs-social-housing/; Center on Budget and Policy Priorities, "Policy Basics: Public Housing," June 16, 2021, https://www.cbpp.org/research/public-housing#%3A~%3Atext%3DThe%20nation%27s%20958%2C000%20public%20housing%2Cof%20them%20in%20rural%20areas.

42. Roma Luciw, "Canadians Spend More Income on Housing than Almost Anyone in the World," *Globe and Mail*, October 30, 2014, https://www.theglobeandmail.com/globe-investor/personal-finance/household-finances/canadians-spend-more-of-their-income-on-hous-ing-than-almost-anyone-in-the-world/article21369414/.

43. Credit Counselling Canada, "Housing, Income, Employment Insecurity Affecting Canadians' Wellbeing," October 13, 2021, https://www.globenewswire.com/en/news-release/2021/10/13/2313299/0/en/Housing-income-employment-insecurity-affecting Canadians-mental-wellbeing.html; Stephenson Strobel et al., "Characterizing People Experiencing Homelessness Using Population-Level Emergency Department Visit Data in Ontario, Canada," Statistics Canada, January 20, 2021, https://www150.statcan.gc.ca/n1/pub/82-003-x/2021001/article/00002-eng.htm; Pete Evans, "Rent Increased More than 18% Last Year for New Tenants, New Numbers Show," CBC, January 26, 2023, https://www.cbc.ca/news/business/cmhc-rent-report-1.6726764; Stephen Gaetz et al., "The State of Homelessness in Canada 2016," Homeless Hub, 2016, https://www.homelesshub.ca/SOHC2016.

44. Mumilaaq Qaqqaq, *Sick of Waiting: A Report on Nunavut's Housing Crisis*, 2021, https://www.aptnnews.ca/wp-content/uploads/2021/03/Qaqqaq.HousingReport.2021-1.pdf; "Nunavut Has Highest Rate of Inadequate, Unaffordable Housing: Report," *Nunatsiaq News*, December 16, 2022, https://www.aptnnews.ca/wp-content/uploads/2021/03/Qaqqaq.HousingReport.2021-1.pdf; "Racialized Communities," Homeless Hub, https://www.homelesshub.ca/about-homelessness/popula-tion-specific/racialized-communities; Dylan Simone and Alan Walks, "Immigration, Race, Mortgage Lending, and the Geography of Debt in Canada's Global Cities," *Geoforum* 98 (January 2019), 286–99, https://www.sciencedirect.com/science/article/pii/S0016718517302956.

45. Don Pittis, "COVID-19 Has Made Reading Next Year's Real Estate Market Harder than Ever," CBC, December 14, 2020, https://www.

sciencedirect.com/science/article/pii/S0016718517302956; Daniel Wong, "Landlord Nation: Over 1 in 6 Canadian Homeowners Own Multiple Properties," *Better Dwelling*, April 12, 2022, https://betterdwelling.com/landlord-nation-over-1-in-6-canadian-homeowners-own-multiple-properties/.

46. Emily Blake, "'No One Is Really Taking Care of Us': Little Progress Made on Improving Inuit Housing," CBC, October 17, 2022, https://www.cbc.ca/news/canada/north/inuit-housing-crisis-1.6618940.

47. Tahiat Mahboob, "Housing Is a Human Right: How Finland Is Eradicating Homelessness," CBC, January 24, 2020; Jon Henley, "'It's a Miracle': Helsinki's Radical Solution to Homelessness," *Guardian*, June 3, 2019, https://www.theguardian.com/cities/2019/jun/03/its-a-miracle-helsinkis-radical-solution-to-homelessness.

48. Kirsty Lang, "Lessons from Vienna: A Housing Success Story 100 Years in the Making," *Financial Times*, December 30, 2022, https://www.ft.com/content/05719602-89c6-4bbc-9bbe-5842fd0c3693.

49. As clarified by Housing Rights Watch, "The Right to housing is not constitutionally guaranteed. However, it is established in legislation through the Austrian Social Aid Act (§20); which supports 'homeless people and persons in extraordinary precarious situations' through the 'provision of housing'" (https://www.housingrightswatch.org/page/state-housing-rights-1).

50. In the United Kingdom, to provide another example, the bombing and rationing of World War II created a new sense of cross-class solidarity, opening space for the Labour government to build public housing at an astonishing speed out of the rubble. By 1979, 42 percent of the population lived in council housing—at which point the Conservative Party, led by Margaret Thatcher, began a process that turned millions of units over to private ownership.

51. Rachel M. Cohen, "Democrats Eye New Legislation to Rein In Wall Street Landlords," *Vox*, December 2, 2022, https://www.vox.com/policy-and-politics/2022/12/2/23485957/housing-banks-corporate-single-family-renters-landlord; Martine August, "The Rise of Financial Landlords Has Turned Rental Apartments into a Vehicle for Profit," *Policy Options*, June 11, 2021, https://policyoptions.irpp.org/magazines/june-2021/the-rise-of-financial-landlords-has-turned-rental-apartments-into-a-vehicle-for-profit/; Mathilde Lind Gustavussen, "Corporate Landlords Are Taking Over—But Tenants Can Use Their Monopolies Against Them," *Jacobin*, June 8, 2022, https://jacobin.com/2022/06/corporate-landlords-ca-tenants-unions-finance.

52. Alexander Ferrer, "The Real Problem with Corporate Landlords," *Atlantic*, June 21, 2021, https://www.theatlantic.com/ideas/archive/2021/06/real-problem-corporate-landlords/619244/.

53.   August, "The Rise of Financial Landlords."

54.   Alan Walks and Brian Clifford, "The Political Economy of Mortgage Securitization and the Neoliberalization of Housing Policy in Canada," *Environment and Planning A: Economy and Space* 47, no. 8 (August 2015), https://doi.org/10.1068/a130226p, 1632.

55.   Walks and Clifford, "The Political Economy of Mortgage Securitization and the Neoliberalization of Housing Policy in Canada," https://doi.org/10.1068/a130226p.

56.   "Value of Global Real Estate Rises 5% to $326.5 Trillion," *Savills Impacts*, September 2021, https://www.savills.us/insight-and-opinion/savills-news/319145/value-of-global-real-estate-rises-5--to-$326.5-trillion/; Robert Hackett, "How Critical Real Estate Is to the Global Economy—In One Chart," *Fortune*, January 26, 2016, https://fortune.com/2016/01/26/rea-estate-global-economy/.

57.   Debt Collective, *Can't Pay Won't Pay; The Case for Economic Disobedience and Debt Abolition* (Chicago: Haymarket Books, 2020), 58–63.

58.   Ted Rutland, *Displacing Blackness: Planning, Power, and Race in Twentieth-Century Halifax* (Toronto: University of Toronto Press, 2018).

59.   Dan Darrah, "We Need Public Housing, Not Affordable Housing," *Jacobin*, April 17, 2022, https://jacobin.com/2022/04/us-canadian-social-housing-affordability-ownership-speculation.

60.   Lawrence Scanlan, "We Have Grown Unacceptably Indifferent to Poverty's Pain," *Globe and Mail*, January 21, 2023, https://www.theglobeandmail.com/opinion/article-we-have-grown-unacceptably-indifferent-to-povertys-pain/.

61.   Amee Chew, *Social Housing for All: A Vision for Thriving Communities, Renter Power, and Racial Justice*, Center for Popular Democracy and Renters Rising, March 2022, 7.

62.   I got this data point from David Hulchanski; Blake, "'No One Is Really Taking Care of Us.'"

63.   As journalist Ryan Holeywell explains, eliminating regressive tax exemptions is key: "Vienna gets about 450 million euros a year in federal funds earmarked for housing. In addition, the city contributes its own funding to the effort, upping its total public housing spending to about 600 million euros per year. Vienna officials are quick to point out that they don't spend more than the US on housing as a percentage of GDP. In addition, there is no mortgage interest deduction as there is in the US—Vienna chooses to subsidize developments rather than residents. Consequently, city officials say, they can exert vastly more influence on housing than their American counterparts." Ryan Holeywell, "Haus Beautiful," *Governing Magazine*, February 2013, 33.

Chapter 3: Consumed by Curiosity

1. The documentary aired on the CBC as part of the series "This Land."

2. Street graffiti quoted in Andrew Feenberg and Jim Freedman, *When Poetry Ruled the Streets: The French May Events of 1968* (Albany: State University of New York Press, 2001). Excerpted at https://www.sfu.ca/~andrewf/books/When_Poetry_Ruled_the_Streets.pdf.

3. "Transcript: Ezra Klein Interviews Pippa Norris," *New York Times*, November 1, 2022, https://www.nytimes.com/2022/11/01/podcasts/transcript-ezra-klein-interviews-pippa-norris.html.

4. The study began with France, West Germany, Belgium, the Netherlands, Italy, Denmark, Ireland, Switzerland, and the US (World Values Survey, https://www.worldvaluessurvey.org/WVSContents.jsp).

5. "'A Chicken in Every Pot' Political Ad and Rebuttal Article in *New York Times*," 1928, US National Archives, https://catalog.archives.gov/id/187095.

6. Ronald Inglehart, *The Silent Revolution: Changing Values and Political Styles Among Western Publics* (Princeton: Princeton University Press, 1977).

7. Ronald Inglehart, "The Age of Insecurity: Can Democracy Save Itself?" *Foreign Affairs*, May/June 2018, https://www.foreignaffairs.com/united-states/age-insecurity.

8. Todd C. Frankel, "A Majority of the People Arrested for Capitol Riot Had a History of Financial Trouble," *Washington Post*, February 10, 2021, https://www.washingtonpost.com/business/2021/02/10/capitol-insurrectionists-jenna-ryan-financial-problems/.

9. Michael Adams, Ron Inglehart, and David Jamieson, "The Authoritarian Reflex: Will It Manifest in Canada?" Environics Institute, June 15, 2019, https://www.environicsinstitute.org/insights/insight-details/the-authoritarian-reflex-will-it-manifest-in-canada.

10. Léger, "The Freedom Convoy and Federal Politics," February 8, 2022, https://leger360.com/surveys/legers-north-american-tracker-february-8-2022/.

11. Ronald Inglehart and Pippa Norris, "Trump and the Populist Authoritarian Parties: *The Silent Revolution* in Reverse," *Perspectives on Politics* 15, no. 2 (2017).

12. Margaret Thatcher, "Interview for *Sunday Times*," reprinted from *Sunday Times*, May 3, 1981, https://www.margaretthatcher.org/document/104475.

13.   "Margaret Thatcher: A Life in Quotes," *Guardian*, April 8, 2013, https://www.theguardian.com/politics/2013/apr/08/margaret-thatcher-quotes.

14.   Shanti Escalante-De Mattei, "Archaeologists Discover 'Oldest' Jewelry Ever, Shedding Light on Early Ways of Expressing Identity," *ARTnews*, November 22, 2021, https://www.artnews.com/art-news/news/oldest-jewelry-discovered-1234611028/. The aesthetic impulse is not unique to *Homo sapiens*, though: the oldest known piece of art is a set of zigzags carved on a mussel shell likely made by our ancestor *Homo erectus* some 540,000 years ago: Helen Thompson, "Zigzags on a Shell from Java Are the Oldest Human Engravings," *Smithsonian Magazine*, December 3, 2014, https://www.smithsonianmag.com/science-nature/oldest-engraving-shell-tools-zigzags-art-java-indonesia-humans-180953522/.

15.   Marilyn Jensen, "Our Story: A Historical Reflection of the Carcross/Tagish First Nation's Land Claims Process," Carcross/Tagish First Nation Ratification Committee, 2005, https://www.ctfn.ca/media/documents/land_claims_book mon.pdf.

16.   Globally, we collectively produce 2.3 billion tons of municipal solid waste per year, enough, it is said, to fill 822,000 Olympic-sized pools. Niall Smith, "US Tops List of Countries Fuelling the Waste Crisis," Verisk Maplecroft, July 2, 2019, https://www.maplecroft.com/insights/analysis/us-tops-list-of-countries-fuelling-the-mounting-waste-crisis/; Joe McCarthy, "Americans Produce 3 Times as much Garbage as the Global Average," Global Citizen, July 3, 2019, https://www.globalcitizen.org/en/content/americans-produce-most-waste/.

17.   Stephen Mitchell, trans., *Tao Te Ching* (New York: HarperCollins, 2006), 36.

18.   Frank Trentmann, *Empire of Things: How We Became a World of Consumers, from the Fifteenth Century to the Twenty-First* (London: Allen Lane, 2016), 8, 21, 30, 34, 37–43, 46–48

19.   "Consumption is the sole end and purpose of all production; and the interest of the producer ought to be attended to, only so far as it may be necessary for promoting that of the consumer": Adam Smith, *An Inquiry into the Nature and Causes of the Wealth of Nations* (London, 1776), bk. 4, chap. 8.

20.   Adam Smith, *The Theory of Moral Sentiments* (London, 1759), pt. IV, chap. I.

21.   Smith, *Theory of Moral Sentiments*, part IV, chap. I; Glory M. Liu, "How Adam Smith Became a (Surprising) Hero to Conservative Economists, *Aeon*, June 10, 2019, https://aeon.co/ideas/how-adam-smith-became-a-surprising-hero-to-conservative-economists.

22.   John Kenneth Galbraith, *The Affluent Society* (1958; pbk. repr., Boston: Houghton Mifflin, 1998), 213

23.   Vince Packard, *The Waste Makers* (1960; repr., Brooklyn: Ig, 2011), 82–83.

24.   Evan T. Sage, "Advertising among the Romans," *The Classical Weekly*, May 6, 1916, vol. 9, no. 26 (May 6, 1916), pp. 202–08; Fred K. Beard, "The Ancient History of Advertising: Insights and Implications for Practitioners," *Journal of Advertising Research*, September 2017, 57 (3), 239-244.

25.   Sara Fischer, "Ad Industry Growing at Record Pace," *Axios*, December 7, 2021, https://www.axios.com/2021/12/07/advertising-industry-revenue.

26.   Jinyan Zang, "Solving the Problem of Racially Discriminatory Advertising on Facebook," Brookings Institution, October 9, 2021, https://www.brookings.edu/research/solving-the-problem-of-racially-discriminatory-advertising-on-facebook/.

27.   Chronic loneliness has been shown to heighten anxiety, fear, and hypervigilance, making some people "more receptive to far-right ideology that relies on fear of the 'other,' fear of radical social change, and promises security"—ideology they often first encounter online. Alexander Sherer, "America the Lonely: Social Isolation, Public Health, and Right-Wing Populism," *Berkeley Political Review*, March 25, 2021, https://bpr.berkeley.edu/2021/03/25/america-the-lonely-social-isolation-public-health-and-right-wing-populism/; Ben Popken, "Age, Not Politics, Is Biggest Predictor of Who Shares Fake News on Facebook, Study, Finds," NBC, January 10, 2019, https://www.nbcnews.com/tech/tech-news/age-not-politics-predicts-who-shares-fake-news-facebook-study-n957246.

28.   "A Review of the Data Broker Industry: Collection, Use, and Sale of Consumer Data for Marketing Purposes," Staff Report for Chairman Rockefeller, United States Senate Committee on Commerce, Science, and Transportation, December 18, 2013; Frank Pasquale, *The Black Box Society: The Secret Algorithms That Control Money and Information* (Cambridge, MA: Harvard University Press, 2015).

29.   Rebecca J. Rosen, "Is This the Grossest Advertising Strategy of All Time?" *Atlantic*, October 3, 2013, https://www.theatlantic.com/technology/archive/2013/10/is-this-the-grossest-advertising-strategy-of-all-time/280242/.

30.   Lucia Moses, "Marketers Should Take Note of When Women Feel Least Attractive," *Adweek*, October 2, 2013, https://www.adweek.com/brand-marketing/marketers-should-take-note-when-women-feel-least-attractive-152753/.

31. *Deadly by Design*, Center for Countering Digital Hate, December 15, 2022, https://counterhate.com/wp-content/uploads/2022/12/CCDH-Deadly-by-Design_120922.pdf.

32. "'Facebook Weakens Our Democracy, Harms Kids': Top Quotes from Whistleblower Frances Haugen's Testimony," WION, October 6, 2021, https://www.wionews.com/world/facebook-weakens-our-democracy-harms-kids-top-quotes-from-whistleblower-frances-haugens-testimony-418489.

33. Tim Kasser, *The High Cost of Materialism* (Cambridge, MA: MIT Press, 2002), 11.

34. Shaun Callaghan et al., "Feeling Good: The Future of the $1.5 Trillion Wellness Market," McKinsey, April 8, 2021, https://www.mckinsey.com/industries/consumer-packaged-goods/our-insights/feeling-good-the-future-of-the-1-5-trillion-wellness-market.

35. Stephanie Alice Baker, "Alt. Health Influencers: How Wellness Culture and Web Culture Have Been Weaponised to Promote Conspiracy Theories and Far-Right Extremism during the COVID-19 Pandemic," *European Journal of Cultural Studies* 25, no.1 (2022), 3–24.

36. "Brené Brown's Top 10 Rules for Self-Love," Mindspo, August 10, 2020, https://mindspo.com/2020/08/10/brene-browns-top-10-rules-for-self-love/.

37. Frédéric Simon and Kira Taylor, "Brussels Targets Greenwashing, Planned Obsolescence in New EU Consumer Rules," Euractiv, March 30, 2022, https://www.euractiv.com/section/circular-economy/news/brussels-targets-greenwashing-planned-obsolescence-in-new-eu-consumer-rules/; "EU Right to Repair: All You Need to Know about Recent Policy Developments," HQTS blog, April 19, 2022, https://www.hqts.com/right-to-repair-electronics/.

38. Sarah McGrath, "Examining the 'Wellness'-to-Far-Right-Conspiracy Pipeline," *Brown Political Review*, November 15, 2021, https://brownpoliticalreview.org/2021/11/examining-the-wellness-to-far-right-conspiracy-pipeline/.

39. Stacy Lee Kong, "Looks Like the Wellness-to-White-Supremacy Pipeline Is Alive and Well," *Friday Things*, February 4, 2022, https://www.fridaythings.com/recent-posts/angela-liddon-oh-she-glows-canada-trucker-convoy-2022.

40. Dan Berrett, "The Day the Purpose of College Changed," *Chronicle of Higher Education*, January 26, 2015, https://www.chronicle.com/article/the-day-the-purpose-of-college-changed/.

41. Ronald Inglehart, *The Silent Revolution: Changing Values and Political Styles Among Western Publics* (Princeton: Princeton University Press, 1977), 7.

42. John Vanderkamp, "University Enrolment in Canada 1951–83 and Beyond," *The Canadian Journal of Higher Education,* vol. XIV-2, 1984, 51.

43. Alexander W. Astin et al., *The American Freshman: Thirty-Year Trends,* Higher Education Research institute, Graduate School of Education & Information Studies, University of California, 1997, 13, https://www.heri.ucla.edu/PDFs/pubs/TFS/Trends/Monographs/ TheAmericanFreshman30YearTrends.pdf.

44. Judy Steed, "Crisis in the Schools: Not Everyone Sees Back-to-Basics as the Way to Go," *Globe and Mail,* January 15, 1983.

45. Joel Hardin, "The Case for Renewal in Post-Secondary Education," Canadian Centre for Policy Alternatives, March 2017, 3. Hardin's white paper eloquently states the general problem: "There was once a time when Canadians could get a post-secondary education without upfront costs, or with nominal fees ... when workers in the post-secondary education sector enjoyed decent wages and full-time employment, and campus leaders were considered equal colleagues, not unapproachable executives armed with battalions of staff. That era ended in the 1990s when tax cuts and austerity took precedence over the delivery of quality public services like education. As elsewhere, Canadian decision makers embraced neoliberal ideas that promoted lower taxes, greater 'personal responsibility' (for education, training, etc.) and the reduced scope of social programs. Post-secondary education was often framed as an individual investment, a private service for which students must bear a far higher cost. International students were aggressively recruited as a high revenue stream for colleges and universities (through differential fees), not as valued sources of knowledge."; Statistics Canada, "Financial Information of Universities for the 2018/19 School Year," October 8, 2020, https://www150. statcan.gc.ca/n1/daily-quotidien/201008/dq201008b-eng.htm.

46. *Budget for Current Operations: Context for the Budget Request 2020–21,* University of California, Office of the President, Budget Analysis and Planning, https://www.ucop.edu/operating-budget/_ files/rbudget/2020-21-budget-detail.pdf.

47. "Transcript: Interview: Carl Sagan, Jan 30, 1995," TVO, https://www. tvo.org/transcript/005584.

48. Kasser, *High Cost,* 49.

49. Johnny Johns, a survivor who attended Choutla in the 1960s, still remembers how children would cry all night long, hungry and cold. "'Like a Big Jail': Yukoners Reflect on Painful Residential School Legacy on Orange Shirt Day," CBC, September 30, 2020, https:// www.cbc.ca/news/canada/north/orange-shirt-day-yukon-1.5743957.

50. Ken Coates, "Betwixt and Between: The Anglican Church and the

Children of the Carcross (Chooutla) Residential School, 1911–1954,"
BC Studies, no. 64, Winter 1984, 32.

51. Toby Rollo, "Beyond Curricula: Colonial Pedagogies in Public Schooling," chap. 7 in *Troubling Truth and Reconciliation in Canadian Education: Critical Perspectives*, ed. Sandra D. Styres and Arlo Kempf (Edmonton: University of Alberta Press, 2022).

52. "Elijah Smith, Father of Modern Day Land Claims in Yukon, Remembered as Veteran," APTN, 2022, https://www.youtube.com/watch?v=TFbXa5D7_II.

53. Council for Yukon Indians, *Together Today for Our Children Tomorrow*, 1977, 51–52, https://cyfn.ca/wp-content/uploads/2013/10/together_today_for_our_children_tomorrow.pdf.

54. Of the fourteen distinct First Nations in the Yukon Territory today, eleven have negotiated self-government agreements that support greater autonomy and self-determination, including over land and resources, transforming Indigenous life and education in the north.

55. *Yukon Poverty Report Card 2020*, Campaign 2000 and Yukon Anti-Poverty Coalition, March 25, 2021, https://campaign2000.ca/wp-content/uploads/2021/03/Yukon-Poverty-Report-Card-2020web.pdf.

56. Leanne Betasamosake Simpson, "Land As Pedagogy: Nishnaabeg Intelligence and Rebellious Transformation," *Decolonization: Indigeneity, Education & Society* 3, no. 3 (2014), 9.

57. Simpson, "Land as Pedagogy," 11.

58. Leanne Betasamosake Simpson, *Dancing on Our Turtle's Back: Stories of Nishnaabeg Re-Creation, Resurgence and a New Emergence* (Winnipeg: ARP Books, 2011) 43.

59. Simpson, "Land as Pedagogy," 11.

60. Carcross Community Education Centre Fonds, Yukon Archives Accession 79/63, https://yukon.ca/sites/yukon.ca/files/tc/tc-inventory-carcross-community-education-centre-fonds.pdf.

61. James Baldwin, *Notes of a Native Son* (1955; repr., Boston: Beacon Press, 2012), 103.

Chapter 4: Beyond Human Security

1. *Global Trends: Paradox of Progress*, National Intelligence Council, January 2017, https://www.dni.gov/files/documents/nic/GT-Full-Report.pdf.

2.   *Global Trends 2040: A More Contested World*, National Intelligence
        Council, March 2021, https://www.dni.gov/files/documents/nic/GT-
        Full-Report.pdf.

3.   United Nations Intergovernmental Panel on Climate Change, "Sum-
        mary for Policymakers of IPCC Special Report on Global Warming
        of 1.5°C Approved by Governments," October 8, 2018, https://www.
        ipcc.ch/2018/10/08/summary-for-policymakers-of-ipcc-special-re-
        port-on-global-warming-of-1-5c-approved-by-governments/.

4.   Dinah Voyles Pulver, "If April Showers Bring May Flowers, Why Are
        Blooms Appearing So Early? Climate Change," *USA Today*, March 9,
        2023, https://www.usatoday.com/story/news/2023/03/09/early-spring-
        2023-flower-blooms-show-climate-change-impact/11373671002/.

5.   Emily Chung, Tashauna Reid, and Alice Hopton, "In the Arctic, 'Ev-
        erything Is Changing,' Massive Animal Tracking Study Finds," CBC,
        November 6, 2020, https://www.cbc.ca/news/science/arctic-animal-
        archive-climate-1.5790992.

6.   Ziya Tong, *The Reality Bubble: How Science Reveals the Hidden Truths
        that Shape Our World* (Toronto: Penguin Canada, 2019), 229–32.

7.   Molly Peterson, "How to Calm Your Climate Anxiety," *New York
        Times*, July 23, 2021, https://www.nytimes.com/2021/07/23/well/
        mind/mental-health-climate-anxiety.html.

8.   Similar to the legislated right to housing discussed in Chapter
        2, Canadians now have domestic right to a healthy environment
        thanks to the 2023 passage of the Canadian Environmental Protec-
        tion Act (CEPA). This is welcome news, but the fight to broaden
        the scope of Section 7 remains imperative for reasons outlined by
        law professor David Boyd: "Although the difference may not be
        immediately apparent, constitutional and legislated environmental
        rights are like Siberian tigers and Siamese cats – related, but with
        dramatically different degrees of strength. A constitution is the su-
        preme law of a nation, meaning that all other laws and regulations
        must be consistent with it or face being struck down. Ordinary leg-
        islation, in contrast, does not override other laws." David Richard
        Boyd, *The Right to a Healthy Environment: Revitalizing Canada's
        Constitution* (Vancouver: UBC Press, 2012), 55.

9.   Katharina Rall and Rachel LaFortune, *"My Fear Is Losing Ev-
        erything": The Climate Crisis and First Nations' Right to Food
        in Canada*, Human Rights Watch, 2020, https://www.hrw.org/
        report/2020/10/21/my-fear-losing-everything/climate-crisis-and-
        first-nations-right-food-canada; Corey Mintz, "The History of Food
        in Canada Is the History of Colonialism," *The Walrus*, April 2019,
        https://thewalrus.ca/the-history-of-food-in-canada-is-the-history-of-

colonialism/; Natasha Beedie, David Macdonald. and Daniel Wilson, "Towards Justice: Tackling Indigenous Child Poverty in Canada," Assembly of First Nations, July 2019.

10. The United Nations Department of Economic and Social Affairs states, "Climate change poses threats and dangers to the survival of Indigenous communities worldwide, even though Indigenous peoples contribute the least to greenhouse gas emissions." https://www.un.org/development/desa/indigenouspeoples/climate-change.html.

11. *Mathur v. His Majesty the King in Right of Ontario*, 2023 ONSC 2316, 37, 42.

12. Aimée Craft, *Breathing Life into the Stone Fort Treaty: An Anishinabe Understanding of Treaty One* (United States: Purich Publishing Limited, 2013), 95–100.

13 John Schwartz, "In 'Strongest' Climate Ruling Yet, Dutch Court Orders Leaders to Take Action," *New York Times*, December 20, 2019, https://www.nytimes.com/2019/12/20/climate/netherlands-climate-lawsuit.html.

14. For an excellent account of some of these cases and the rights of nature movement, see David R. Boyd, *The Rights Of Nature: A Legal Revolution That Could Save the World* (Toronto: ECW, 2017).

15. Michael Safi and agencies, "Ganges and Yamuna Rivers Granted Same Legal Rights as Human Beings," *Guardian*, March 21, 2017, https://www.theguardian.com/world/2017/mar/21/ganges-and-yamuna-rivers-granted-same-legal-rights-as-human-beings.

16. Nicole Pallotta, "Federal Judge Strikes Down 'Lake Erie Bill of Rights,'" Animal Legal Defense Fund, May 4, 2020, https://aldf.org/article/federal-judge-strikes-down-lake-erie-bill-of-rights/; "Lake Erie Algae Blooms," Alliance for the Great Lakes, https://greatlakes.org/campaigns/lake-erie-algae-blooms/.

17. Winona LaDuke, "The White Earth Band of Ojibwe Legally Recognized the Rights of Wild Rice," *YES!*, February 1, 2019, https://www.yesmagazine.org/environment/2019/02/01/the-white-earth-band-of-ojibwe-legally-recognized-the-rights-of-wild-rice-heres-why.

18. Alliance Muteshekau-shipu, "For the First Time, a River Is Granted Official Rights and Legal Personhood in Canada," news release, February 23, 2021, https://www.prnewswire.com/news-releases/for-the-first-time-a-river-is-granted-official-rights-and-legal-personhood-in-canada-301233731.html; Chloe Rose Stuart-Ulin, "Quebec's Magpie River Becomes First in Canada to Be Granted Legal Personhood," *Canada's National Observer*, February 24, 2021, https://www.nationalobserver.com/2021/02/24/news/quebecs-magpie-river-first-in-canada-granted-legal-personhood.

19. Chloe Berge, "This Canadian River Is Now Legally a Person. It's Not the Only One," *National Geographic*, April 15, 2022, https://www.nationalgeographic.com/travel/article/these-rivers-are-now-considered-people-what-does-that-mean-for-travelers.

20. Sunaura Taylor and Sara E. S. Orning, "Being Human, Being Animal: Species Membership in Extraordinary Times," *New Literary History* 51, no. 4 (2020), 663–85, https://muse.jhu.edu/article/781675/summary. For more on my sister's work on cross-species solidarity, read her book *Beasts of Burden: Animal and Disability Liberation* (New York: New Press, 2017).

21. Rebecca Solnit, *Orwell's Roses* (New York: Viking, 2021), 133–46; Sam Kean, "The Soviet Era's Deadliest Scientist Is Regaining Popularity in Russia," *The Atlantic*, December 19, 2017, https://www.theatlantic.com/science/archive/2017/12/trofim-lysenko-soviet-union-russia/548786/.

22. Judith Shapiro. *Mao's War Against Nature: Politics and the Environment in Revolutionary China* (United Kingdom: Cambridge University Press, 2001); Jeremiah Steinfeld, "China's Deadly Science Lesson," *Index on Censorship*, volume 47, issue 3, 2018.

23. R. Daniel Bressler, "The Mortality Cost of Carbon," *Nature Communications* 12, no. 4467 (2021), https://www.nature.com/articles/s41467-021-24487-w; Joseph Guzman, "New Study Says Global Warming Could Kill 83M People by the End of the Century," *Changing America*, July 30, 2021, https://thehill.com/changing-america/sustainability/climate-change/565626-new-study-says-global-warming-could-kill-83/.

24. Qi Zhao et al., "Global, Regional, and National Burden of Mortality Associated with Non-Optimal Ambient Temperatures from 2000 to 2019," *Lancet* 5, no. 7 (July 2021), https://doi.org/10.1016/S2542-5196(21)00081-4.

25. *Drought in Numbers, 2022*, United Nations Convention to Combat Desertification, https://www.unccd.int/resources/publications/drought-numbers; Sean McAllister, "There Could Be 1.2 Billion Climate Refugees by 2050," *Zurich*, January 13, 2023, https://www.zurich.com/en/media/magazine/2022/there-could-be-1-2-billion-climate-refugees-by-2050-here-s-what-you-need-to-know; Chi Xu et al., "Future of the Human Climate Niche," *Proceedings of the National Academy of Sciences* 117, no. 21 (2020), https://doi.org/10.1073/pnas.1910114117.

26. Joëlle Gergis, "A Climate Scientist's Take on Hope," in *Not Too Late: Changing the Climate Story from Despair to Possibility*, ed. Rebecca Solnit and Thelma Young Lutunatabua (Chicago: Haymarket Books, 2022), 40.

27. Astra Taylor, "Who Speaks for the Trees?" *The Baffler*, September

2016, https://thebaffler.com/salvos/speaks-trees-astra-taylor; Colin Jerolmack, "A Tiny Pennsylvania Town of 700 People Declared War on the Fracking Industry in 2014. They're Finally Getting Their Day in Court," *New Republic*, July 26, 2022, https://newrepublic.com/article/167163/grant-township-fracking-home-rule.

28. Jerolmack, "Tiny Pennsylvania Town."

29. Utopians in More's tale are contradictory: dogmatic and open-minded, rigidly egalitarian but also slave-holding; More seemed to believe slavery as punishment was superior to the English habit of executing people for petty theft. (Eventually, More would be executed himself, though for treason, not theft.) Their unusual attitudes extend to animals, whom they consume sparingly, killing only for necessity and not for sport. The Utopians regard hunting for pleasure with contempt and worry that slaughtering numbs people's sense of compassion. But instead of abstaining from animal flesh, they assign the job of butchering to those they hold in bondage.

30. Thomas More, *Utopia*, ed. Stephen Duncombe (1516; Wivenhoe, UK: Minor Compositions, 2012), 44.

31. More, *Utopia*, 44.

32. Gerrard Winstanley, *The True Levellers Standard Advanced: Or, The State of Community Opened, and Presented to the Sons of Men* (London, 1649).

33. Additionally, going back to the thirteenth century, the word *cattle* was synonymous with all moveable property, a meaning captured by the related word *chattel*.

34. European and settler fortunes were amassed through loot, land, and labour. Furs, silver, gold, and valuable crops were part of the bounty colonizers seized while Indigenous land was stolen and kidnapped Africans were forced to work in cotton-growing fields.

35. Allan Greer, "Commons and Enclosure in the Colonization of North America," *American Historical Review* 117, no. 2 (April 2012), 382; Scott M. Strickland et al., *Defining the Indigenous Cultural Landscape for the Nanjemoy and Mattawoman Creek Watersheds* (St. Mary's City, MD: St. Mary's College of Maryland, 2015), https://www.nps.gov/cajo/learn/upload/ICL-Piscataway_Nanjemoy-508.pdf.

36. Virginia DeJohn Anderson, *Creatures of Empire: How Domestic Animals Transformed Early America* (New York: Oxford University Press, 2004), 7–8.

37. Kenneth A. Lockridge, *A New England Town: The First Hundred Years* (New York, 1970), 82, quoted in Greer, "Commons and Enclosure," 373.

38.   Greer, "Commons and Enclosure," 373.

39.   Quoted in William Cronon, *Changes in the Land: Indians, Colonists, and the Ecology of New England*, rev. ed. (New York: Farrar, Straus & Giroux, 2003), 130.

40.   Allan Greer, *Property and Dispossession: Natives, Empires and Land in Early Modern North America* (New York: Cambridge University Press, 2018), 247.

41.   For a rich account of Locke's activities in this period and their larger context, see David Armitage, "John Locke, Carolina, and the *Two Treatises of Government*," *Political Theory* 32, no. 5 (October 2004). It's also worth noting that some scholars have tried to absolve Locke, insisting that he was little more than a gun for hire; see, for example, Holly Brewer, "Slavery-Entangled Philosophy," *Aeon*, September 12, 2018, https://aeon.co/essays/does-lockes-entanglement-with-slavery-undermine-his-philosophy.

42.   No matter that North America's temperate zones had been dense with farming people before European illnesses struck, as Ronald Wright notes in *A Short History of Progress* (Toronto: House of Anansi Press, 2004), 113.

43.   This dynamic was contingent on local ecology. As Greer shows, conflicts over livestock were less intense in northern New France, in what we now call Canada, largely because cold winters meant animals had to be kept close to home and stall-fed—a contributing factor, he speculates, to the comparatively peaceful relations between settlers and Indigenous peoples (though it should go without saying that the bar is very low).

44.   Anderson, *Creatures of Empire*, 116.

45.   Anderson, *Creatures of Empire*, 7. The phrase "ungulate irruption" originally came from Elinor Melville, *A Plague of Sheep: Environmental Consequences of the Conquest of Mexico* (United Kingdom: Cambridge University Press, 1994).

46.   Derek Gow, *Bringing Back the Beaver: The Story of One Man's Quest to Rewild Britain's Waterways* (White River Junction, CT: Chelsea Green, 2020), 18–19.

47.   Hudson's Bay Company History Foundation, "Beaver Hats," https://www.hbcheritage.ca/things/fashion-pop/beaver-hats.

48.   Cronon, *Changes in the Land*, 91.

49.   Jennifer Ott, "'Ruining' the Rivers in the Snake Country: The Hudson's Bay Company's Fur Desert Policy," *Oregon Historical Quarterly* 104, no. 2 (Summer 2003), 172.

50.   Ott, "'Ruining' the Rivers," 179.

51.   Leila Philip, *Beaver Land: How One Weird Rodent Made America* (New York: Twelve, 2022), 261–62; Liz McKenzie, "Beaver—Ecology," Encounters North, August 2, 2017, https://www.encountersnorth. org/beaver-summary/2017/8/2/beaver-ecology.

52.   Ben Goldfarb, *Eager: The Surprising, Secret Life of Beavers and Why They Matter* (White River Junction, VT: Chelsea Green, 2018), 6; on the landscape after beavers disappeared, Cronon, *Changes in the Land*, 106.

53.   Adam Hadhazy, "Rivers Will Become a Bigger Boon to River Water Quality as US West Warms," *Stanford Earth Matters Magazine*, November 8, 2022, https://earth.stanford.edu/news/beavers-will-become-bigger-boon-river-water-quality-us-west-warms.

54.   Chris Jordan and Emily Fairfax, "Want to Fight Climate Change and Drought at the Same Time? Bring Back Beavers," *Los Angeles Times*, July 25, 2022, https://www.latimes.com/opinion/story/2022-07-25/climate-change-beavers-wetland-restoration.

55.   Hadhazy, "Rivers."

56.   Isobel Whitcomb, "Beaver Dams Help Wildfire-Ravaged Ecosystems Recover Long after Flames Subside," *Scientific American*, February 7, 2022, https://www.scientificamerican.com/article/beaver-dams-help-wildfire-ravaged-ecosystems-recover-long-after-flames-subside/. Beaver dams help populations rebound by staving off fire-related water contamination.

57.   Michelle Nijhuis, "The Miracle of the Commons," *Aeon*, May 4, 2021, https://aeon.co/essays/the-tragedy-of-the-commons-is-a-false-and-dangerous-myth.

58.   Erik Nordman, *The Uncommon Knowledge of Elinor Ostrom* (Washington, DC: Island Press, 2021), 15.

59.   Amanda Huron, *Carving Out the Commons: Tenant Organizing and Housing Cooperatives in Washington, D.C.* (Minneapolis: University of Minnesota Press, 2018), 35–36.

60.   "In Spain, 1,000-Year-Old Court Settles Water Disputes," Agence France-Presse, July 10, 2017, https://www.ndtv.com/world-news/in-spain-1-000-year-old-court-settles-water-disputes-1722770.

61.   Nordman, *Uncommon Knowledge*, 61–80.

62.   Elinor Ostrom, Marco A. Janssen, and John M. Anderies, "Going Beyond Panaceas," PNAS 104, no. 39 (September 2007), https://doi.org/10.1073/pnas.0701886104; Elinor Ostrom, "Beyond Markets and States: Polycentric Governance of Complex Economic Systems," Nobel Prize lecture, Stockholm, December 8, 2009, https://www.nobelprize.org/uploads/2018/06/ostrom_lecture.pdf.

63. This is a complicated and murky point, as activist and professor Shiri Pasternak reminded me. In the 2014 decision *Tsilhqot'in Nation v. British Columbia*, the Supreme Court repudiated *terra nullius*. But the justices never gave another basis for Canadian sovereignty, which means the rationale still hangs in the shadows as a justification for underlying Crown title.

64. Arthur Manuel and Grand Chief Ronald Derrickson, *The Reconciliation Manifesto: Recovering the Land, Rebuilding the Economy* (Toronto: James Lorimer, 2017), 102.

65. John Borrows, *Recovering Canada: The Resurgence of Indigenous Law* (Toronto: University of Toronto Press, 2017), 89.

66. Robert T. Anderson, "Aboriginal Title in the Canadian Legal System: The Story of *Delgamuukw v. British Columbia*," in *Indian Law Stories*, ed. Carole E. Goldberg, Kevin K. Washburn, and Philip P. Frickey (St. Paul, MN: Foundation, 2011).

67. Leslie Hall Pinder, "Carriers of No: After the Land Claims Trial," *Index on Censorship* 28, no. 4 (1999), 65–75.

68. Ian Gill, "Delgamuukw: The Man and the Momentous Ruling," *Tyee*, January 12, 2022, https://thetyee.ca/Analysis/2022/01/12/Delgamuukw-Man-Momentous-Ruling/.

69. Shiri Pasternak, "25 Years On, the Battle to Enforce a Monumental Supreme Court Decision Rages On," *Canada's National Observer*, December 10, 2022, https://www.nationalobserver.com/2022/12/10/opinion/25-years-supreme-court-delgamuukw-decision.

70. Martin Lukacs and Shiri Pasternak, "Industry, Government Pushed to Abolish Aboriginal Title at Issue in Wet'suwet'en Stand-off, Docs Reveal," *Narwhal*, February 7, 2020, https://thenarwhal.ca/industry-government-pushed-to-abolish-aboriginal-title-at-issue-in-wetsuweten-stand-off-docs-reveal; Arthur Manuel and Grand Chief Ronald M. Derrickson, *Unsettling Canada: A National Wake-Up Call* (Toronto: Between the Lines, 2015), 59.

71. According to research by the Yellowhead Institute, Indigenous and Northern Affairs Canada spends over one hundred million public dollars a year to undermine Indigenous sovereignty, making it one of the Canadian government's biggest consumers of legal services and a telling indication of the government's commitment to keeping the extractive economy churning. Yellowhead Institute, *Cash Back*, May 2021, 46, https://cashback.yellowheadinstitute.org/wp-content/uploads/2021/05/Cash-Back-A-Yellowhead-Institute-Red-Paper.pdf.

72. Pasternak, "25 Years On."

73. Unist'ot'en, "No Pipelines: Background of the Campaign," https://unistoten.camp/no-pipelines/background-of-the-campaign/.

74. Manuel and Derrickson, *Unsettling Canada*, 116, 185.

75. Manuel is clear that he's not anti-development but maintains that projects must respect the integrity of land and prioritize clean energy. For more on these issues, read the *Land Back* and *Cash Back* reports from the Yellowhead Institute.

76. Emily Atkin, "Why Animal Rights Is the Next Frontier for the Left," *New Republic*, March 14, 2019, https://newrepublic.com/article/153302/animal-rights-next-frontier-left.

77. Rochelle Baker, "Unchecked Climate Change Puts Canada's West Coast in Hot Water," *Canada's National Observer*, March 23, 2023, https://www.nationalobserver.com/2023/03/23/news/unchecked-climate-change-puts-canada-west-coast-hot-water.

78. Creating such a system would present plenty of challenges, to be sure, but trustees or proxies could effectively advocate on the behalf of life forms that lack sentience or speech, as the example of the Magpie River guardians shows.

79. United Nations Environment Programme and International Livestock Research Institute, *Preventing the Next Pandemic: Zoonotic Diseases and How to Break the Chain of Transmission* (Nairobi: United Nations Environment Programme, 2020), 22; Andrew P. Dobson et al., "Ecology and Economics for Pandemic Prevention," *Science* 369, no. 6502 (July 2020), https://www.science.org/doi/10.1126/science.abc3189; Caroline Chen, Irena Hwang, and Al Shaw, "On the Edge," ProPublica, February 27, 2023, https://www.propublica.org/article/pandemic-spillover-outbreak-guinea-forest-clearing.

80. UN Environment Programme, *Preventing the Next Pandemic.*

81 Sheila Wertz-Kanounnikoff, "Preventing Future Pandemics Starts with Protecting Our Forests," Sustainable Development Goals Knowledge Hub, July 6, 2021.

82. Jeff Sebo, *Saving Animals, Saving Ourselves: Why Animals Matter for Pandemics, Climate Change, and Other Catastrophes* (New York: Oxford University Press, 2022), 48. Information on antibiotic use in Canada can be found here: http://omafra.gov.on.ca/english/livestock/animalcare/amr/index.html.

83. Michael Greger, "Primary Pandemic Prevention," *American Journal of Lifestyle Medicine* 15, no. 5 (September–October 2021), https://www.ncbi.nlm.nih.gov/pmc/articles/PMC8504329/.

84. American Public Health Association, "Precautionary Moratorium on New and Expanding Concentrated Animal Feeding Operations," November 5, 2019, https://www.apha.org/policies-and-advocacy/public-health-policy-statements/policy-database/2020/01/13/precautionary-moratori-

um-on-new-and-expanding-concentrated-animal-feeding-operations.

85.   One movement trying to precipitate this shift is One Health.

86.   Oliver Milman and Nina Lakhani, "Atlanta Shooting Part of Alarming US Crackdown on Environmental Defenders," *Guardian*, February 2, 2023, https://www.theguardian.com/environment/2023/feb/02/atlanta-shooting-manuel-teran-crackdown-environmental-defenders; Animal Justice, "'Ag Gag' Laws," https://animaljustice.ca/issues/ag-gag-laws.

87.   J. H. Dales, *Pollution Property & Prices: An Essay in Policy-Making and Economics* (Toronto: University of Toronto Press, 1968).

88.   Lisa Song, "Cap and Trade Is Supposed to Solve Climate Change, but Oil and Gas Company Emissions Are Up," ProPublica, November 15, 2019, https://www.propublica.org/article/cap-and-trade-is-supposed-to-solve-climate-change-but-oil-and-gas-company-emissions-are-up.

89.   Troy Gabriel Wesley Vettese, "Limits and Cornucopianism: A History of Neo-Liberal Environmental Thought, 1920–2007," (PhD dissertation, New York University, 2019), 128.

90.   Naomi Klein, *On Fire: The (Burning) Case for a Green New Deal* (Toronto: Knopf Canada, 2019), 269.

91.   Astra Taylor and Leah Hunt-Hendrix, "One for All," *New Republic*, August 26, 2019, https://newrepublic.com/article/154623/green-new-deal-solidarity-solution-climate-change-global-warming. For more on the concept of a solidarity state see our forthcoming book *Solidarity: The Past, Present, and Future of a World-Changing Idea*.

92.   Patricia Lane, "How an Anishinaabe Lawyer Is Helping Indigenous Communities Strengthen Their Legal Traditions," *Canada's National Observer*, December 14, 2020, https://www.nationalobserver.com/2020/12/14/opinion/anishinaabe-lawyer-lindsay-keegitah-borrows-legal-tradition-reconciliation.

93.   Government of the Netherlands, "Circular Dutch Economy by 2050," https://www.government.nl/topics/circular-economy/circular-dutch-economy-by-2050.

94.   Plato, *Critias*, trans. Robert Gregg Bury (Cambridge, MA: Harvard University Press, 1929), http://www.perseus.tufts.edu/hopper/text?doc=Plat.+Criti.+111.

95.   Rivka Galchen, "The Myth of the Alpha Wolf," *New Yorker*, March 25, 2023, https://www.newyorker.com/science/elements/the-myth-of-the-alpha-wolf.

95.   Luis P. Villarreal, "Are Viruses Alive?," *Scientific American*, Au-

gust 8, 2008, https://www.scientificamerican.com/article/are-viruses-alive-2004/; for more on my father's work, see Ethan Will Taylor, ResearchGate, https://www.researchgate.net/profile/Ethan-Taylor-2; Ethan Will Taylor, UNC Greensboro faculty page, https://chem.uncg.edu/person/e-will-taylor/.

Chapter 5: Escaping the Burrow

1.   Franz Kafka Museum, "The Workers' Accident Insurance Institute," https://kafkamuseum.cz/en/franz-kafka/employment/the-workmens-accident-insurance-institute/.

2.   M. Wasserman, "Changing Minds, Saving Lives: Franz Kafka as a Key Industrial Reformer," *East European Quarterly* 35, no. 4 (2001), 473–82, PMID: 18286740; Steele D. Burrow, "Risk and Insurance in the Writings of Franz Kafka" (PhD dissertation, University of California, 1994), 77.

3.   For Kafka's collected professional works, see *Franz Kafka: The Office Writings*, ed. Stanley Corngold, Jack Greenberg, and Benno Wagner, trans. Eric Patton and Ruth Hein (Princeton: Princeton University Press, 2008). For the 720,000-worker figure, see Louis Begley, "Before the Law," *New Republic*, May 6, 2009, https://newrepublic.com/article/64034/the-law.

4.   Burrow, "Risk and Insurance," 3–4.

5.   Burrow, "Risk and Insurance," 91.

6.   Quoted in Bernard Lahire, "Kafka et le travail de la domination," *Actuel Marx* 49, no. 1 (2011), 46–59, https://www.cairn-int.info/journal-actuel-marx-2011-1-page-46.htm.

7.   *Kafka: The Office Writings*, 20.

8.   Quoted in François Ewald, "Insurance and Risk," in *Embracing Risk: The Changing Culture of Insurance and Responsibility*, ed. Tom Baker and Jonathan Simon (Chicago, University of Chicago Press, 2002), 208.

9.   Quoted in Deborah Stone, "Beyond Moral Hazard: Insurance as Moral Opportunity," in *Embracing Risk*, 60.

10.   Ulrich Beck, *Risk Society: Towards a New Modernity* (Newbury Park, CA: Sage, 1992), 46.

11.   Grant McCool, "AIG 2008 Bonuses Spawned 73 Millionaires: Cuomo," Reuters, March 18, 2009, https://www.reuters.com/article/us-aig-bonuses-cuomo-sb-idUSTRE52G5AP20090318.

12.   At some point, the word may have been fused with the Arabic word *rizq*, which means provision or wealth.

13.   Hannah Farber, *Underwriters of the United States: How Insurance Shaped the American Founding* (Chapel Hill: University of North Carolina Press, 2021), 6.

14.   Guy Faulconbridge, "Some Facts About London's Role in Insuring the Slave Trade," *Insurance Journal*, June 19, 2020, https://www.insurancejournal.com/news/international/2020/06/19/572859.htm.

15.   Guy Faulconbridge and Kate Holton, "Lloyd's of London to Pay for 'Shameful' Atlantic Slave Trade Role," Reuters, June 18, 2020, https://www.reuters.com/article/us-minneapolis-police-protests-lloydsofl/lloyds-of-london-to-pay-for-shameful-atlantic-slave-trade-role-idUSKBN23P0SM.

16.   Yusra Murad, "As Coronavirus Surges, 'Medicare for All' Support Hits 9-Month High," Morning Consult, April 1, 2020, https://morningconsult.com/2020/04/01/medicare-for-all-coronavirus-pandemic/.

17.   Council of Canadians, "New Data Shows Pharmaceutical Lobbying of the Federal Government Has Quadrupled Since NDP-Liberal Confidence-and-Supply Agreement," February 9, 2023, news release, https://canadians.org/media/pharmaceutical-lobbying-press-release/; Sharon Batt, *The Big Money Club: Revealing the Players and Their Campaign to Stop Pharmacare* (Ottawa: Canadian Federation of Nurses Unions, 2019), https://nursesunions.ca/wp-content/uploads/2019/03/CFNU_bigmoneyclub_low.pdf.

18.   Vivek Agrawal et al., *Global Insurance Report 2023: Reimagining Life Insurance*, McKinsey, November 16, 2021, https://www.mckinsey.com/industries/financial-services/our-insights/global-insurance-report-2023-reimagining-life-insurance.

19.   Reclaim Finance, "Lloyd's of London Still on a Fossil Fuel Diet," press release, April 26, 2023, https://reclaimfinance.org/site/en/2023/04/06/lloyds-of-london-still-on-a-fossil-fuel-diet/. This report comes with a disclaimer noting that, shortly before its release, one of Lloyd's of London's major managing agents announced it would no longer underwrite certain energy projects, possibly reducing that 40 percent number; an updated estimate was forthcoming at the time of writing.

20.   BlackRock, "BlackRock Study: Global Insurers Are Future-Proofing Portfolios Amidst Shifting Markets," news release, September 27, 2022, https://www.blackrock.com/corporate/newsroom/press-releases/article/corporate-one/press-releases/global-Insurers-are-future-proofing-portfolios-amidst-shifting-markets.

21. Geoff Dembicki, "The $1 Trillion Storm: How a Single Hurricane Could Rupture the World Economy," *Vice*, March 3, 2019, https://www.vice.com/en/article/wjm78x/the-dollar1-trillion-storm-how-a-single-hurricane-could-rupture-the-world-economy.

22. Quoted in Dembicki, "The $1 Trillion Storm."

23. Amanda Cantrell, "Backstopping Catastrophes Was a Quiet Business—Then Came the Hurricanes," *Institutional Investor*, April 4, 2018, https://www.institutionalinvestor.com/article/b17mmbhxyk9g-pc/backstopping-catastrophes-was-a-quiet-business-then-came-the-hurricanes.

24. Kate Aronoff, "Florida and the Insurance Industry Weren't Built to Withstand a Flooded World," *New Republic*, October 12, 2022, https://newrepublic.com/article/168103/florida-flood-insurance-hurriane-ian.

25. Susie Cagle and Vivian Ho, "'Not Our Mission': Private Fire Crews Protect the Insured, Not the Public," *Guardian*, November 3, 2019, https://www.theguardian.com/us-news/2019/nov/03/not-our-mission-private-fire-crews-protect-the-insured-not-the-public; Naomi Klein, *This Changes Everything: Capitalism vs. the Climate* (Toronto: Knopf Canada, 2014), 45.

26. Beck, *Risk Society*, 23.

27. Carl Meyer, "Trans Mountain Wins Approval to Keep Insurers Secret," *Canada's National Observer*, April 29, 2021, https://www.nationalobserver.com/2021/04/29/news/trans-mountain-approval-keep-insurers-secret.

28. The Stand.earth website has a chart tracking which insurance companies have and have not ruled out insuring Trans Mountain: https://stand.earth/resources/un-insuring-trans-mountain/.

29. Ian Hacking, *The Emergence of Probability: A Philosophical Study of Early Ideas about Probability, Induction and Statistical Inference* (Cambridge: Cambridge University Press, 2006).

30. Blaise Pascal, *Pensées* (1670), trans. W. F. Trotter (London: Dover, 2003), 66.

31. Viviana A. Rotman Zelizer argues that these concerns slowed the growth of life insurance markets in the US and France in the nineteenth century in *Morals and Markets: The Development of Life Insurance in the United States* (New York: Columbia University Press, 2017).

32. John Fabian Witt, *The Accidental Republic: Crippled Workingmen, Destitute Widows, and the Remaking of American Law* (Cambridge, MA: Harvard University Press, 2009), 44.

33. US Social Security Administration, "Social Security History: Otto von Bismarck," https://www.ssa.gov/history/ottob.html.

34. Sarah Laskow, "How Retirement Was Invented," *Atlantic*, October 24, 2014, https://www.theatlantic.com/business/archive/2014/10/how-retirement-was-invented/381802/; Michael Sainato, "'At 75, I Still Have to Work': Millions of Americans Can't Afford to Retire," *Guardian*, December 13, 2021, https://www.theguardian.com/money/2021/dec/13/americans-retire-work-social-security; Benefits Canada, "Just a Third of Older Canadians Believe They Can Financially Afford to Retire: Survey," December 21, 2022, https://www.benefitscanada.com/pensions/retirement/just-a-third-of-older-canadians-believe-they-can-financially-afford-to-retire-survey/.

35. Gregory P. Guyton, "A Brief History of Workers' Compensation," *Iowa Orthopaedic Journal* 19 (1999), https://www.ncbi.nlm.nih.gov/pmc/articles/PMC1888620/.

36. R. Blake Brown and Noelle Yhard, "'The Harshness and Injustice of the Common Law Rule ... Has Frequently Been Commented Upon': Debating Contributory Negligence in Canada, 1914–1949," *Dalhousie Law Journal* 36, no. 1 (2013), 144.4.

37. Association of Workers' Compensation Boards of Canada, "Workers Compensation," https://awcbc.org/en/about/workers-compensation/.

38. Crystal Eastman, *Work-Accidents and the Law*, vol. 2 of *The Pittsburgh Survey*, ed. Paul Underwood Kellogg (New York: Charities Publication Committee, 1910), 80.

39. Joanna Scutts, "How Crystal Eastman Fought for Equality," *New Republic*, January 13, 2020, https://newrepublic.com/article/156180/crystal-eastman-fought-equality.

40. Quoted in Amy Aronson, *Crystal Eastman: A Revolutionary Life* (New York: Oxford University Press, 2020), 96; see also Bruce Dearstyne, "Crystal Eastman and New York's Workers' Compensation Law," *New York Almanac*, January 5, 2022.

41. For Perkins's remarkable life story, see Kirstin Downey, *The Woman Behind the New Deal: The Life of Frances Perkins, FDR's Secretary of Labor and His Moral Conscience* (New York: Nan A. Talese, 2009); for more on how workers' compensation programs laid the groundwork for other social insurance programs, see Price V. Fishback and Shawn Everett Kantor, *A Prelude to the Welfare State: The Origins of Workers' Compensation* (Chicago: University of Chicago Press, 2000).

42. Franklin D. Roosevelt, "FDR's Statements on Social Security," Social Security Administration, https://www.ssa.gov/history/fdrstmts.html.

43. Michael Powell, "Bank Accused of Pushing Mortgage Deals on

Blacks," *New York Times*, June 6, 2009, https://www.nytimes.com/2009/06/07/us/07baltimore.html.

44.   Jacob S. Hacker, *The New Economic Insecurity and the Decline of the American Dream* (New York: Oxford University Press, 2019).

45.   PressProgress, "Canada's Social Spending Is Still Among the Lowest in the Industrialized World," March 16, 2019, https://pressprogress.ca/canadas-social-spending-is-still-among-the-lowest-in-the-industrialized-world/.

46.   Canadians owe approximately $1.83 for each $1 they have of disposable income. Canada's total credit card debt now exceeds $100 billion for the first time. Ephraim Vecina, "Canadian Credit Card Debt Continues to Surge," *Canadian Mortgage Professional Magazine*, March 10, 2023, https://www.mpamag.com/ca/mortgage-industry/industry-trends/canadian-credit-card-debt-continues-to-surge/439117; Christin Dobby, "Overwhelmed by Debt': Canadians are Hurting as Their Debt Problems Mount," *Toronto Star*, May 26, 2023, https://www.thestar.com/business/2023/05/26/can-we-pay-our-bills-new-reports-shed-light-on-the-depth-of-canadians-debt-problems.html. Trading Economics, "Canada Households Credit Market Debt to Disposable Income," https://tradingeconomics.com/canada/households-debt-to-income.

47.   Francesca Ortegren, "State of Retirement Finances: 2021 Edition," Clever Real Estate, April 10, 2023, https://listwithclever.com/research/retirement-finances-2021/#debt; Sharanjit Uppal, "Debt and Assets among Senior Canadian Families," *Insights on Canadian Society*, April 3, 2019, https://www150.statcan.gc.ca/n1/pub/75-006-x/2019001/article/00005-eng.htm.

48.   Erika Shaker, "What to Know about Student Debt," *Maclean's*, August 11, 2022, https://macleans.ca/economy/canadian-economy-guide-2022-student-debt/; Hoyes, Michalos & Associates, "Student Debt Crisis—A Generation Buried in Student Debt," Annual Bankruptcy Study, 2021, https://www.hoyes.com/press/joe-debtor/the-student-debtor/; Emma Kerr and Sarah Wood, "See How Average Student Loan Debt Has Changed," *US News and World Report*, September 13, 2022, https://www.usnews.com/education/best-colleges/paying-for-college/articles/see-how-student-loan-borrowing-has-changed. American borrowers have fewer protections available to them. In Canada, student debt drives a significant number of insolvencies; in the US, student loans are not dischargeable in bankruptcy.

49.   Lori Culbert, "How High Variable-Rate Mortgages Cripple Homeowners, Hobble Housing Market," *Vancouver Sun*, April 29, 2023, https://vancouversun.com/business/mortgages/how-high-variable-rate-mortgages-cripple-homeowners-hobble-housing-market.

50. Ipsos, "Nearly Half of Canadians (48%) Are $200 or Less Away from Financial Insolvency," October 28, 2019, https://www.ipsos.com/en-ca/news-polls/Canadians-and-Bankruptcy-Oct-2019.

51. David Parkinson, "Mortgage Debt a 'Ticking Time Bomb' as Renewals Come Up, Economists Warn," *Globe and Mail*, May 18, 2023, https://www.theglobeandmail.com/business/commentary/article-mortgage-debt-crisis-renewals/; Rachelle Younglai and Mark Rendell, "Bank of Canada Says Mortgage Payments Could Spike as Much as 40 Per Cent," *Globe and Mail*, May 18, 2023, https://www.theglobeandmail.com/business/economy/article-bank-of-canada-mortgage-payments/; Kayla Rosen, "Many Manitoba Residents Regret the Amount of Debt They've Taken On: Report," CTV News, January 16, 2023, https://winnipeg.ctvnews.ca/many-manitoba-residents-regret-the-amount-of-debt-they-ve-taken-on-report-1.6232339.

52. Zoë Richards, "White House Shines Light on Republicans Who Are Criticizing Student Debt Cancellation after Getting Their PPP Loans Forgiven," NBC, August 25, 2022, https://www.nbcnews.com/politics/white-house/white-house-shines-light-republicans-are-criticizing-student-debt-canc-rcna44904; Andy Nguyen, "Businesses Associated with GOP Politicians Had Pandemic Government Loans Forgiven," Austin-American Statesman, September 6, 2022, https://www.statesman.com/story/news/politics/politifact/2022/09/06/fact-check-ppp-loans-forgiven-republicans-matt-gaetz-marjorie-taylor-greene/65470173007/.

53. The racial politics of debt are complex and beyond the scope of this chapter. While debt has historically been deployed to maintain racial hierarchies, there is also a long and disturbing tradition of anti-Semitism directed against creditors.

54. Aristotle, *The Politics*, trans. Benjamin Jowett, Book 1, Chapter 10.

55. Alex Mayyasi, "Of Money and Morals," *Aeon*, July 7, 2017, https://aeon.co/essays/how-did-usury-stop-being-a-sin-and-become-respectable-finance; see also Edward L. Glaeser and José Scheinkman, "Neither a Borrower Nor a Lender Be: An Economic Analysis of Interest Restrictions and Usury Laws," *Journal of Law & Economics* 41, no. 1, 1998, 1–36, https://doi.org/10.1086/467383.

56. These restrictions vary, of course, and yet lenders are rarely if ever lionized. In Islamic finance, charging interest is also subject to strict moral prohibitions.

57. Edward Chancellor, *The Price of Time: The Real Story of Interest* (Washington, DC: Atlantic Monthly Press, 2022), 25.

58. Quoted in Chancellor, *Price of Time*, 26. The English Parliament eliminated the last prohibitions on charging interest in 1623.

59. Bruce H. Mann, *Republic of Debtors: Bankruptcy in the Age of American Independence* (Cambridge, MA: Harvard University Press, 2009).

60. Astra Taylor, "Make Americans' Crushing Debt Disappear," *New York Times*, July 2, 2021, https://www.nytimes.com/2021/07/02/opinion/student-loan-medical-debt-forgiveness.html.

61. Brian Gettler, *Colonialism's Currency: Money, State, and First Nations in Canada, 1820–1950* (Montreal: McGill-Queen's University Press, 2020), 102.

62. *The Other Side of the Ledger: An Indian View of the Hudson's Bay Company*, directed by Martin Defalco and Willie Dunn, National Film Board of Canada, 1972, 42 min., https://www.nfb.ca/film/other_side_of_the_ledger/.

63. In this way, the mortgage offered an appealing means of circumventing the prohibition on charging interest, as noted by K-Sue Park in "Money, Mortgages, and the Conquest of America," *Law & Social Inquiry* 41, no. 4 (2016), 1006–1035. For an in-depth discussion of credit during the colonial period, see Claire Priest, *Credit Nation: Property Laws and Institutions in Early America* (Princeton: Princeton University Press, 2022).

64. "Indigenous debt created through colonial lending practices, often predatory in nature, enabled the seizure of indigenous land. Land therefore became a money equivalent not through positive sale, but through debt and loss; foreclosure was a tool of indigenous dispossession": Park, "Money, Mortgages," 1009; K-Sue Park, "Race, Innovation, and Financial Growth: The Example of Foreclosure," in *Histories of Racial Capitalism*, ed. Destin Jenkins and Justin Leroy (New York: Columbia University Press, 2021).

65. Park, "Money, Mortgages," 1012.

66. Thomas Jefferson to James Madison, September 6, 1789, https://founders.archives.gov/documents/Jefferson/01-15-02-0375-0003.

67. Thomas Jefferson to William Henry Harrison, February 27, 1803, https://founders.archives.gov/documents/Jefferson/01-39-02-0500.

68. Jefferson died owing around US$2 million, adjusted for inflation. During his lifetime, Jefferson used enslaved people as collateral to negotiate better terms with his European creditors, a common practice. In Canada, stolen land, and even not-yet-stolen land, was used as collateral, with loans issued on the "future promise of expansion and Indigenous removal" on the London Stock Exchange. In the US, plundered wealth helped pay back the young country's debts to England. And, of course, there was the enslaved labour of African people, whose lives were routinely used as securities. Before the US Civil

War, an entire financial services industry was built on slave-backed debt, including the Bank of Charleston, which eventually became part of Wells Fargo—the bank that issued subprime mortgages to "mud people." At the same time, a variety of companies sold insurance policies to cover the enslaved human beings backing all of these money-making bonds and loans, including Aetna, New York Life, and, predictably, AIG.

69.   Katherine Aske, *Finance in the Fields: Investors, Lenders, and the Future of Farmland in Alberta* (Edmonton: Parkland Institute, 2022), 2, https://assets.nationbuilder.com/parklandinstitute/pages/1979/attachments/original/1654755581/parkland-report-finance-in-the-fields.pdf?1654755581.

70.   Darrin Qualman et al., "Forever Young? The Crisis of Generational Renewal on Canada's Farms," *Canadian Food Studies* 5, no. 3 (September 2018), 100–27. As they say on page 104: "Looking over a longer period—the 31 years encompassing 1986 to 2016, inclusive—the picture is only slightly better. During that time, farmers were able to retain only two percent of their gross revenues from the markets (i.e., with state subsidies subtracted out); inputs makers and other corporations captured the other 98 percent."

71.   Stats Canada, "Farm Debt Outstanding, classified by lender," https://www150.statcan.gc.ca/t1/tbl1/en/tv.action?pid=3210005101.

72.   Qualman et al., "Forever Young?"

73.   Lauren Foster, "Farmland Is an Inflation Hedge. How to Invest," *Barron's*, July 29, 2022, https://www.barrons.com/articles/farmland-inflation-hedge-how-to-invest-51659043559.

74.   Ian James and Geoff Hing, "Investors Are Buying Up Rural Arizona Farmland to Sell the Water to Urban Homebuilders," *Arizona Republic*, November 26, 2021, https://www.azcentral.com/story/news/local/arizona-environment/2021/11/25/investors-buying-up-arizona-farmland-valuable-water-rights/8655703002/; Lucy Kafanov, "Wall Street Is Thirsty for Its Next Big Investment Opportunity: The West's Vanishing Water," CNN, March 22, 2023, https://www.cnn.com/2023/03/22/business/southwest-water-colorado-river-wall-street-climate/index.html.

75.   A 2023 study published in the *Industrial Relations Journal* analyzed fifty years of data from around the world to come to this conclusion (Giorgos Gouzoulis, "What Do Indebted Employees Do? Financialisation and the Decline of Industrial Action," January 2, 2023, https://doi.org/10.1111/irj.12391).

76.   Tony Davis, "PCs, NDP, Greens Promise to Create Land Bank to Preserve Island Farming Industry," CBC, April 4, 2019, https://www.cbc.ca/news/canada/prince-edward-island/pei-farmbank-promise-1.5084933.

77. Lee O. Sanderlin, "'Being Poor Is Not a Crime': Mississippi Residents among 20,000 to Get Probation Debt Erased," *Mississippi Clarion Ledger*, October 29, 2021, https://www.clarionledger.com/story/news/politics/2021/10/29/rolling-jubilee-fund-debt-collective-pay-off-private-probation-debt-mississippi-florida/6180764001/.

78. Rachel M. Cohen, "How to Cancel $3.2 Million of Debt for 20,000 People Who Went Through the Carceral System," *Intercept*, October 29, 2021, https://theintercept.com/2021/10/29/debt-cancellation-carceral-bail/.

79. We devised the Rolling Jubilee in 2012, during the aftershocks of the global financial crisis. Millions had lost their homes, and the economy was in shambles. It was hugely popular, but we always knew it wasn't a solution to the social problems we were highlighting. You cannot buy and abolish all the predatory debt in the country—we need structural change. So we put Rolling Jubilee to rest and founded the Debt Collective, which organizes to build debtor power. We briefly revived the Rolling Jubilee due to the Covid-19 pandemic.

80. Georgetown Law Civil Rights Clinic and Campaign Legal Center, *Can't Pay, Can't Vote*, 2019, 20, https://campaignlegal.org/document/cant-pay-cant-vote-national-survey-modern-poll-tax.

81. Lucero Herrera et al., *Work, Pay, or Go to Jail: Court-Ordered Community Service in Los Angeles* (Los Angeles: UCLA Labor Center, 2019), https://www.labor.ucla.edu/publication/communityservice/.

82. According to Stephanie Ben-Ishai and Arash Nayerahmadi, US and Canadian systems are largely comparable, with two key differences: probation services are not privatized in Canada, and "provinces do not charge interest on court fees and fines, nor do they add late penalties." Stephanie Ben-Ishai and Arash Nayerahmadi, "Over-Indebted Criminals in Canada," *Manitoba Law Journal* 42, no. 4 (2019), 222, https://themanitobalawjournal.com/wp-content/uploads/articles/MLJ_42.4/42.4_Ben-Ishai.pdf

83. Emily Knox, "Poverty Is Not a Crime—So Why Is Montreal Still Ticketing the Unhoused?" CBC, October 27, 2021, https://www.cbc.ca/amp/1.6221531

84. Emily Knox et al, "Ticketing Poverty: An Analysis of the Discriminatory Impacts of Public Intoxication By-Laws on People Experiencing Homelessness in Montreal," *Dalhousie Journal of Legal Studies* 32, no. 6 (2023), 157.

85. Knox, "Poverty Is Not a Crime."

86. Knox, "Poverty Is Not a Crime"; see also Ben-Ishai and Nayerahmadi, "Over-Indebted Criminals."

87. Simon Kent, "Policing Toronto's Panhandlers," *Toronto Sun*, October 7,

2012, https://torontosun.com/2012/10/07/policing-torontos-panhan-dlers. For more info on the budget, here is the breakdown: "We esti-mate that the actual cost to the Toronto Police Service of issuing the SSA tickets was $189,936 in 2009, and $936,0191 over the past eleven years. Note that this does not include the cost of processing tickets, or any follow-up overhead (for instance if a ticket is challenged in court, or if a bench warrant is issued for non-payment of tickets). This also amounts to 16,847 hours of police time, which begs the question: Is this a reasonable use of resources, and may there be other crimes de-serving of more attention? These costs have been incurred by the City for the collection of only $8,086.56 in fines paid over this eleven year period": Bill O'Grady, Stephen Gaetz, and Kristy Buccieri, *Can I See Your ID? The Policing of Youth Homelessness in Toronto* (Toronto: JFCY & Homeless Hub, 2011), 10. See also this article, which men-tions a more recent study: *Star* Editorial Board, "Ontario Should Re-peal the Safe Streets Act," *Toronto Star*, July 10, 2019, https://www.thestar.com/opinion/editorials/2019/07/10/ontario-should-repeal-the-safe-streets-act.html.

88.   *Star* Editorial Board, "Ontario Should Repeal."

89.   The average annual inmate expenditure for federal correctional services in Canada in 2019 was $120,589. For slightly older figures, see "Update on Costs of Incarceration," Office of the Parliamentary Budget Officer, March 22, 2018. Numbers vary across American states and municipali-ties. In New York City it costs an eye-watering $556,539.00 per inmate per year, or over $1,500 a day, to jail someone, https://comptroller.nyc. gov/newsroom/comptroller-stringer-cost-of-incarceration-per-person-in-new-york-city-skyrockets-to-all-time-high-2/.

90.   Tom Cardoso and Molly Hayes, "Canadian Cities' Police Spending Ranges from One-10th to Nearly a Third of Total Budgets, Globe Analysis Finds," *Globe and Mail*, August 16, 2020, https://www.the-globeandmail.com/canada/article-canadian-cities-police-spending-ranges-from-one-10th-to-nearly-a/; Lam Thuy Vo, "More on Cops and Less on Housing: Here's How Minneapolis Spends Its Money," Buzzfeed News, May 29, 2020, https://www.buzzfeednews.com/arti-cle/lamvo/minneapolis-spends-a-hell-of-a-lot-on-policing-and-much.

91.   Defund the Police Coalition, "The People's Vision: Community Re-sponses to the City of Montreal's 2021 Budget," November 26, 2020.

92.   Felisha Adam, "Montreal Police to Receive Another Budget Boost, Community Groups Call on Citizens to Take Action," CityNews Mon-treal, December 12, 2022, https://montreal.citynews.ca/2022/12/12/ spvm-budget-boost/; Bob Becken, "'Defund the Police' Calls in Canada Began in 2020. Today, Budgets Continue to Climb," CBC, February 12, 2023, https://www.cbc.ca/radio/day6/defund-police-2023-budgets-grow-1.6741711.

93. Mariame Kaba and Andrea J. Ritchie, "Reimagining the Commons Is One Step Toward a Future Without Police," *Truthout*, September 16, 2022, https://truthout.org/articles/reimagining-the-commons-is-one-step-toward-a-future-without-police/.

94. White Bird Clinic, "What Is CAHOOTS?" October 29, 2020, https://whitebirdclinic.org/what-is-cahoots/.

95. John Locke, *Second Treatise on Civil Government* (London, 1690), ch. 17, *§123*.

96. William Blackstone, *Commentaries on the Laws of England* (Oxford, 1765–70), ch. 16.

97. Smith, *Wealth of Nations*, bk. 5, chap. 1.

98. Karl Marx, "Debates on Law on Thefts of Wood," *Rheinische Zeitung*, 1842; quoted in Daniel Bensaïd, *The Dispossessed: Karl Marx's Debates on Wood Theft and the Right of the Poor*, trans. Robert Nichols (Minneapolis: University of Minneapolis Press, 2021), 25.

99. Thomas More, *Utopia*, ed. Stephen Duncombe (1516; Wivenhoe, UK: Minor Compositions, 2012), 45.

100. Quoted in Jay Walljasper, "'Stealing the Common from the Goose': A 17th-Century Rhyme That Stands the Test of Time," *Commons Magazine*, January 18, 2013, https://www.onthecommons.org/magazine/"stealing-common-goose".

101. James Hudsonh Maurer, *Report of the Pennsylvania Commission on Old Age Pensions*, United States, J. L. L. Kuhn, Printer to the Commonwealth, 1919, 226.

102. Robert Wardhaugh, "Productivity and Popular Attitudes toward Welfare Recipients in Saskatchewan, 1970–1990," University of Regina SIPP Public Policy Paper 14, https://ourspace.uregina.ca/handle/10294/6666?show=full.

103. Rebecca Shabad et al., "Manchin Privately Raised Concerns That Parents Would Use Child Tax Credit Checks on Drugs," NBC, December 20, 2021, https://www.nbcnews.com/politics/congress/manchin-privately-raised-concerns-parents-would-use-child-tax-credit-n1286321.

104. Lindsey M. Burke, "Why Biden's Student Loan Bailout Is Unfair," Heritage Foundation, August 29, 2022, https://www.heritage.org/education/commentary/why-bidens-student-loan-bailout-unfair.

105. Here's one more example: Before the great risk shift, a higher proportion of workers had defined-benefit pensions that provided a reliable income in old age. Today, workers are incentivized to invest in the stock market by contributing to an RRSP or 401K. Not only does this make retirement

far more vulnerable to economic volatility, it also means that our ability to survive in old age is invested in things that undermine democratic and planetary stability—fossil fuels, big tech, or corporate ownership of farmland in the prairies. In other words, things that increase overall insecurity.

106. Galbraith, *Affluent Society*, 94.

107. Galbraith, *Affluent Society*.

108. James Mulvale and Sid Frankel, "Next Steps on the Road to Basic Income in Canada," *The Journal of Sociology & Social Welfare*, vol. 43, issue 3, September 2016, 34.

109 David Cox, "Canada's Forgotten Universal Basic Income Experiment," BBC, June 24, 2020, https://www.bbc.com/worklife/article/20200624-canadas-forgotten-universal-basic-income-experiment.

110. D. Calnitsky, "'More Normal than Welfare': The Mincome Experiment, Stigma, and Community Experience." *Canadian Review of Sociology* 53, no. 1 (February 2016), 26–71, doi: 10.1111/cars.12091.

111. Quoted in Sarah Gardner, "On the Canadian Prairie, a Basic Income Experiment," *Marketplace*, December 20, 2016, https://www.marketplace.org/2016/12/20/dauphin/.

112. Gardner, "On the Canadian Prairie."

113. David Calnitsky and Pilar Gonalons-Pons, "The Impact of an Experimental Guaranteed Income on Crime and Violence," *Social Problems* 68, no. 3 (August 2021), 778–98.

114. Evelyn L. Forget, "The Town with No Poverty: The Health Effects of a Canadian Guaranteed Annual Income Field Experiment," *Canadian Public Policy* 37, no. 3 (September 2011), 290; see also Whitney Mallett, "The Town Where Everyone Got Free Money," *Vice*, February 4, 2015, https://www.vice.com/en/article/nze99z/the-mincome-experiment-dauphin.

115. Cox, "Canada's Forgotten Universal Basic Income Experiment."

116. For a discussion of business opposition to universal basic income programs and a discussion of MINCOME, see David Calnitsky, "If the Work Requirement Is Strong": The Business Response to Basic Income Proposals in Canada and the US," *Canadian Journal of Sociology* 43, no. 3 (2018), 291–315.

117. All quotes from "The Burrow" are from *Franz Kafka: The Complete Stories*, trans. Nahum Norbet Glatzer (New York: Schocken Books, 1971), 325–59.

118. Seneca, *Moral Epistles* (c. 65 AD), trans. Richard M. Gummere, letter 5.

119. Beck, *Risk Society*, 76.

120. Quarries: *Kafka: The Office Writings*, 273–30. Wood-planing: *Kafka: The Office Writings*, 109–15.

121. Jessie Singer, *There Are No Accidents: The Deadly Rise of Injury and Disaster—Who Profits and Who Pays the Price* (New York: Simon & Schuster, 2022).

122. Pew Charitable Trusts, "Americans' Financial Security: Perception and Reality," March 5, 2015, https://www.pewtrusts.org/en/research-and-analysis/issue-briefs/2015/02/americans-financial-security-per-ceptions-and-reality.

Coda: Accepting Cura's Gift

1. William Butler Yeats, "The Second Coming," in *Selected Poetry* (London: Macmillan, 1962), 99–100.

2. Karl Marx and Friedrich Engels, *Manifesto of the Communist Party*, Chapter 1, https://www.marxists.org/archive/marx/works/1848/com-munist-manifesto/ch01.htm.

3. Yeats, "The Second Coming."

4. Rebecca Solnit, "The Ideology of Isolation," *Harper's*, July, 2016.

5. W. J. McCormack, *Blood Kindred: W. B. Yeats, the Life, the Death, the Politics* (London: Random House, 2011); for a more sympathetic take on Yeats, see Roy Foster, "Philosophy and a Little Passion," *Irish Times*, June 10, 2015, https://www.irishtimes.com/culture/books/philosophy-and-a-little-passion-roy-foster-on-wb-yeats-and-politics-1.2241504.

6. Søren Kierkegaard, *The Concept of Anxiety: A Simple Psychologically Oriented Deliberation in View of the Dogmatic Problem of Hereditary Sin* (1844), trans. Alastair Hannay (New York: Liveright, 2014), 75.

7. Martin Heidegger, *Being and Time: A Revised Edition of the Stam-baugh Translation*, trans. Joan Stambaugh, rev. Dennis J. Schmidt (Albany: State University of New York Press, 2010), 199.

8. Simone de Beauvoir, *The Ethics of Ambiguity* (1947), trans. Bernard Frechtman (New York: Open Road, 2018), 9.

9. Beauvoir, *Ethics of Ambiguity*, 169.

10. Suzanne Simard, *Finding the Mother Tree: Uncovering the Wisdom and Intelligence of the Forest* (London: Penguin, 2021).

11. David Graeber, *The Utopia of Rules: On Technology, Stupidity, and the Secret Joys of Bureaucracy* (Brooklyn: Melville House, 2015), 89.

BIBLIOGRAPHY

Anderson, Virginia DeJohn. *Creatures of Empire: How Domestic Animals Transformed Early America*. New York: Oxford University Press, 2004.

Aronson, Amy. *Crystal Eastman: A Revolutionary Life*. New York: Oxford University Press, 2020.

Beck, Ulrich. *Risk Society: Towards a New Modernity*. Newbury Park, CA: Sage, 1992.

Boyd, David R. *The Rights Of Nature: A Legal Revolution That Could Save the World*. Toronto: ECW, 2017.

Canada, Truth and Reconciliation Commission of. *A Knock on the Door: The Essential History of Residential Schools from the Truth and Reconciliation Commission of Canada*, Edited and Abridged. Winnipeg, MB: University of Manitoba Press, 2015.

Case, Anne, and Angus Deaton. *Deaths of Despair and the Future of Capitalism*. Princeton: Princeton University Press, 2021.

Cicero. *On Obligations: De Officiis*. Translated by P. G. Walsh. London: Oxford University Press, 2008.

Corngold, Stanley, Jack Greenberg, and Benno Wagner, eds. *Franz Kafka: The Office Writings*. Translated by Eric Patton and Ruth Hein. Princeton: Princeton University Press, 2008.

Council for Yukon Indians. *Together Today for Our Children Tomorrow*. 1977.

Cronon, William. *Changes in the Land: Indians, Colonists, and the Ecology of New England*. New York: Farrar, Straus & Giroux, 2003.

Debt Collective. *Can't Pay, Won't Pay: The Case for Economic Disobedience and Debt Abolition*. Chicago: Haymarket Books, 2020.

Defalco, Martin, and Willie Dunn, dir. *The Other Side of the Ledger: An Indian View of the Hudson's Bay Company*. National Film Board of Canada, 1972. 42 min.

Downey, Kirstin. *The Woman Behind the New Deal: The Life of Frances Perkins, FDR's Secretary of Labor and His Moral Conscience*. New York: Nan A. Talese, 2009.

Ewen, Stuart. *Captains of Consciousness: Advertising and the Social Roots of the Consumer Culture*. New York: McGraw-Hill, 1976.

Ehrenreich, Barbara. *Fear of Falling*. New York: Pantheon, 1989.

Forget, Evelyn L. "The Town with No Poverty: The Health Effects of a Canadian Guaranteed Annual Income Field Experiment." *Canadian Public Policy* 37, no. 3 (September 2011).

Fraser, Nancy. *Cannibal Capitalism: How Our System Is Devouring Democracy, Care, and the Planet and What We Can Do About It*. London: Verso, 2022.

Galbraith, John Kenneth. *The Affluent Society*. Pbk. repr. Boston: Houghton Mifflin, 1998.

Gettler, Brian. *Colonialism's Currency: Money, State, and First Nations in Canada, 1820–1950*. Montreal: McGill-Queen's University Press, 2020.

Globensky, Peter André. "The Life of a Canadian Internationalist: Dr. John Peters Humphrey and the Universal Declaration of Human Rights." *University of New Brunswick Law Journal* 47 (1998).

Graeber, David. *Debt: The First 5,000 Years*. Brooklyn: Melville House, 2011.

Greer, Allan. *Property and Dispossession: Natives, Empires and Land in Early Modern North America*. New York: Cambridge University Press, 2018.

Hacker, Jacob. *The Great Risk Shift: The New Economic Insecurity and the Decline of the American Dream*. New York: Oxford University Press, 2019.

Hacking, Ian. *The Emergence of Probability: A Philosophical Study of Early Ideas about Probability, Induction and Statistical Inference*. Cambridge: Cambridge University Press, 2006.

Hamilton, John T. *Security: Politics, Humanity, and the Philology of Care*. Princeton: Princeton University Press, 2013.

Hobbes, Thomas. *Leviathan*. 1651. Cambridge: Cambridge University Press, 1904.

Hobbins, A. J. "Eleanor Roosevelt, John Humphrey and Canadian Opposition to the Universal Declaration of Human Rights: Looking Back on the 50th Anniversary of UNDHR," *International Journal* 53, no. 2 (1998).

Hunt-Hendrix, Leah, and Astra Taylor. *Solidarity: The Past, Present, and Future of a World-Changing Idea*. New York: Pantheon, 2024.

Inglehart, Ronald. *The Silent Revolution: Changing Values and Political Styles Among Western Publics*. Princeton: Princeton University Press, 1977.

Klein, Naomi. *On Fire: The (Burning) Case for a Green New Deal*. Toronto: Knopf Canada, 2019.

Linebaugh, Peter. *The Magna Carta Manifesto: Liberties and Commons for All*. Berkeley: University of California Press, 2009.

———. *Stop, Thief! The Commons, Enclosures, and Resistance*. Binghamton, NY: PM Press, 2012.

Locke, John. *Two Treatises of Government*. 1690.

Mann, Bruce H. *Republic of Debtors: Bankruptcy in the Age of American Independence*. Cambridge, MA: Harvard University Press, 2009.

Manuel, Arthur, and Grand Chief Ronald M. Derrickson. 2021. *Unsettling Canada: A National Wake-Up Call*. Toronto: Between the Lines, 2015.

———. *The Reconciliation Manifesto: Recovering the Land, Rebuilding the Economy*. Toronto: James Lorimer, 2017.

Marmot, Michael. *Status Syndrome: How Your Social Standing Directly Affects Your Health and Life Expectancy*. London: Bloomsbury, 2005.

Maté, Gabor, and Daniel Maté. *The Myth of Normal*. Toronto: Knopf Canada, 2022.

Maynard, Robyn. *Policing Black Lives: State Violence in Canada from Slavery to the Present*. Halifax: Fernwood, 2017.

More, Thomas. *Utopia*. 1516. Edited by Stephen Duncombe. Wivenhoe, UK: Minor Compositions, 2012.

Neeson, J. M. *Commoners: Common Right, Enclosure and Social Change in England, 1700–1820*. Cambridge: Cambridge University Press, 1993.

Neocleous, Mark. *Critique of Security*. Edinburgh: Edinburgh University Press, 2008.

Pasternak, Shiri, Kevin Walby, and Abby Stadnyk, eds. *Disarm, Defund, Dismantle: Police Abolition in Canada*. Toronto: Between the Lines, 2022.

Pickett, Kate, and Richard Wilkinson. *The Spirit Level: Why Greater Equality Is Better for Everyone*. London: Allen Lane, 1989.

Porter, Bruce, and Martha Jackman, eds. *Advancing Social Rights in Canada*. Toronto: Irwin Law, 2014.

Qaqqaq, Mumilaaq. *Sick of Waiting: A Report on Nunavut's Housing Crisis*. 2021. https://www.aptnnews.ca/wp-content/uploads/2021/03/Qaqqaq. HousingReport.2021-1.pdf.

Rigakos, George. *Security/Capital: A General Theory of Pacification*. Edinburgh: Edinburgh University Press, 2016.

Rutland, Ted. *Displacing Blackness: Planning, Power, and Race in Twentieth-Century Halifax*. Toronto: University of Toronto Press, 2018.

Sebo, Jeff. *Saving Animals, Saving Ourselves: Why Animals Matter for Pandemics, Climate Change, and Other Catastrophes*. New York: Oxford University Press, 2022.

Seneca. *Moral Epistles*. Circa 65 AD. Translated by Richard M. Gummere. London, 1917.

Sherman, Rachel. *Uneasy Street: The Anxieties of Affluence*. Princeton: Princeton University Press, 2017.

Simpson, Leanne Betasamosake. *Dancing on Our Turtle's Back: Stories of Nishnaabeg Re-creation, Resurgence and a New Emergence*. Winnipeg: ARP Books, 2011.

Singer, Jessie. *There Are No Accidents: The Deadly Rise of Injury and Disaster—Who Profits and Who Pays the Price*. New York: Simon & Schuster, 2022.

Smith, Adam. *An Inquiry Into the Nature and Causes of the Wealth of Nations*. London, 1776.

———. *The Theory of Moral Sentiments*. London, 1759.

Suttor, Gregory. *Still Renovating: A History of Canadian Social Housing Policy*. Montreal: McGill-Queen's University Press, 2016.

Taylor, Astra. *Democracy May Not Exist, But We Will Miss It When It's Gone*. New York: Henry Holt, 2019.

Taylor, Sunaura. *The People's Platform: Taking Back Power and Culture in the Digital Age*. New York: Henry Holt, 2014.

————. *Beasts of Burden: Animal and Disability Liberation*. New York: New Press. 2017.

Thompson, Edward Palmer. *Customs in Common*. New York: New Press, 1993.

Tong, Ziya. *The Reality Bubble: How Science Reveals the Hidden Truths that Shape Our World*. Toronto: Penguin Canada, 2019.

Trentmann, Frank. *Empire of Things: How We Became a World of Consumers, from the Fifteenth Century to the Twenty-First*. London: Allen Lane, 2016.

United Nations. Universal Declaration of Human Rights, adopted December 10, 1948. https://www.un.org/en/about-us/universal-declaration-of-human-rights.

United Nations Environment Programme and International Livestock Research Institute. *Preventing the Next Pandemic: Zoonotic Diseases and How to Break the Chain of Transmission*. Nairobi: United Nations Environment Programme, 2020.

Watts, Alan. *The Wisdom of Insecurity: A Message for an Age of Anxiety*. New York: Vintage Books, 2011.

Witt, John Fabian. *The Accidental Republic: Crippled Workingmen, Destitute Widows, and the Remaking of American Law*. Cambridge, MA: Harvard University Press, 2009.

Yellowhead Institute. *Cash Back*. May 2021. https://cashback.yellowheadin stitute.org.

————. *Land Back*. October 2019. https://redpaper.yellowheadinstitute.org.

(THE CBC MASSEY LECTURES SERIES)

Laughing with the Trickster
Tomson Highway
978-1-4870-1123-9

Out of the Sun
Esi Edugyan
978-1-4870-0986-1

Reset
Ronald J. Deibert
978-1-4870-0805-5 (CAN)
978-1-4870-0808-6 (US)

Power Shift
Sally Armstrong
978-1-4870-0679-2 (CAN)
978-1-4870-0682-2 (US)

All Our Relations
Tanya Talaga
978-1-4870-0573-3 (CAN)
978-1-4870-0574-0 (US)

In Search of a Better World
Payam Akhavan
978-1-4870-0200-8 (CAN)
978-1-4870-0339-5 (US)

Therefore Choose Life
George Wald
978-1-4870-0320-3 (CAN)
978-1-4870-0338-8 (US)

The Return of History
Jennifer Welsh
978-1-4870-0242-8

History's People
Margaret MacMillan
978-1-4870-0137-7

Belonging
Adrienne Clarkson
978-1-77089-837-0 (CAN)
978-1-77089-838-7 (US)

Blood
Lawrence Hill
978-1-77089-322-1 (CAN)
978-1-77089-323-8 (US)

The Universe Within
Neil Turok
978-1-77089-015-2 (CAN)
978-1-77089-017-6 (US)

Winter
Adam Gopnik
978-0-88784-974-9 (CAN)
978-0-88784-975-6 (US)

Player One
Douglas Coupland
978-1-4870-1146-8

The Wayfinders
Wade Davis
978-0-88784-842-1 (CAN)
978-0-88784-766-0 (US)

Payback
Margaret Atwood
978-1-4870-0697-6

The City of Words
Alberto Manguel
978-0-88784-763-9

More Lost Massey Lectures
Bernie Lucht, ed.
978-0-88784-801-8

The Lost Massey Lectures
Bernie Lucht, ed.
978-0-88784-217-7

The Ethical Imagination
Margaret Somerville
978-0-88784-747-9

Race Against Time
Stephen Lewis
978-0-88784-753-0

A Short History of Progress
Ronald Wright
978-1-4870-0698-3

The Truth About Stories
Thomas King
978-0-88784-696-0

Beyond Fate
Margaret Visser
978-0-88784-679-3

The Cult of Efficiency
Janice Gross Stein
978-0-88784-678-6

The Rights Revolution
Michael Ignatieff
978-0-88784-762-2

The Triumph of Narrative
Robert Fulford
978-0-88784-645-8

The Elsewhere Community
Hugh Kenner
978-0-88784-607-6

The Unconscious Civilization
John Ralston Saul
978-0-88784-731-8

On the Eve of the Millennium
Conor Cruise O'Brien
978-0-88784-559-8

Democracy on Trial
Jean Bethke Elshtain
978-0-88784-545-1

Twenty-First Century Capitalism
Robert Heilbroner
978-0-88784-534-5

The Malaise of Modernity
Charles Taylor
978-0-88784-520-8

Biology as Ideology
R. C. Lewontin
978-0-88784-518-5

The Real World of Technology
Ursula M. Franklin
978-0-88784-636-6

Necessary Illusions
Noam Chomsky
978-0-88784-574-1

Compassion and Solidarity
Gregory Baum
978-0-88784-532-1

Prisons We Choose to Live Inside
Doris Lessing
978-0-88784-521-5

Latin America
Carlos Fuentes
978-0-88784-665-6

Nostalgia for the Absolute
George Steiner
978-0-88784-594-9

Designing Freedom
Stafford Beer
978-0-88784-547-5

The Politics of the Family
R. D. Laing
978-0-88784-546-8

The Real World of Democracy
C. B. Macpherson
978-0-88784-530-7

The Educated Imagination
Northrop Frye
978-0-88784-598-7